The World Atlas of Treasure

Derek Wilson

The World Atlas of Treasure

Pan Books   London and Sydney

First published 1981 by William Collins Sons & Co. Ltd
This edition published 1982 by Pan Books Ltd,
Cavaye Place, London SW10 9PG
© Derek Wilson 1981
ISBN 0 330 26450 8

Set, printed and bound in Great Britain by
Fakenham Press Limited, Fakenham, Norfolk

Contents

6 · Contents

Illustration Acknowledgements

12 bottom right, Mansell Collection; **13** top centre, Ronald Sheridan; centre right, Metropolitan Museum of Art, New York; bottom left, Ronald Sheridan; **14** top right, Ronald Sheridan; bottom right, Mansell Collection; **15** top right, Mansell Collection; bottom, Mansell Collection; **16** bottom left, MacQuitty Collection; bottom right, MacQuitty Collection; **17** top left, MacQuitty Collection; **18** bottom left, Reproduced by courtesy of the Trustees of the British Museum; bottom left, Peter Clayton; **19** top left, Peter Clayton; bottom left, MacQuitty Collection; bottom right, Peter Clayton; **20** bottom left, Peter Clayton; **21** top, Mansell Collection; **23** top right, Werner Forman Archive; bottom right, Ronald Sheridan; **24** top right, Ronald Sheridan; bottom right, BBC Hulton Picture Library; **25** top right, Werner Forman Archive; bottom left, Ronald Sheridan; **26** centre right, Mansell Collection; **27** left, John Hillelson Agency, photo Marc Ribout; **29** top right, William MacQuitty and Camera Press; bottom right, Robert Harding; **32** bottom, Ing Associates; top right, Robert Harding; **33** top, Camera Press; bottom left, Camera Press; **34** bottom left, Peter Clayton; **35** top left, BBC Hulton Picture Library; middle left, Ronald Sheridan; bottom right, Peter Clayton; **36** bottom right, Reproduced by courtesy of the Trustees of the British Museum; **37** bottom left, Reproduced by courtesy of the Trustees of the British Museum; **38** top, Reproduced by courtesy of the Trustees of the British Museum; middle right, Reproduced by courtesy of the Trustees of the British Museum; **39** bottom left, Dean and Chapter of Durham Cathedral; bottom right, Dean and Chapter of Durham Cathedral; **40** top right, Janet and Colin Bord; bottom, Janet and Colin Bord; **41** bottom left, Ashmolean Museum, Oxford; bottom right, Ashmolean Museum, Oxford; **42** top right, Reproduced by courtesy of the Trustees of the British Museum; bottom left, National Museum, Copenhagen; **43** top left, Reproduced by courtesy of the Trustees of the British Museum; bottom left, Reproduced by courtesy of the Trustees of the British Museum; **44** bottom left, Ronald Sheridan; bottom right, Ronald Sheridan; **45** top right, Reproduced by courtesy of the Trustees of the British Museum; centre, Reproduced by the Trustees of the British Museum; bottom left, Peter Clayton; **46** top right, Ronald Sheridan; top right, Sonia Halliday; **47** right, Sonia Halliday; **48** top right, Peter Clayton; centre right, Peter Clayton; bottom right, Peter Clayton; **49** top left, Ken Smith; **50** bottom left, Ronald Sheridan; bottom right, Ronald Sheridan; **51** top centre, Ronald Sheridan; top right, Ronald Sheridan; **52** right, Ronald Sheridan; **53** top left, Ronald Sheridan; **55** top left, Lennart Larsen; bottom left, Lennart Larsen; bottom right, Ronald Sheridan; **57** top right, National Museum, Copenhagen; bottom, National Museum, Copenhagen; **58** top left, Ulster Museum, Belfast; bottom right, Ulster Museum, Belfast; **59** centre right, National Museum of Antiquities, Scotland; bottom, National Museum of Antiquities, Scotland; **61** top right, Ronald Sheridan; **62** top right, Mansell Collection; **63** top, Mansell Collection; right, BBC Hulton Picture Library; **64** bottom right, Mary Evans Picture Library; **65** top, BBC Hulton Picture Library; bottom, BBC Hulton Picture Library; **67** top, Metropolitan Museum of Art, New York; centre right, Metropolitan Museum of Art, New York; **68** bottom, Karl Meyer; **69** top right, BBC Hulton Picture Library; centre right, Reproduced by courtesy of the Trustees of the British Museum; **70** left, Karl Meyer; top right, Karl Meyer; bottom right, Werner Forman Archive; **71** top right, Philippe Halsman; **72** top right, Peter Clayton; bottom right, Peter Clayton; **73** top left, Peter Clayton; bottom, National Museum of Antiquities, Scotland; **77** centre, J. Allan Cash; bottom, The Warburg Institute; **78** top left, Reproduced by courtesy of the Trustees of the British Museum; centre, Reproduced by courtesy of the Trustees of the British Museum; bottom right, Reproduced by courtesy of the Trustees of the British Museum; **79** bottom, Mansell Collection; **80** centre, Reproduced by courtesy of the Trustees of the British Museum; bottom, Aerofilms Ltd; **81** left, Peter Clayton; **83** top right, Ronald Sheridan; **84** top left, Werner Forman Archive; top centre, Ronald Sheridan; top right, Antikvarisk-topogrfiskaarkivet (ATA), Stockholm; centre left, Ronald Sheridan; bottom right, Ronald Sheridan; **85** top left, Werner Forman Archive; bottom left, University of Oslo, Norway; **86** bottom, BBC Hulton Picture Library; **87** left, Peter Clayton; top right, Reproduced by courtesy of the Trustees of the British Museum; **88** top right, BBC Hulton Picture Library; **89** top, Giraudon; bottom left, John Topham; **90** top, Camera Press; **91** top right, The Museum of London; bottom right, Reproduced by courtesy of the Trustees of the British Museum; **92** centre, Victoria and Albert Museum; bottom right, Victoria and Albert Museum; **93** top left, Edwin Smith; top right, Norman Thompson; **94** bottom right, Giraudon; **95** top left, Giraudon; bottom, Giraudon; **96** bottom left, Peter Newark's Historical Pictures; **97** left, Peter Clayton; bottom left, Peter Clayton; **98** centre, Peter Newark's Historical Pictures; bottom, Peter Newark's Historical Pictures; **100** right, Peter Newark's Historical Pictures; **101** bottom, Bettmann Archive Inc.; **102** top, Peter Newark's Historical Pictures; bottom, Peter Newark's Historical Pictures; **103** top right, Peter Newark's Historical Pictures; **105** Popperfoto; **108** top right, Werner Forman Archive; bottom right, Werner Forman Archive; **109** top right, Ronald Sheridan; bottom right, Ronald Sheridan; **110** bottom, Geoff Harwood; **111** bottom left, Camera Press; top right, Ronald Sheridan; bottom right, Ronald Sheridan; **113** centre top, David Allen; top right, BBC Hulton Picture Library; **115** centre left, BBC Hulton Picture Library; bottom left, BBC Hulton Picture Library; **118** top right, Karen McKee; centre right, Karen McKee; bottom right, Karen McKee; bottom left, Karen McKee; **119** centre left, Forlasta Bureau; bottom left, Karen McKee; **120** centre right, John Topham; bottom right, Karen McKee; **121** bottom left, Camera Press; top right, Reproduced by courtesy of the Trustees of the British Library; **122** top right, Mary Evans Picture Library; bottom, Mansell Collection; **123** bottom left, BBC Hulton Picture Library; centre, BBC Hulton Picture Library; top right, BBC Hulton Picture Library; **124** top right, Camera Press; centre right, Camera Press; **127** top right, Camera Press; centre right, Ken Smith; **128** bottom, Peter Newark's Historical Pictures; **130** bottom left, Ulster Museum, Belfast; centre right, Ulster Museum, Belfast; bottom right, Ulster Museum, Belfast; **131** centre left, Ulster Museum, Belfast; bottom left, Ulster Museum, Belfast; top right, Keystone Press; **132** bottom, The Connoisseur; **133** bottom, Victoria and Albert Museum; **134** bottom, National Maritime Museum; **135** centre right, East India Office; **137** bottom right, John Topham; top right, Camera Press; bottom left, Rijksmuseum, Amsterdam; **139** bottom right, BBC Hulton Picture Library; centre left, Mary Evans Picture Library; **141** bottom right, Western Australia Newspapers; bottom left, Western Australia Newspapers; **143** bottom left, National Maritime Museum; **144** bottom, Seaphot, Mike Ross; **145** bottom, Public Record Office, London; **146** top left, Seaphot, Mike Ross; top right, Keystone Press; bottom, Seaphot, Mike Ross; **147** bottom, Keystone Press; **148** bottom, Keystone Press; **149** top left, BBC Hulton Picture Library; top right, BBC Hulton Picture Library; **151** John Topham; **152** bottom right, Keystone Press; **154** bottom, Peter Clayton; **155** top left, Peter Clayton; centre left, Peter Clayton; **156** top, BBC Hulton Picture Library; **158** bottom, BBC Hulton Picture Library; **159** top centre, BBC Hulton Picture Library; top right, BBC Hulton Picture Library; bottom centre, BBC Hulton Picture Library; **160** Reproduced by courtesy of the Trustees of the British Museum; **161** top left, BBC Hulton Picture Library; bottom right, Reproduced by courtesy of the Trustees of the British Museum; **162** centre top, National Portrait Gallery; top left, Ken Smith; centre, Ken Smith; bottom right, Ken Smith; bottom centre, Ken Smith; **163** top left, BBC Hulton Picture Library; bottom left, Popperfoto; **164** top left, Marion and Tony Morison; top right, Camera Press; bottom right, Peter Newark's Historical Pictures; **165** centre, Ronald Sheridan; **166–7** J. Allan Cash Ltd; **167** top centre, BBC Hulton Picture Library; top right, BBC Hulton Picture Library; **169** top left, BBC Hulton Picture Library; bottom, Mansell Collection; **170** bottom left, Museum of Zambia; top right, Werner Forman Archive; bottom right, Werner Forman Archive; **171** top, BBC Hulton Picture Library; bottom right, BBC Hulton Picture Library; **172** bottom right, BBC Hulton Picture Library; **173** bottom left, BBC Hulton Picture Library; **174** bottom, British Library; **175** bottom, Daily Telegraph Colour Library, P. Thurston; **176** bottom, The Associated Press Ltd; **177** top, Daily Mail; **178** top, Daily Express; **180** bottom, Popperfoto; **182** bottom left, Peter Newark's Historical Pictures; top right, Popperfoto; **183** top left, Popperfoto; bottom left, Popperfoto; **184** bottom, BBC Hulton Picture Library; **185** top left, BBC Hulton Picture Library; bottom right, BBC Hulton Picture Library; top right, Popperfoto; **187** top left, Cambridge University Library; **189** top, BBC Hulton Picture Library; bottom, BBC Hulton Picture Library; **190** top left, BBC Hulton Picture Library; bottom right, Illustrated London News; **191** centre left, Camera Press; centre right, Camera Press; bottom right, Illustrated London News; **192** bottom right, Camera Press; **193** Camera Press; **194** top left, Camera Press; **195** top right, Camera Press; **196** top right, Popperfoto; **197** top left, National Maritime Museum; centre left, BBC Hulton Picture Library; bottom left, Popperfoto; top right, R. I. Nesmith, New York; centre right, R. I. Nesmith, New York; **198** bottom, National Maritime Museum; **199** bottom right, Mary Evans Picture Library; **200** bottom, Jamaica Tourist Board; **201** Institute of Jamaica; **203** bottom right, BBC Hulton Picture Library; **204** bottom, Popperfoto; **205** bottom right, Popperfoto; **207** bottom, National Maritime Museum; **209** top right, Die Klenodien; centre right, Die Klenodien; **210** centre left, Keystone Press; bottom right, National War Museum; **211** bottom right, John Topham; **212** bottom left, Keystone Press; centre right, Keystone Press; **213** centre left, Keystone Press, right, Keystone Press; **214** centre left, Keystone Press; centre right, Keystone Press; bottom right, Keystone Press; **216** top, Keystone Press; bottom, John Topham; **217** top right, John Topham; bottom, Keystone Press; **219** top left, Popperfoto; top right, Popperfoto; bottom right, BBC Hulton Picture Library; bottom, Keystone Press; **221** top, Keystone Press; **224** bottom, Giraudon; **225** top, Giraudon; **226** bottom left, Giraudon; bottom right, Giraudon; **227** top, Giraudon; bottom right, Giraudon; **229** bottom right, Giraudon; **230** bottom, Illustrated London News; **231** Illustrated London News; **232** top right, Illustrated London News; top right, Illustrated London News; bottom right, Illustrated London News; **233** bottom left, Illustrated London News; top right, Illustrated London News; **234** bottom right, President and Fellows of Harvard College; **235** top, President and Fellows of Harvard College; bottom left, President and Fellows of Harvard College; **236** bottom, Ann Kendall; **237** top right, National Geographical Society; **239** British Library; **240** top left, John Topham; centre right, John Topham; bottom right, John Topham; **241** top right, Peter Clayton; bottom right, Keystone Press; **242** bottom left, BBC Hulton Picture Library; **243** bottom right, John Topham; **245** bottom right, BBC Hulton Picture Library; **246** bottom right, Keystone Press; top right, Keystone Press; centre right, Keystone Press; **247** centre left, Stan Teasdale; bottom left, Savo Electronics; top right, Keystone; **249** right, Mary Evans Picture Library.

The publishers have made every effort to trace the copyright holders, but if they have inadvertently overlooked anybody they will be pleased to make the necessary arrangements at the first opportunity.

Introduction

£135,000 FOR TREASURE-FINDER

BID TO RAISE *TITANIC* GOLD

JAPANESE BUSINESSMAN IN £20,000,000 RUSSIAN
TREASURE ROW

These are just some of the headlines which appeared in newspapers during the last few days that I spent writing this book. They were added to the thick file of cuttings accumulated over the last few years. Not a single month and scarcely a week passes without someone somewhere finding treasure. It may be a Norfolk gravedigger accidentally coming upon a bundle of Saxon silver brooches. It may be an American consortium finding the coral-encrusted wreck of a Spanish bullion ship after months of patient searching. It may be an archaeological team opening the rich, intact grave of a third-century BC Macedonian king. It may be an amateur with a metal detector unearthing 60,000 Roman coins in a Wiltshire field. However it is found, whatever form it takes, it is treasure. Over the centuries its discovery has made countless men and women rich beyond their wildest imaginings. It has claimed the lives of many poor wretches who have gone in its pursuit. It has become a glittering obsession, tempting others to forsake all, in the hope of sudden wealth.

It is not possible to write the story of all the gold, silver, gems, ivory, jade and other precious items lost by accident or design beneath tons of earth or water without telling also of the men and women who have gone in search of it. And this takes us into a strange world indeed; a world of adventurers and scholars, criminals and necromancers, of desperados destroyed by the lure of gold, and pragmatic businessmen prepared to invest heavily in expensive expeditions in the hope of high dividends.

The quest for hidden wealth has always attracted both the professional and the amateur. The origins of grave-robbing are obscured in the depths of antiquity. There is scarcely a pyramid or rock tomb in the whole of Egypt which was not looted thousands of years ago. The tumuli of the Balkans and southern Russia have almost all been plundered over the centuries. In the Middle Ages, British and European treasure-hunters sought the aid of spirits in discovering the wealth of the dead. Nowadays more scientific methods are used to locate and rifle ancient tombs, and the craft of the *tomboroli* and *huaqueros* (professional grave-robbers) flourishes as never before. From Turkey, Italy, Latin America and other regions a steady stream of looted grave goods comes on to the international art market. Beside these professionals we must set the organizers of the highly capitalized consortia which are set up every year to find and market the hidden riches of antiquity, and most of these are concerned with locating and salvaging the wrecks of ancient treasure ships. The development of scuba diving and the perfection of techniques of deep water search have transformed undersea treasure-hunting into a boom industry in the last two decades. Over the centuries countless thousands of richly loaded vessels – Spanish silver galleons, East Indiamen laden with gems and ivory, Mediterranean galleys carrying classical statuary – have foundered, and now, for the first time, the raising of their precious cargoes becomes a possibility. Nor must we forget the professionals of a different kind, the archaeologists for whom articles rescued from obscurity have value, not for their market price but for what they can tell us about the past. The archaeologist's craft has developed over the last two hundred years from the dilettantism of a coterie of wealthy curio collectors into a highly specialized science involving several academic disciplines.

To whom does buried treasure belong? It is an unresolved question or, rather, one to which different interest-groups give different answers – answers which bring them into inevitable conflict. Warren Stearns, American banker and backer of underwater quests, is quite certain about his businesslike approach to treasure-hunting:

> This isn't the Holy Grail . . . We're going to do this again and again and again. We're going to find treasure all over the world. We're a business.
>
> (P. Earle, 'Why it Pays to Send Good Money After Old',
> *Daily Telegraph Colour Magazine*, 27 April 1979)

One of his fellow countrymen, Dr G. F. Bass, is equally forthright in claiming for the world of scholarship the right to the heritage of the past:

> If we, as archaeologists, are truly interested in artefacts as evidence for ancient history, rather than as possessions to be selfishly prized because of their rarity, it is time to take a firm stand. The clandestine excavator and antiquities smuggler are criminals to be abhorred.
>
> ('A Hoard of Trojan and Sumerian Jewellery',
> *American Journal of Archaeology*, 1970, p. 341)

The ire of the archaeologist is also raised against the amateur, a category which includes the holiday diver who claps on scuba gear and scans inshore waters for old cannon, clumps of coins and other valuable artefacts. It also includes the 'T.H.er'. 'T.H.ing', as members of the fastest growing modern hobby call it, is treasure-hunting with the aid of metal detectors. Millions of people have taken up this pastime in recent years. Weekends and holidays find them on beaches and farmland, in parks and woods sweeping the ground with their machines, hoping for the high-pitched signal which will tell them that metal lies just below the surface. They band together into clubs to discuss their finds, to compare notes on various sites and to study local history. Most are serious students of the past who share the archaeologist's excitement in making tangible contact with former epochs. But there are those who see T.-H.ing as simply a more energetic alternative to doing the football pools. A small investment and the minimum of thought may lead them to a lucky find. Like treasure-seekers throughout history, it is the prospect of sudden wealth which provides the main motivation for their activities. Most of them never discover anything of any consequence, but a steady trickle of 'lucky strike' stories in the national press is sufficient to maintain the momentum of enthusiasm. Unfortunately, archaeological sites and protected areas are prime targets and this creates bad blood between the scholars and the whole treasure-hunting fraternity. Finds made with metal detectors have been compared to pages torn at random from an encyclopaedia; when, in 1978, an unprecedentedly large hoard of Roman coins was found in Wiltshire, one archaeologist sourly remarked, 'It would have been better left in the ground.'

Over the last two decades many countries have introduced new laws aimed at curbing the activities of amateur and professional treasure-hunters. Some have been brought in at the instigation of scholars and museum authorities, others by governments alarmed at the clandestine outflow of valuable objects. But they are fighting a losing battle, since in today's art market, buyers abound and prices move steadily upward. As a result there is more digging and diving for treasure than at any other period in history. It is ironic that the modern interest in archaeology and ancient civilizations fostered by scholars and experts should have led to renewed plundering and damaging of sites, which creates enormous problems for the researcher. For example, though most Egyptian tombs have long since been emptied of all objects of intrinsic value, they are now being consistently revisited for the removal of papyri, pottery and even wall paintings. There are large sums of money involved and it is easy to bribe officials. Overworked police forces do not place the apprehension of tomb-robbers at the top of their list of priorities and the laws are difficult to enforce. Nor do they usually have the cooperation of the public. Even the professional archaeologists who spearhead the campaign against illicit excavation are in a weak position to make convincing protest; by and large they lack the funds to carry out properly the work that treasure-hunters do improperly.

Not all people who uncover long-hidden objects of value, of course, are on the criminal fringe of society. Apart from professional archaeologists, there are those who stumble by accident on pots of coins, torcs, brooches and other items of value; scarcely a week passes without some such find being reported in the press.

Why is it that so many valuable objects still lie concealed? Some were deliberately interred with the dead, and some were lost by accident, principally shipwreck. These categories we have already mentioned. Another motive for the hiding of treasure was fear:

> Just think: in those so frightful times
> When hordes the land o'erflooded, and its people,
> How this man, that man – as it frightened him –
> Did hide his treasure, hither and yon.
> Thus 'twas in powerful Roman days,
> And on to yesterday, e'en till today;
> And all this lieth buried in the earth.
>
> (Goethe, *Faust*)

Banks, vaults and safes are relatively modern inventions. Throughout the millennnia that went before, it was the common practice for men to secure their wealth by hiding it in the earth, in riverbeds, under stones, beneath floors, in marshes. War, rebellion, plague – all these provided dramatic reasons for the hiding of gold and silver. But they were not the only reasons. In uncertain times and times when life was simpler men kept their wealth in an easily portable form – coins, armlets, leg bangles, ingots – and what they could not carry about their person they concealed. It is not surprising that several of these caches remain where they were placed centuries ago, their owners having succumbed to peaceful or violent death, or flight.

Thus, the scope for a book like this one is vast. What I have tried to do is to bring together as much information as possible about the world's buried and sunken treasures. They fall basically into two categories: those that have been found and those that have not been found. The former category is relatively easy to deal with. I have gathered the information, located the treasure site on a map and, if the story is an interesting one, retold it. With undiscovered hoards many more imponderables come into play. Is this just an old wives' tale or could it be true? Is there any documentary evidence to support it? If this site has been known about for generations why has no one found the treasure? Is it possible that someone has found it and secretly removed it without disturbing the lengend . . . ? Here I have had to use my judgement in deciding whether or not to accord a particular hoard a place in the maps as a 'legendary treasure site'. Inevitably my opinion on this will not coincide with every reader's, and some will perhaps be disappointed not to discover their own favourite treasure story in these pages. Equally inevitably there will be some true stories that have slipped through the net of my research. All I can say is that I have tried to make this atlas not comprehensive but representative. I shall always be delighted to receive information about sites and treasures that do not appear in the book.

The greatest pleasure I have derived from writing *The World Atlas of Treasure* has been meeting and corresponding with large numbers of people who have had fascinating stories to tell and who have been extremely helpful in providing information. It would be quite impossible in the space available to acknowledge them all but there are some to whom special thanks are due. Karl Meyer, Caroline Beshers and Karen McKee provided valuable information from across the Atlantic, as did the Director of the Institute of Texan Cultures. David Allen was enormously helpful in allowing me to dip into his vast store of knowledge and experience of South African shipwrecks. Douglas King in Japan and A. L. Moore in Australia both opened up important areas of research to me. In this country I was inundated with information from scores of kind correspondents. Mr P. Brightman supplied many items from his own library of newspaper cuttings. J. R. M. Heppell opened up fascinating areas of local history, and Henry Cleere, Director of the Council for British Archaeology, gave me guidance on the vexed question of official versus unofficial excavation. In addition to these there were the staffs of museums, libraries and archive offices the world over.

A book such as this is obviously the result of teamwork and I have been fortunate in having a creative, industrious and sympathetic group of colleagues to work with: Faith Perkins, who scoured the world for pictures; Ken Smith who somehow turned my notes and jottings into accurate maps; Simon Bell who designed the book so splendidly; Hetty Thistlethwaite who coordinated all our efforts; and Kyle Cathie who masterminded the whole project. My wife, Ruth, as always, typed the script. My thanks to them all.

It remains only for me to let you read this chronicle full of examples of human bravery, corruption and folly

> As is the owse and bottom of the sea
> With sunken wreck and sumless treasuries . . .
>
> (Shakespeare, *Henry V*)

Treasures of the Tomb

Houses of the Dead

To be rich; to be immortal: there can be few who have not indulged one or both of those dreams. There have been whole civilizations which believed it possible to combine the two. Take, for example, the Etruscans.

Long before Rome had conquered most of the known world, in northern Italy flourished a sophisticated, commercially astute, luxury-loving people called the Etruscans. Much of their way of life is still a mystery to us because no one has yet been able to decipher the Etruscan language, but their way of death is very revealing. At the height of this civilization (*c.* 700–400 BC), the wealthy built dwellings to lie in after death similar to those they had occupied in life. Stone vaults – whole villages and towns of them – were built and, after occupation, covered by mounds of earth. The internal walls were painted with scenes from the lives of the dead. While bodies rapidly mouldered in elegant sarcophagi their owners were immortalized in funerary sculpture. Handsome ladies and gentlemen reclined in effigy on alabaster couches.

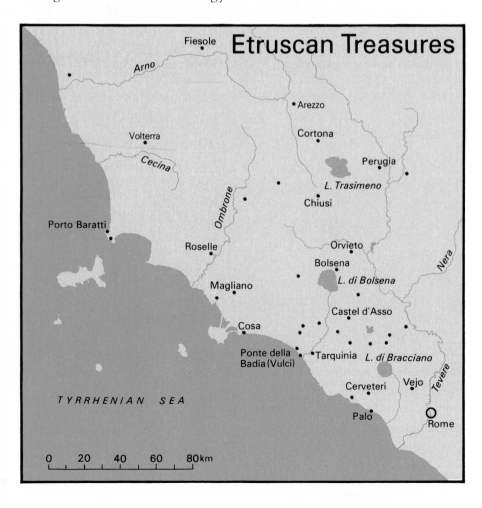

Etruscan Treasures

One of the most hauntingly beautiful treasures from antiquity is this woman's head modelled in clay, from an Etruscan temple. Greek influence here is obvious but the work has a warmth and naturalness which unmistakably declares its origin. Women had considerably more independence in Etruscan society than was allowed to their counterparts of Greece and Rome. This piece from the ancient town of Falerii dates from the third to second century BC.

One of the tombs in the large Etruscan cemetery of Cerveteri.

The work of Etruscan goldsmiths was both delicate and elaborate. This fourth- or third-century BC necklace has for its clasp two finely-carved lions' heads. It is now on display in the Metropolitan Museum of Art, New York.

It is the fascination of antiquities that they give us information about long-vanished civilizations. Items like this terracotta warrior may not strike some observers as beautiful but they command high prices on the international art market. Perhaps it is as well that they do for it is this that sometimes ensures their survival. Earlier generations of grave-robbers often destroyed such objects in their frenzied search for gold and silver.

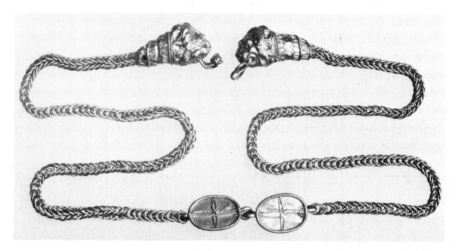

Also into their new homes the Etruscan dead took their household goods, tools, weapons and jewellery. Items of gold, silver, bronze, marble, and terracotta were packed in jars and boxes. The works of art were in a variety of styles but they all had a forthrightness and a vigour which distinguishes them quite clearly from other classical artefacts. There were silver mirror-backs engraved with mythological scenes; there were silver death masks; there were bronze statues of warriors, and even models of humble ploughmen; there were painted vases; there were golden goblets, rings, brooches, necklaces and earrings; there were elaborate incense burners and offerings. In short, below the soil of Tuscany lay a wealth of objects intrinsically valuable, and priceless as indicators of a lost civilization.

For Etruria was indeed a lost civilization for centuries. It was engulfed by Rome. It shared the neglect of all things ancient throughout the Middle Ages, and when the Renaissance rediscovered the classical world it remained overshadowed by the splendours of Greece and Rome. Unlike most tombs of antiquity, the deserted Etruscan tumuli were not persistently looted by grave-robbers. Occasionally a Tuscan peasant would break through into one of the chambers while ploughing. Such an incident was an occasion for annoyance rather than excitement. Stone slabs and pottery shards had to be cleared away so that the serious work of agriculture could continue. Not until the eighteenth century – epoch of the Enlightenment and the dilettante scholar – did the Etruscan civilization come under serious investigation. In 1728 amateur archaeologists excavated the necropolis and town of Volterra. To their amazement, they discovered a treasure house of artefacts that proved Volterra to be one of the greatest cities of the ancient world. Eagerly the sites were stripped. Jewellery, bronzes, pottery and statuettes were soon on their way to private and public collections all over Europe.

When the Princess of Canino attended embassy functions in Rome wearing two-thousand-year-old jewellery she created a sensation. All the ladies admired the chains of fine-spun gold, the chased ornament, the polished gemstones – work which, it was confidently declared, 'excelled the *chefs d'oeuvres* of Paris or Vienna'. Naturally they, too, pestered their husbands to acquire Etruscan trinkets. More of these beautiful antiquities were readily available, and their owner the Prince of Canino was quite prepared to supply them – at a price.

The Prince was none other than Lucien Bonaparte, brother of the Emperor Napoleon, and it was he who was responsible for the rape of Etruria. He lived a largely non-political life and concentrated on exploiting his North Italian estates. By far the most lucrative of his assets was the rich concentration of Etruscan tombs on his land. Bonaparte rifled every site and peddled his antiquities all over Europe.

In 1828 he had a stroke of good fortune. A peasant was ploughing his fields when the earth suddenly gave way beneath him and he found himself in a stone-built chamber, a subterranean house with decorated walls and furniture. When news of this new Etruscan site was brought to Bonaparte he came and personally supervised the excavation, if 'excavation' is the right word. The necropolis of Vulci, which was what had come to light, contained some six thousand graves. Most of these were systematically pillaged by the Prince. His only concern was the removal of saleable treasures. He cared nothing for Etruscan civilization and the gathering of information about it. This was made quite clear to the overseers supervising the teams of peasant labourers who dug into the tombs and brought out their contents. Each overseer kept his gun at the ready to deter the workmen from pocketing items of value. Bonaparte examined each piece that came out. Jewellery, painted pottery, curiously wrought vessels, bronze incense burners, statuary, golden bowls, swords, helmets and coins were carefully put on one side. Anything else, deemed to have no market value, was deliberately smashed and thrown into the excavation. Then all the earth was shovelled back, destroying human remains and causing irreparable damage to magnificent frescoes and decorated columns. Bonaparte disposed of thousands of beautiful, intriguing artefacts through dealers in Rome and directly to royal and noble customers who came to him from all over Europe. He made some attempt to control the flow of Etruscan goods on to the market but could scarcely avoid flooding it. Thousands of visitors came away from Italy with rare pieces of gold, bronze, terracotta or alabaster in their luggage for which they had paid very modest sums.

The trail pioneered by an emperor's brother has been well trodden by generations of treasure-hunters over the last century and a half, despite the efforts of the Italian authorities. When Dr Carlo Lerici, an eminent archaeologist, examined 550 tombs at Cerveteri he discovered that almost 400 had been looted.

Another piece which shows even more clearly the skill of Etruscan goldsmiths is this earring, dating from the third century BC. Thousands of similar pieces of exquisite jewellery were placed in the tombs of wealthy Etruscan ladies. Most of these tombs have been looted over the centuries and their precious contents have ended up in private or public collections. Some, unfortunately, have been melted down for their metal value.

Lucien Bonaparte was Napoleon's younger brother. At quite an early stage the two Corsicans fell out and Lucien played little part in his brother's empire building. Sufficient wealth and influence came his way to enable him to acquire considerable estates in Tuscany and to style himself 'Prince' of Canino.

The rich Etruscan culture shows itself in a wide variety of grave goods. Even those articles which now exist only in fragmentary form, such as these decorative motifs from a bronze urn, reveal the skill and imagination of the craftsmen who fashioned them over 2,300 years ago.

Inside an Etruscan tomb at Caere.

Trappings of Immortality

The Etruscans were not the only people whose beliefs about the afterlife encouraged them to think that they could take their worldly treasures with them. Although the interment of grave goods was by no means a universal practice in antiquity, it appears to have been a very common one ever since man emerged from a Neolithic hunter-gatherer into a settled farmer living in village and town communities.

Unlike his predecessors, man the settler became man the acquisitive. For survival he had to own and stake a permanent claim to an area of land where he could sow and reap. He had to be fiercely possessive in order to ward off other farming communities and nomadic neighbours who resented the 'earth-scratchers' and the restrictions they imposed on their lordship of the plains. As its population increased so did a society's needs – and wants. These were met by conquest.

> I extended all the boundaries of Egypt ... I slew the Denyen in their isles, the Tjeker and the Peleset were made ashes. The Shardana and the Weshesh of the sea, they were made as those that exist not, taken captive at one time, brought as captives to Egypt, like the sand of the shore. I settled them in strongholds bound in my name. Numerous were their classes like hundred-thousands. I taxed them all, in clothing and grain from the store-houses and granaries each year...

Such was the boast of Rameses III, and his words may stand as representative of the pride of all those ancient rulers who successfully dominated the lives and goods of millions of subjects. Conquering societies, or, at least, the wealthier sections of those societies, accumulated material possessions as the constant symbols of their power and prestige. Discerning patrons valued certain natural substances – gold, silver, cornelian, amethyst, lapis lazuli, turquoise, etc. – for their rarity, their innate beauty, and the yet more beautiful shapes and patterns into which they could be fashioned. They employed craftsmen to pander to their tastes. Clothes, weapons, furniture, cups, pots and all the necessities of life were

Many Han dynasty tombs are rich in clay figures like these tumblers (below left). By placing such effigies with the honoured dead, relatives believed they were ensuring constant entertainment for the departed.

Grave goods laid out in a Han dynasty tomb (below).

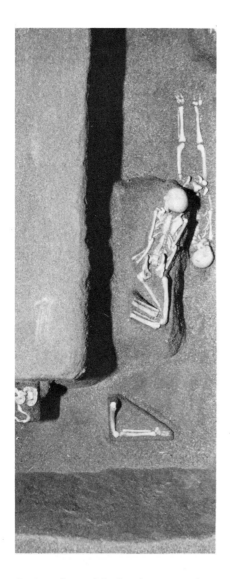

Section of a model of a Shang period royal tomb. The burial pit was dug up to seventy feet deep and had sloping roadways which slaves and servants used to go down to die and be buried with their royal master.

highly ornamented. Precious metal and stone went into the manufacture of elaborate necklaces, brooches and headdresses.

It was inconceivable to these people that all this acquisitive effort should have been for nothing. That at the end of a man's brief life he must leave behind for others to enjoy the material symbols of his wealth and importance, the very expressions of his personality. So they conceived of the next world as an extension of and an improvement upon this one.

For Viking warriors, heaven was Valhalla, the palace of Odin, where brave men feasted daily with the god and kept themselves in training for Ragnarök, the final battle. Of course, they took their gold-hilted swords and their embossed shields with them to the hall of the war god.

A more sophisticated belief seems to have pertained in Minoan Crete. The *tholos* graves at Kamilari were above ground, domed mausolea used as places of interment for families or clans. Each body was laid with its head towards the east, accompanied by personal adornments and necessities, some of them valuable and beautifully wrought. But later generations seem to have had no compunction about shovelling bones unceremoniously out of the way to make room for new occupants, or about removing grave goods. Presumably, after the corpse had decomposed its owner was supposed to have entered the spirit realm and to have taken with him 'in spirit' all his treasured possessions.

In some societies religious beliefs demanded that priests or members of the deceased's family be allowed access to his tomb. In 1927 archaeologists investigating Ur, the great Sumerian city (in modern Iraq), came upon the grave of King A-bar-gi, who ruled in about 3000 BC. The chamber contained the bodies of sixty-three servants and courtiers who had voluntarily accompanied their lord to the next world. The grave had been looted, but apparently the thieves had only had time for a hurried visit. Adornments and vessels of gold, lapis lazuli and precious stones glowed and twinkled in the lamplight. One important item, however,

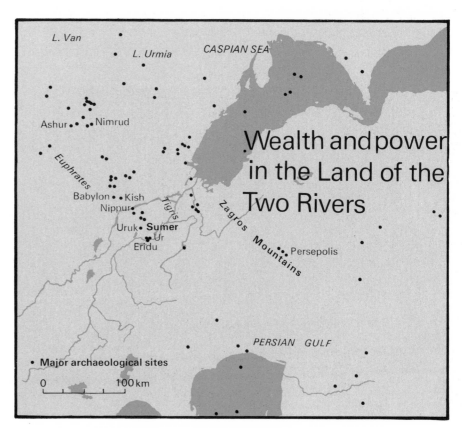

was missing: the body of the King. But A-bar-gi was not the victim of some macabre theft; the Sumerians believed that after death their sovereign achieved divinity and was united with the sun god. After a prescribed period of time, therefore, the priests broke into the tomb and symbolically passed the royal corpse out into the realm of eternal light.

The story of the excavation of the royal tombs of Ur is one of the most remarkable in the history of archaeology – remarkable both for the treasure unearthed and the professionalism of the archaeologist who discovered it. Sir Leonard Woolley led the team which began excavation at Tell el Muqayyar, to the west of the Euphrates, in 1922. Working in the graveyard of the old city, his men came upon a set of walled tombs towards the end of the first season's dig. They were obviously of an early date and potentially of great importance. Most archaeologists would have pressed ahead eagerly. Woolley marked the area on his site map, filled in the trenches and proceeded to dig elsewhere. Not for five years did he return to the spot where, he felt sure, remains and grave goods of enormous importance were awaiting discovery.

Most magnificent of all Sir Leonard Woolley's finds at Ur was the golden helmet of Mes-kalam-dug. Fashioned rather like a wig, it shows in fine detail a headband and long hair, plaited round the head and tied in a knot at the back.

Sir Leonard Woolley's excavations into the great Tell at Ur in the 1920s extended over many years. Centuries of blown sand had to be removed as the archaeologist descended to the outline of houses, temples and tombs that were the remains of a once great city.

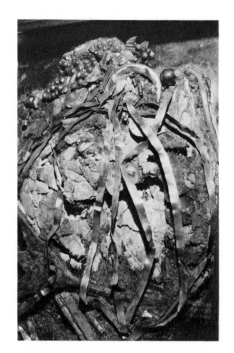

Careful excavation in the tomb of Queen Shub-ad at Ur revealed this exquisite headdress. Even in the fragmentary form in which it was found it was impressive. Skilfully reconstructed, it could be seen in its full glory: strips of gold to which were fixed golden flowers inlaid with white enamel.

One of Woolley's more remarkable finds was the 'Standard of Ur', a mosaic of lapis lazuli, red limestone and pearl. The wooden frame that had originally held it had long-since rotted and it was an arduous task retrieving the pattern intact. The story depicted in the plaque, which resembled a banner, was of soldiers going to war and returning victorious.

His action was not a gesture of pointless self-abnegation. Woolley knew that his Arab workforce was not yet fully trained in the handling of delicate, fragile artefacts wrought five thousand years before by Sumerian craftsmen. He knew that he had yet to win their complete loyalty. He knew that a partial excavation would release a flood of stories and rumours about great buried wealth and bring a horde of rival archaeologists and treasure-seekers to Tell el Muqayyar. He must wait until his team had the necessary expertise to be able to complete work on the royal tombs (as he suspected they were) in one season.

The staggering series of finds he made in the winter of 1927 proved Woolley's wisdom beyond measure. The first tomb he entered was that of a warrior prince – Mes-kalam-dug. In the centre of the chamber was a coffin studded with beads and precious stones. Around it were weapons of copper with gold mounts and lapis-lazuli ornamentation, bowls of silver, jugs and urns of alabaster and terracotta which had once held offerings of food and wine. Staggering as these finds were, objects of even more breathtaking beauty lay inside the coffin. The body had been laid to rest wearing a silver belt from which a gold dagger hung. Bowls of gold, earrings, bracelets, amulets, lamps and an axe all lay beside him. Ready to hand was his golden helmet, beautifully fashioned in the form of a wig tied around with a woven band.

Yet all this was only a prelude to the discoveries that were to come. Woolley's men now uncovered shafts leading to the complex of tombs built for King A-bar-gi and his queen, Shub-ad. The corridors contained the remains of richly decorated men and women, servants who voluntarily accompanied their sovereign to the next world. Carriages were also ready to transport the royal couples on their journey. The remains of the oxen and asses which had drawn these highly decorated vehicles were still there, slaughtered within the tomb in order to continue rendering in death the service they had given in life. The carts themselves were piled with more tools, weapons and vessels of precious metal and alabaster. One of the most beautiful finds was a harp or lyre, much decayed but still bearing a sounding-box sparkling with red and blue mosaic and a bull's head boss of gold with beard and eyes of lapis lazuli. There were two

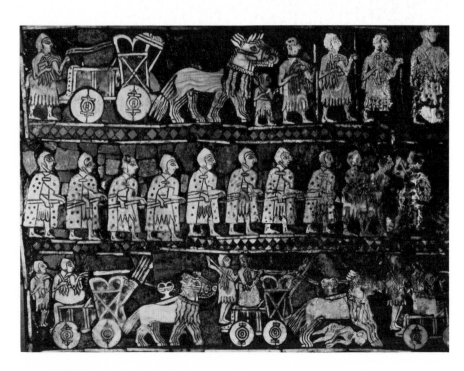

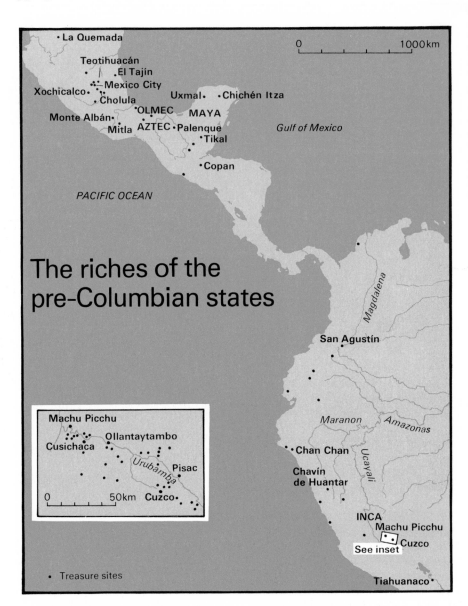

The riches of the pre-Columbian states

La Quemada
Teotihuacán
El Tajín
Mexico City
Xochicalco
Cholula
OLMEC
MAYA
Uxmal
Chichén Itza
Monte Albán
Mitla
AZTEC
Palenque
Tikal
Gulf of Mexico
Copan

PACIFIC OCEAN

Magdalena

San Agustín

Maranon
Amazonas

Chan Chan
Ucayali
Chavín
de Huantar

INCA
Machu Picchu
See inset
Cuzco

Tiahuanaco

0 1000km

Machu Picchu
Ollantaytambo
Cusichaca
Urubamba
Pisac
0 50km
Cuzco

• Treasure sites

The religion of the ancient Egyptians required the preservation of the body after death so that it could one day rise from the dead and live again. The mummy here shows the skill of the embalmers who were a combination of surgeons and priests. The process required the removal of the organs through a slit in the left side and their preservation with natron.

high-prowed boats modelled in silver and a curiously wrought gaming board. The king's tomb had suffered from a visitation by grave-robbers at some time but Queen Shub-ad had been protected from such desecration by the collapse of the tomb chamber roof. When stones and dust had been painstakingly removed the royal skeleton was discovered lying on an open bier. The fabric of her richly ornamented clothing had long since rotted but the body was surrounded with a profusion of beads, gold pins and semi-precious stones. There were two elaborate headdresses, one of golden flowers with inlaid petals of white; the other had a row of exquisitely fashioned golden animals – stags, gazelles, bulls and goats – leaves, fruit and flowers against a radiant background of lapis lazuli.

Sixteen such royal graves were eventually excavated, all of which added to the immense haul of buried treasure. More important, they added enormously to our knowledge of the culture and beliefs of ancient Sumeria. Here was a civilization which held its ruler and its gods in such awe that men and women counted it a privilege to serve in life and death. Hundreds of them, some mere children, adorned themselves in their finest clothes and processed into the darkness of the tomb, chanting and playing harps. There they drank poisoned wine, and as the potent drug overcame them, they passed peacefully and joyfully into eternity.

Access of the living to the gilded resting places of the dead was

Inca Death Palaces
The Incas of Peru believed in a two-way contact between this world and the next. Good people went to Hanac-paca, the realm of the sun, and took with them the tools of their trade as well as their most treasured possessions. Yet they also maintained contact with their descendants. Regularly their mummified bodies were brought out from their tombs. Their counsel was sought through their kinsmen and descendants. So richly were the 'death palaces' of Inca rulers and others equipped, and so great was the waste of precious metal on them, that the empire was eventually faced with a grave economic crisis. Respect for and fear of the spirits of the dead were apparently so strong that no one seriously thought of recovering treasure from the tombs.

unusual. Most societies went to elaborate lengths to preserve the graves of their rulers and great men from violation. The people of the Colombian highlands, where the legend of El Dorado originated, buried the wealthy dead in chambers at the foot of deep shafts. When the mummified body and its grave goods had been placed in position, the chamber was sealed and the shaft filled with earth and rock, thus concealing from the gaze and cupidity of men the golden diadems, pendants, grotesque masks, pectorals, nose ornaments, emerald necklaces, and other examples of craftsmanship which seem to western eyes bizarre but strangely compelling.

The successive pre-Columbian cultures of Central America practised a variety of inhumation rights, but thousands of tombs exist containing artefacts of great variety and beauty. Tomb robbers are constantly occupied in locating and rifling these sites. For example, in 1969–70 an Olmec cemetery was discovered, which brought on to the international art market thirty-two jade masks, three mirrors, various carved figures, and over a thousand jade implements dating from about 1200 BC.

Splendours of the Boy King

The incredible wealth of the pharaohs was revealed to an astonished twentieth century with the discovery of Tutankhamen's virtually undisturbed tomb in 1922. Until then archaeologists and historians had only been able to guess at the riches enjoyed by ancient Egypt's rulers. Contemporary literature as well as occasional finds amid the debris of long-ransacked rock and pyramid tombs hinted at the wealth accumulated by trade and conquest throughout an area extending from India to the Pillars of Hercules.

The many thousands of tombs which survive from the period of ancient Egyptian greatness (*c.* 3000–*c.* 1000 BC) reveal two apparently contradictory facts: these people were obsessed with death and the need to provide for the comfort and well-being of the departed; yet, at the same time, large numbers of them were involved in robbing tombs and were thereby jeopardizing those who had gone to the next world.

The afterlife beliefs of the Egyptians were complex and developed gradually over the centuries. Put very simply, the faith, as it had emerged by the time of the New Kingdom, was as follows: man is made up of body; *ka,* which we may loosely interpret as spirit; and *ba* or moral sense. These three had to be held together after death. For this reason, bodies were embalmed and mummified, and food and drink were placed alongside them in the tomb. Also lifelike statues of the dead were placed inside or outside the burial chamber to assist the *ka* in locating the body. Since life hereafter was a continuation of life here it was but a short step from providing the body with food to equipping it with everything else necessary for a full and happy existence. Thus, as time went by, tombs (especially those of the wealthy – royalty, nobility, officials and priests) became larger and more elaborate. The table below indicates, roughly, the main stages of development.

BC

3000–2700	Early dynastic period	Simple inhumation. Early burial chambers
2700–2200	Old Kingdom	Pyramid
2200–2000	Intermediate period (a time of foreign invasion)	
1991–1778	Middle Kingdom	Elaborate burial chambers and temple complexes
1778–1550	Intermediate period (more foreign invaders, principally the Hyksos)	
1570–1310	Dynasty XVIII ⎫ New	Cliff tombs in the Valley
1310–1200	Dynasty XIX ⎭ Kingdom	of the Kings
1180–1066	Dynasty XX	

Originally bodies were laid in simple graves in the dry desert sand, which acted as an excellent preservative, but later more sophisticated beliefs made it necessary to build an underground chamber. Here the body and grave goods were laid. Then the entrance was sealed and the shaft which gave access to it was filled in. Over the tomb a *mastaba* was erected. This

The Wealth of the Pharaohs

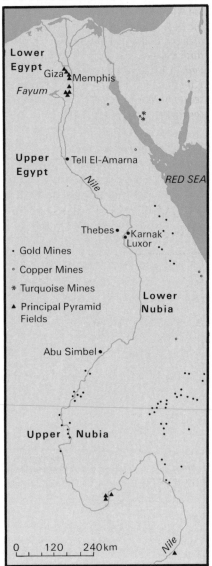

Western Thebes had long since been the resting place of Egypt's kings, aristocrats and priests but the tomb cut into cliffs close to the Nile had proved too vulnerable to robbers so the rulers of the New Kingdom elected to have themselves interred in a new location further from the river. The complex of valleys known as the Valley of the Kings would, it was thought, be more secure in that it could be policed by a comparatively small force of men.

The inner sarcophagus containing Tutankhamen's coffin.

Royal Tombs of Thebes

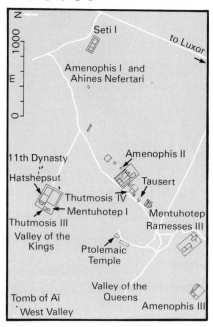

was a stone structure containing the statue of the deceased and rooms decorated with wall paintings where the *ka* could take its ease. Space was also made for a shrine. The pyramids of the Old and Middle Kingdoms are an extension of the *mastaba* idea, the burial chambers being either within or beneath the massive stone structures. Temple complexes were attached to the pyramids and *mastabas* of the great, and funds were provided for the perpetual offering of worship on behalf of the dead.

Despite the most elaborate attempts to stop thieves rifling the tombs and removing their treasure, every single one (as far as we know) was broken into, probably within a short period of the burial. It was probably for this reason that Pharaoh Thutmose I initiated a new custom. Instead of having his tomb built in the great royal necropolis at Thebes he ordered a secret grave to be tunnelled out of the hillside in the lonely valley of Biban el-Moluk, now known as the Valley of the Kings. He thus separated his tomb and mortuary chapel, which must have created problems for his *ka* but would, he hoped, preserve his treasure. His example was followed by his successors, but the ruse did not thwart the highly professional robbers. The time came when the royal sarcophagi of the Valley of the Kings lay alone amid the chaos of overturned furniture and broken pots left by thieves who had removed everything of intrinsic value. Some desecrators even daubed the walls with defiant graffiti before leaving the scene of the crime. The confession of one robber who was caught gives us only a fleeting glimpse of the enormously valuable plunder carried off from just one tomb. He describes how he and his seven accomplices opened the sarcophagus and

> found the august mummy of this pharaoh … There were several strings of amulets and ornaments of gold at its throat. Its head had a mask of gold upon it. The … mummy … was completely overlaid with gold. Its coverings were fashioned of gold and silver … and set with every type of costly stone. We stripped off the gold … amulets and ornaments … and the covering … We found the pharaoh's wife. We stripped off all that we found on her. We set fire to their coverings. We stole their furniture, which we found with them, being vases of gold, silver and bronze …

The ancient art of tomb-robbing received a new lease of life in the sixteenth century of our era. From then onwards an increasing number of wealthy Europeans visited Egypt, eager to see the remains of an ancient civilization and to bring home curiosities for their collections. Local initiative scoured the crevices of the long-ruined tombs to produce scarabs, rings, amulets, pottery and statuettes for the dilettante collectors to put into their private galleries. By the early nineteenth century, the age of the amateur archaeologist had arrived. With virtually no official restrictions on their activities, enthusiasts from Germany, France, Britain and America processed to the Valley of the Kings and hired labourers who plied picks and shovels until the floor of the valley was feet deep in rubble. By the beginning of the present century it was confidently asserted in archaeological circles that every tomb in the area had been opened and thoroughly examined. The pharaohs had no more secrets.

That was the situation when in 1917 Howard Carter, colleague of the wealthy enthusiast Lord Carnarvon, set to work to find the tomb of Tutankhamen, an insignificant king who ruled briefly in the mid-fourteenth century BC. Carter had seen a faience cup and various other items belonging to Tutankhamen which an earlier American archae-ologist, Theodore Davis, had found. Since this pharaoh's resting place had not been recorded, Carter assumed that it was still awaiting discovery. With little more than this hunch to go on, he began work. Six years later his men had found nothing. With Carnarvon's approval, Carter resolved upon one last season's work.

He explored a pile of rubble below the entrance to the tomb of Rameses VI and immediately came upon a series of steps. These led down to a door which was still sealed. He had a small hole broken in the door and shone a torch inside. He saw that the corridor beyond was filled

This elaborate alabaster vase with incised decoration stands 50 cm high and is one of about fifty which were placed in Tutankhamen's tomb and which contained sweet-smelling unguents. Almost all of them had been emptied by grave-robbers who had not bothered with objects of gold and gems lying to hand. Presumably the perfumed oils were equally valuable and more easily disposable.

The dead appear to walk in this picture which shows a carved head of the pharaoh being carried from the excavation by one of Howard Carter's workmen.

In Egyptian mythology the scarab was a symbol for the sun god. In this magnificent necklace of lapis lazuli, cornelian, felspar and turquoise in a gold setting, the scarab is shown pushing the sun before it.

The god Ptah was one of the more important members of the Egyptian pantheon and was regarded in some traditions as the original creator. This wooden statue (52.8 cm high) is covered in gold and has a skull cap of dark blue faience.

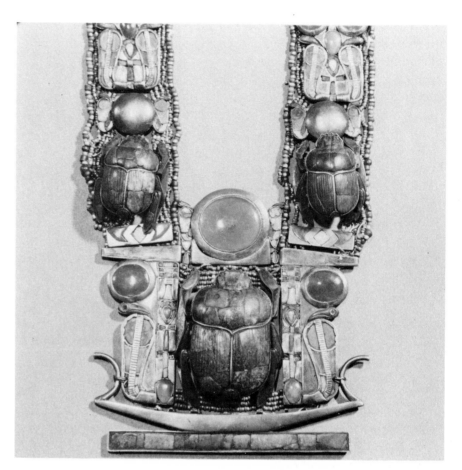

with boulders – exactly as it would have been by the priests who first filled it to protect it from intruders. Carter immediately telegraphed Carnarvon: 'AT LAST HAVE MADE WONDERFUL DISCOVERY IN VALLEY. A MAGNIFICENT TOMB WITH SEALS INTACT. RE-COVERED SAME FOR YOUR ARRIVAL. CONGRATULATIONS.' He then had an agonizing wait of three weeks while his colleague travelled from England. When he was able to resume, his hopes were immediately dashed: there were signs that this grave had been visited by robbers. At last the excavators were on the brink of discovery or disappointment. Carter made another hole and thrust a candle inside. Carnarvon and others crowded around him. 'Can you see anything?' they inquired. 'Yes,' breathed the awestruck archaeologist, 'wonderful things.'

Carter and Carnarvon discovered a four-chamber complex. The central object was a shrine, 5 m × 4 m × 3.5 m, covered in gold, inlaid with faience. Within lay three similar gilded shrines, one inside another, before the yellow quartzite sarcophagus was revealed. Within that lay a coffin covered with an effigy of pure gold decorated with lapis lazuli, aragonite and obsidian. Around the shrine and in the other chambers were stacked hundreds upon hundreds of precious objects – a gilded throne, four chariots overlaid with gold, statues clothed in gold, couches, dishes and ewers, toys and ornaments, vases of polychromed glass and, within the folds of the mummy itself, 143 pieces of jewellery.

Today this treasure gleams in the glare of electric lights in Cairo Museum, never failing to impress visitors, none of whom has ever seen anything so splendid. Yet it raises in the mind one last question: if this represents the wealth of an eighteen-year-old king who died after a mere six years as a puppet ruler, would not the wealth with which any of the really great pharaohs was laid to rest have been far more impressive?

Marching to Eternity

The largest and most extraordinary tomb of antiquity so far discovered is in the valley of China's Yellow River. It was found accidentally by peasants digging a well in 1974 and is still in the process of excavation. Yet what has already been revealed is quite staggering. The burial place of the Emperor Ch'in Shih Huang-ti, builder of the Great Wall, is a fifty-metre mound known as Mount Li. But the chamber itself is at the heart of a complex that dwarfs the pyramids in the extravagance of its conception. An area perhaps six and a half kilometres square was dug out in the third century BC and peopled with an immense procession – thousands of soldiers, servants, wagons and horses – all made of terracotta. Each figure was modelled from the life and its features carefully painted. We know from an early written account just what was involved in this massive operation:

> As soon as the First Emperor became king of Chin, excavations and building had been started at Mount Li, while after he won the empire more than seven hundred thousand conscripts from all parts of the country worked there. They dug through three subterranean streams and poured molten copper for the outer coffin, and the tomb was filled with models of palaces, pavilions and offices, as well as fine vessels, precious stones and rarities ... All the country's streams, the Yellow River and the Yangtse were reproduced in quicksilver and by some mechanical means made to flow into a miniature ocean. The heavenly constellations were shown above and the regions of the earth below. The candles were made of whale oil to ensure their burning for the longest possible time after the burial and sealing up of the treasures, the middle gate was shut and the outer gate closed to imprison all the artisans and labourers, so that no one came out. Trees and grass were planted over the mausoleum to make it seem like a hill.

Every effort was made to ensure that the Emperor's journey to the next world should not be interrupted. Crossbow booby traps were set up within the passages around the burial chamber. Before the tomb was finally sealed all those who had worked on it and who knew its secrets were walled up inside. Finally trees and grass were planted on the mound to make it look like a hill. Despite all these precautions looters broke into the complex within years of its completion. Archaeologists found many of the figures disturbed or broken, objects removed and the timber roof and walls burned to cover the robbers' traces.

Yet enough items have been found to give a foretaste of the incredible treasure partly described by the chronicler – ornaments of gold and jade, bronze swords, pottery, iron implements, even fragments of linen and silk.

It will be years before the excavations are completed and we know for certain whether or not Shih Huang-ti's tomb itself has been violated. If not, one of the greatest treasures of the ancient world is certain to come to light. For the founder of modern China wielded enormous power and commanded vast wealth. Whatever items of intrinsic worth, rarity and craftsmanship he wanted, he took. And what he took he intended to enjoy for eternity. That is why he devoted much of his attention over thirty-six years to the building of his tomb. It is also why an army several thousands strong accompanied him on his march to eternity.

Shih Huang-ti was the ruler of Ch'in, one of many feudal states in eastern Asia. By persistent and ruthless warfare he had made himself master of a vast empire by 221 BC. He ruled that empire as a tyrant, completing the construction of the Great Wall (at a cost, it is said, of a million lives) to keep out enemies, destroying possible rivals, creating a large, impressive centralized government. He lived in constant fear of assassination and was always on the move. However, he died peacefully on one of his journeys and was laid to rest in the enormous tomb he had had built. Like many despots, he was highly superstitious, and the tomb, like his many palaces, was built to principles established by astrology and magic.

Shih Huang-ti's terracotta army extending 70 metres by 140 metres consists of at least 6,000 life-size figures and 100 horse-drawn chariots (perhaps many more). It was probably created to replace the ancient custom of burying the ruler with live attendants. Perhaps even the bloodthirsty Shih Huang-ti baulked at such wholesale slaughter, though more likely he could not afford to sacrifice his army. Below, an aerial view of the site; the circular enlargement indicates how the columns are composed of horses, chariots and foot soldiers.

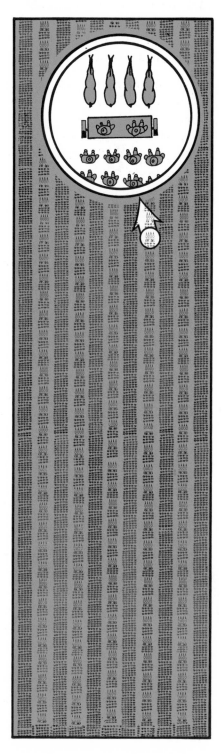

Jade Panoply

The vast country we know today as China achieved its political shape very slowly. For long periods of time much of it was ruled as a unified whole by strong emperors, but at other epochs it was divided among warring feudal states. Yet certain features were constant. The ruling castes possessed themselves of great wealth. Much of this wealth they took with them into the realm of death.

Until the middle of the nineteenth century China was a closed country; little was known about its history or culture. The development of commercial and diplomatic links with the West encouraged the inevitable looting of ancient graves to supply the international art market. It was not until the establishment of the People's Republic that a serious programme of archaeological research was set in motion. Already this has brought back into the light of day a large quantity of buried treasures which now make it possible to survey over five thousand years of the cultural development of a remarkable people. That development is astonishingly smooth. If we take, for example, the growth of Chinese ceramic art we find that it had its beginnings in the late Stone Age. Already in the fifth millennium BC pottery bowls and vases were being fired in simple but beautiful shapes. Many of them were painted, and an amphora of c. 2200 BC carries a representation of the dragon which was to be so important in Chinese art and myth. A few hundred years later potters of Shantung province were creating three-legged vessels whose lines clearly derived their inspiration from the animal world. It is not an enormous leap to the beautiful horses and camels so often found in tombs of the Han and T'ang dynasties. By this time craftsmen had mastered the techniques of glazing their wares. The steady development of these skills resulted in the delicate, gleaming, multicoloured porcelain of the Ming dynasty.

Pottery, even some of the more elaborate pieces, was for everyday use. Raw metal was in short supply, and expensive. For serving the spirits, however, pottery was inadequate. For that purpose bronze was used. This metal was introduced during the Shang dynasty and almost immediately Chinese bronzesmiths attained a high degree of skill which allowed them to express a soaring imagination. Leaders of Shang society were buried in cross-shaped underground vaults and most of their kings had their tombs at Yin, the capital. Their religion demanded that all ceremonies be performed with complete precision. If ancient forms were not followed to the letter, they believed, the harmony of earth and heaven would be upset, with evil consequences. Thus, undisturbed graves of the period are rich in ritual implements and vessels of bronze. The object known as a *kuang*, for example, was a jug in the form of a grotesque animal which was used for mixing wine during funeral and other ceremonies. These rites involved the sacrifice of animals, usually bulls, and this is alluded to in the blunted horns often found on the *kuangs*. The tradition of exuberant yet rigidly disciplined workmanship in bronze continued over the centuries, reaching its peak in such items as the ring and mask coffin handle from Yi-hsien which dates from the mid fifth century BC.

Many people would say that out of the profusion of superb treasures from ancient China, the most beautiful are the horses. Cavalry warfare (as opposed to fighting from chariots) was introduced to China about

The Jade Princess

Jade, so the Taoist magicians believed, possessed many wondrous properties. Among other things it could prevent the decay of the body after death. Many wealthy Chinese, therefore, made sure that they were buried with articles of the semi-precious stone. But Prince Liu Sheng and his wife Tou Wan went much further. When they died in the second century BC their bodies were entirely encased in jade. The princess's suit was made up of 2,160 plaques fastened together with gold wire. The suit of Liu Sheng, son of Emperor Ching (pictured here) was even larger. The twin tombs were shafts cut into a hillside at Man-ch'eng, south of Peking. When archaeologists opened them in 1968, they discovered, as well as the spectacular jade suits, 2,800 objects of bronze, jade and pottery. Among the more beautiful objects were four parcel-gilt bronze leopards inlaid with silver and garnets. They were probably used as weights at the four corners of the princess's funeral pall. There were many other representations of animals: bronze daggers and swords; ornate lamps, some in the form of animals; vases of bronze, intricately inlaid with gold and silver; painted dishes and plates, fretted censers, jade rings and tablets; in fact, everything that had been placed in the tombs over two thousand years ago was still there – except the prince and princess. Of their bodies there was little trace. The magnificent jade suits had fallen inwards as the corpses disintegrated, to lie finally flat and unoccupied on the rock floor. The magicians were wrong.

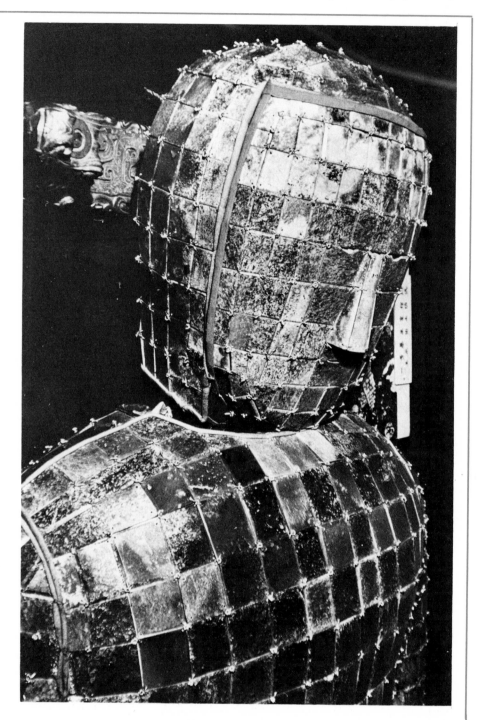

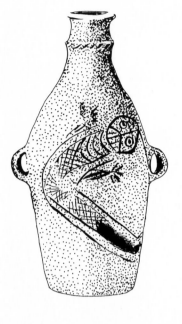

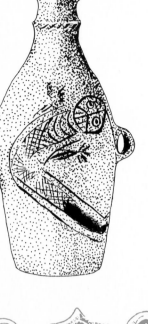

Civilizations of Ancient China		
	Principal states and dynasties	*Cultural characteristics*
7000–1600 BC	Neolithic	Painted and turned pottery
1600–1027 BC	Shang dynasty	Bronze tools and ritual objects
1027–771 BC	Western Chou dynasty	Glazed pottery
771–221 BC	Warring feudal states	Highly intricate bronzes, use of silver and gold inlay
221–206 BC	Ch'in dynasty	Animal models in bronze and pottery
206 BC–8 AD	Western Han dynasty	Magnificent bronze horses, intricate jade work
24–220 AD	Eastern Han dynasty	Spread of Buddhism
220–580 AD	Division of the empire into dynastic states	
580–618 AD	Sui dynasty	Glazed and unglazed pottery horses, porcelain
618–906 AD	T'ang dynasty	
907–960 AD	Division of the empire into dynastic states	
960–1279 AD	Sung dynasty	Highly glazed pottery and porcelain
1280–1368 AD	Yüan dynasty (Mongols)	Very fine, highly ornate porcelain
1368–1644 AD	Ming dynasty	Blue and red coloured porcelain, lacquered furniture, cloisonné enamel work, great influence of Chinese art in Europe

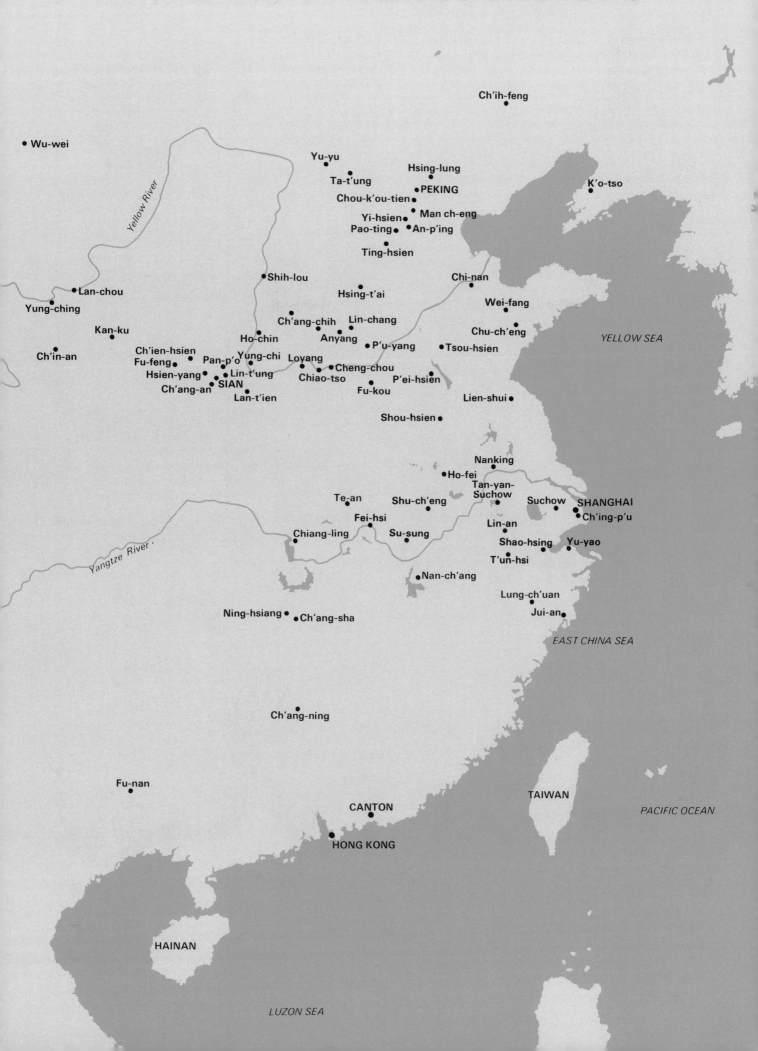

Treasure of ancient China

Wu-wei

Yellow River

Lan-chou

Yung-ching

Kan-ku

Ch'in-an

Ch'ih-feng

Yu-yu

Ta-t'ung

Hsing-lung

PEKING

Chou-k'ou-tien

Yi-hsien

Man ch-eng

Pao-ting

An-p'ing

Ting-hsien

K'o-tso

Shih-lou

Hsing-t'ai

Chi-nan

Wei-fang

YELLOW SEA

Ch'ang-chih

Lin-chang

Ho-chin

Anyang

P'u-yang

Chu-ch'eng

Ch'ien-hsien

Yung-chi

Tsou-hsien

Fu-feng

Pan-p'o

Loyang

Cheng-chou

Hsien-yang

Lin-t'ung

Chiao-tso

P'ei-hsien

Ch'ang-an

SIAN

Fu-kou

Lan-t'ien

Lien-shui

Shou-hsien

Nanking

Ho-fei

Tan-yan-

Suchow

Te-an

Shu-ch'eng

Suchow

SHANGHAI

Fei-hsi

Lin-an

Ch'ing-p'u

Chiang-ling

Su-sung

Shao-hsing

Yu-yao

T'un-hsi

Nan-ch'ang

Lung-ch'uan

Ning-hsiang

Ch'ang-sha

Jui-an

Yangtze River

EAST CHINA SEA

Ch'ang-ning

Fu-nan

TAIWAN

PACIFIC OCEAN

CANTON

HONG KONG

HAINAN

LUZON SEA

500 BC but it was another four hundred years before a superior type of horse was introduced. This was as a result of an expedition to the Oxus valley far to the west. A few of the large, fiery animals of that region were brought back and proved immediately to be superior to the smaller horses from the steppes which had been used until that time. The slow process of breeding now began. For very many years fine war horses were in short supply and highly prized by the warrior nobility of China. Therefore their animals accompanied them to the spirit world – in effigy. Tombs of the Han and T'ang dynasties abound in models of horses – some in unglazed terracotta, some in bronze, some, perhaps the most typical, in boldly painted and glazed pottery. Many were quite small but they were made in all dimensions up to life size. The tomb of General Ho Ch'ü-ping, for example, was guarded by two full-size stone chargers. Horses are depicted in a variety of positions – hunting, playing polo, pulling light carts and chariots – yet all representations reveal a real love and knowledge of the animal. It is small wonder that these figures are highly prized by modern collectors and fetch large sums of money.

Some of the finest examples of pottery horses and other T'ang artefacts come from the tomb of the nineteen-year-old Princess Yung T'ai at Ch'ien-hsien. A sad story lies behind this particular interment. According to the ancient chroniclers, Yung T'ai was executed for unwittingly offending her grandmother, the empress. Moreover, her husband was

Here is an example of comparatively rare Chinese work in precious metal. This eighth-century silver-gilt cup shows considerable Sassanian influence.

The horse was virtually worshipped by noblemen of the Han dynasties. The animals introduced from Central Asia were called 'celestial horses' because of their strength, stamina, speed and grace. All these qualities have been captured by the bronzesmith in this figure of a flying horse, symbolically standing on a swallow. This justly famous work was discovered in a tomb at Wu-wei in 1969.

Glazed pottery camels of the T'ang dynasty. These beautiful models remind us of the growing commerce between imperial China and the lands further west. China trains passed to and fro along the 'silk road' carrying the fine examples of Chinese workmanship to the Levant and Europe.

Whether working in bronze or stone the Chinese craftsmen managed to combine a sense of the intricate with the massive. In this fifth century AD stone pedestal, unearthed in 1966, musicians, dragons, tigers and lotus flowers combine in an elaborate design.

obliged to share the poor girl's fate. Only when Yung T'ai's father ascended the throne were the royal couple accorded a state funeral. They were laid to rest in an underground chamber beneath a twelve-metre mound. After they and their grave goods had been placed in position, the sloping passage leading to the vault was blocked and the young people were left in peace. But not for long: within years, perhaps months, tomb-robbers were at work, digging a tunnel into the mound. Fortunately, they were disturbed at their work. Excavators entering the mausoleum in 1964 found most of the grave goods intact, amidst evidence of plunder and violence. Following the robbers' tunnel to the heart of the tomb, they came upon the sprawled skeleton of one of the thieves. From that point to the chamber itself lay a trail of silver and pottery objects. It requires little imagination to reconstruct the scene of panic within the dim, torchlit corridor as royal guards rushed in upon the wretched malefactors. Thanks to that intervention the twentieth-century visitors to the tomb came upon a spectacular collection of eighth-century AD treasures. There were ritual vessels of bronze and silver and no less than 837 terracotta figures – horses, camels, soldiers, huntsmen, servants and courtiers.

Supplies of precious metal and gemstones were poor in ancient China and reached the empire largely by way of trade. This explains why even the work of native goldsmiths shows considerable foreign influence. However, the skill and artistry of Chinese craftsmen turned materials less intrinsically valuable into treasures no less real.

The Grave of a Hero King

Most archaeologists would be content to make one major *coup* in their professional lifetime. Heinrich Schliemann made two. He is most famous for the discovery of Troy (see below page 154). Yet fresh from his triumphant discovery of Priam's Treasure he began excavations at Mycenae on the Greek mainland. There were at least two good reasons for selecting this site. Mycenae was the capital of Agamemnon, the king who according to Homer conquered Troy. Schliemann hoped to locate the graves of the legendary ruler and his family. Mycenae was also reputed by the ancient writers to be 'rich in gold'.

Schliemann began digging in what transpired to be the royal grave circle. In one season he uncovered and stripped five tombs, revealed the famous Lion Gate and partially excavated other areas. But it was the shaft graves that really excited Schliemann, and with reason. In November 1876 he was able to report to the King of the Hellenes:

> With great joy I announce to Your Majesty that I have discovered the tombs that tradition ... claimed as the sepulchres of Agamemnon, Cassandra, Eurymedon and their comrades all killed during the banquet by Clytemnestra and her lover Aegisthus. I have found in the tombs enormous treasures comprising ancient objects of pure gold. These treasures will be sufficient in themselves to fill a large museum which will be the most marvellous in the world and which throughout centuries to come will bring to Greece thousands of visitors from every country.

It was the most magnificent collection of antique gold, silver, bronze and pottery that the world had seen up to that time. There were cups and goblets, faience vases and jugs, bronze weapons, earrings, necklaces, helmets, crowns and diadems, hundreds of embossed gold plates and buttons, alabaster bowls, rings and armlets. Most remarkable of all were the heavy gold face masks worn by some of the bodies.

Unfortunately, objective research rules out Schliemann's identification of the bodies at Mycenae with Agamemnon and his comrades. The great archaeologist achieved some magnificent feats but he had his faults. One was his determination to use excavation to 'prove Homer right'. Having found his richly adorned graves in the right place he was convinced beyond all doubt about the identity of the remains. Regrettably, he was so anxious to remove the treasure that he destroyed much valuable evidence in the process. The skeletons themselves crumbled to dust as a result of sudden exposure to the air. However, enough has survived at Mycenae to enable scholars to fix the date of grave circle A at *c.* 1550 BC, roughly three hundred years before the time of the semi-mythical Agamemnon.

Discarding the Homeric origins of the Mycenae treasure, however, only leaves us with an unanswered question: who were these wealthy rulers? The graves contained a great wealth of precious metal which has never been mined in southern Greece. The workmanship showed Minoan influence, yet there was no direct contact at this time between Crete and the inland Greek state. It seems, then, that Mycenae was already powerful, dominating its mainland neighbours, who *did* have trading links with Crete, and that by conquest and the levying of tribute its rulers could possess themselves of golden objects in abundance.

This magnificent bronze dagger from Mycenae is inlaid in gold with the representation of a lion hunt.

The area excavated by Schliemann at Mycenae is known by archaeologists as Grace Circle A. It is just inside the Lion Gate of the city and was clearly kept as a shrine to the memory of the royal personages buried within the circle. There were six shaft graves marked by carved stone slabs. The graves themselves contained the remains of nineteen men, women and children of the Mycenaean royal house, all richly adorned and surrounded by objects of gold, silver and bronze. The burial dated from the sixteenth century BC and proves the power, wealth and splendour of the early Mycenaean civilization.

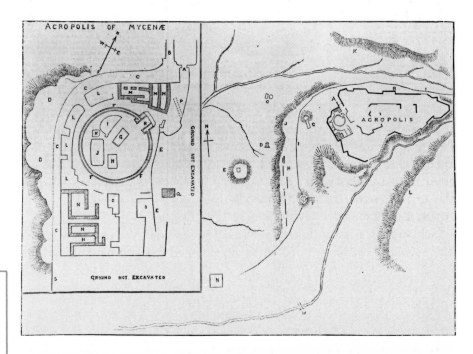

Schliemann called it the mask of Agamemnon and the name has stuck. Scholars now know that the bodies found in Grave Circle *A* were not those of Agamemnon and his companions – always assuming that there ever was a king called Agamemnon – but it is not without a certain regret that the fabulous golden treasure of Mycenae is dissociated from the Homeric myth: it would be nice if it were true. The story of Agamemnon's treacherous murder is a dramatic one and the circumstances surrounding the burial of the bodies at Mycenae seem, circumstantially, to fit in with it. It is not difficult to see how Schliemann could persuade himself that he had proved Homer right.

Agamemnon's tragic history, as recorded in the *Iliad* and the *Odyssey*, is as follows. He was a very powerful king and ruled much of southern Greece. When Paris, son of King Priam of Troy, carried off Helen, his brother's daughter, Agamemnon led the combined Greek forces which sailed for Asia Minor and besieged Priam's capital. During the long war he left his wife, Clytemnestra, in charge of the kingdom. She was seduced by Aegisthus, who thus won both queen and state. Aegisthus now kept a careful watch for Agamemnon's return and when, at length, the king and his weary warriors reappeared Aegisthus organized a banquet to celebrate their safe homecoming. At the feast the heroes were murdered and hastily buried.

The actual graves at Mycenae were not impressive. In Schliemann's words they were 'merely deep, irregular

quadrangular holes, into which the royal victims were huddled by three and even by five'. A half-hearted attempt had been made at cremation but the holes had been filled in before the burning was complete. All this seemed to fit Homer's account of the burial of Agamemnon and his colleagues. Schliemann did not find the wealth of the grave goods a difficult point to argue away: even murderers, he insisted, would find themselves bound by the strong customs of the day to accord the dead full honours. Unfortunately, there are too many strong arguments against Schliemann's hypothesis. Principally, the dating is wrong. Rejection of Homer's stories

presents us with many more problems: who were these people? Why were so many of them buried together? Why was there apparent haste about the interment? Probably we shall never know.

The Radiant and Eager Ship of the Lord

It has been described as 'the richest and most brilliant treasure ever found on British soil'. Whether or not we agree with that judgement, there can be no doubt that no buried hoard stirs the imagination quite so much as the Sutton Hoo ship burial. It takes us back to the world of the Nordic heroes who crossed the sea in their longboats to carve out kingdoms for themselves in France, England, Ireland, Iceland, Greenland and even, perhaps, North America. It is the world of the Norse and Anglo-Saxon sagas. The most famous of these, *Beowulf*, tells how a great hero-king was buried:

> There at the haven stood a ring-prowed ship –
> The radiant and eager ship of the lord.
> They laid down the beloved lord,
> The giver of rings, in the lap of this ship,
> The lord by the mast. They brought from afar
> Many great treasures and costly trappings.
> I have never heard of a ship of this size so richly furnished
> With weapons of war, armour of battles,
> Swords and corselets. Many treasures lay
> Piled on his breast ...

When all the rites had been completed, earth was piled over the ship and the 'beloved lord' was left to make his journey to Valhalla.

Until 1939 scholars had little more than literary evidence to go on. Many long barrows were discovered throughout northern Europe but decay and grave robbers had considerably reduced their value. Then, on the eve of the Second World War, the Sutton Hoo ship burial was discovered in a field near Woodbridge, Suffolk. It was immediately obvious that the archaeologists had found an undisturbed Anglo-Saxon burial of an important and very wealthy man. Necessarily, the work was interrupted by the international crisis and, in any case, the excavation of such an important site had to be carried out methodically, carefully, scientifically. Not until 1967 was the project completed. Then the scholars were able to recreate the events that had occurred 1300 years before.

Sometime in the middle of the seventh century (between 625 and 670), a king of East Anglia died. His people took an old longboat, eighty-six feet long, dragged it on rollers to the royal burial ground overlooking the Deben, and lowered it into a specially dug trench. Then into a cabin, erected amidships, they carried all their beloved leader's possessions – his axe, jewelled sword, knife and spears, magnificent helmet of iron and bronze, shield, stone sceptre tipped with a fine bronze stag, leather and linen parade dress with gold buckles and other accoutrements, a purse decorated with panels of gold and enamel, six-stringed harp, drinking horns mounted in gilt, dishes and bowls of silver, bronze cauldrons and hanging bowls, wooden cups, combs, clothes, a hoard of coins, even his pillow stuffed with goose-down. These they laid around him, before filling in the trench and piling the earth carefully over the dead king.

By the mid-twentieth century, little was left of the boat and the body had decomposed entirely. Cloth, leather and wood had largely perished and objects made of iron were badly corroded. But gold, silver, enamel, bronze and precious stones are more durable. The surviving objects and

A hoo is a small spur of land. Probably the low ridge across the Deben from Woodbridge was once such a spur, jutting into the river. When the mound had been uncovered nothing remained of the ship but marks in the sand. Other materials had also long since perished. But gold and gems are incorruptible, and items remained to dazzle the eyes of the excavators. Mrs E. M. Pretty, the landowner, generously gave the Sutton Hoo Treasure to the nation.

The shoulder clasp used to fix the king's cloak was of gold with cloisonné decoration and typical, intertwined ornaments of semi-naturalistic creatures from the world of Norse myth.

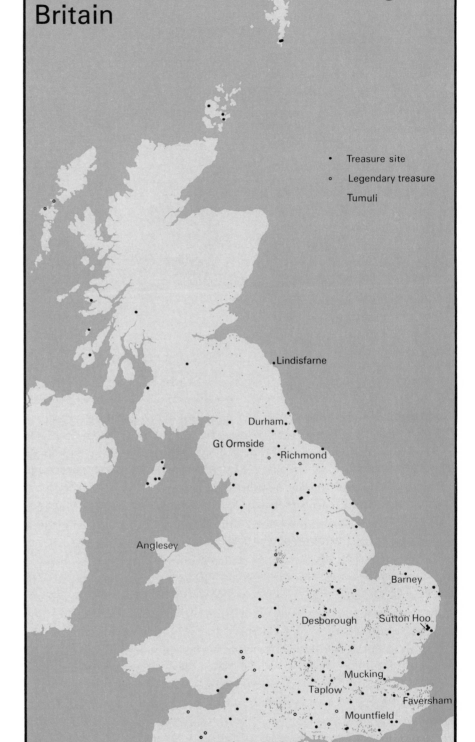

Burials and Hoards in Dark Age Britain

- • Treasure site
- ○ Legendary treasure
-   Tumuli

Lindisfarne

Durham

Gt Ormside

Richmond

Anglesey

Barney

Desborough

Sutton Hoo

Mucking

Taplow

Faversham

Mountfield

fragments were removed with care, treated with preservatives and examined patiently. For these reasons the Sutton Hoo Treasure has become a part of the British national heritage – not just an amazing collection of valuable and beautiful objects but one which tells us a great deal about the way of life of the northern barbarians of the Dark Ages.

First of all, the occupant of the Sutton Hoo burial was a Christian king

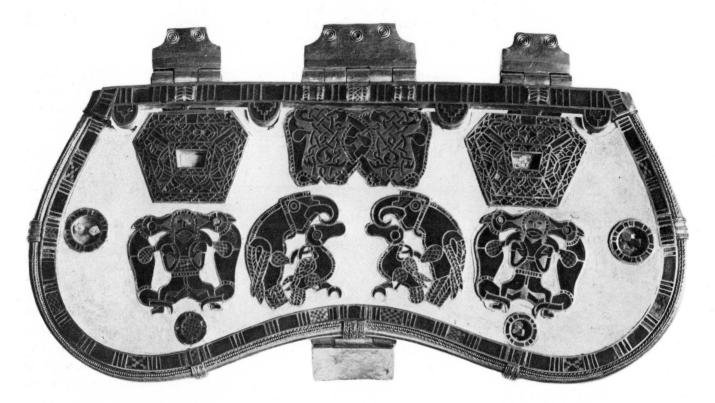

but one who was still much given to the old ways. Perhaps he was Raedwald (c. 599–625), the first Anglo-Saxon ruler of East Anglia, whom we know received Christian missionaries. The existence of two silver christening spoons in the ship suggests that the king had received Christian baptism. The monks would have taught him that the soul had no need of earthly treasures after death, but the belief of the king and his people in their new God was not yet so complete that they felt they could safely ignore the old deities and the old customs.

Secondly, the treasure is made up of pieces from a wide area. There is a silver dish bearing the monogram of the Byzantine Emperor Anastasius and fifteen other pieces of silver which also originated in the eastern Mediterranean. The shield with its gilded mounts came from Sweden, as did the magnificent ceremonial helmet. The coins were from the land of the Franks. Bronze bowls in the burial carry decoration which is definitely Celtic and must have come from western Britain. But the most beautiful items in the find are almost certainly of local craftsmanship. There was a purse of gold and ivory set with garnets and millefiori glass; a pair of shoulder clasps similarly wrought and a magnificent gold belt-buckle ornamented with interlaced animals and snakes.

Finally, there is a connection with the dying empire of Rome suggested by some of the objects. The most enigmatic item is the staff of stone and bronze surmounted by a finely modelled stag. It is believed to be a sceptre. Although the workmanship is northern, the idea of a symbol of authority can only have come from the Roman world. This and other pieces in the collection suggest that the barbarians envied the civilization they were helping to destroy and that they may have had some sense of continuity with it.

Despite what we do know about the discovery, there are further mysteries for solution. Is Sutton Hoo the grave of King Raedwald or one of his successors? Has the body decomposed totally or was it, for some reason, never there?

The Sutton Hoo purse hung from the king's belt and contained thirty-seven gold coins. The leather pouch had decayed, leaving only the purse-lid with gold and garnet decoration, mounted (originally) on walrus ivory. The panels depicting boars, birds, grotesque animals and men all derive from Norse mythology.

Helmets are very rarely found in ancient graves; they were too valuable and too important to warrior peoples. This makes the Sutton Hoo helmet, though badly corroded, particularly interesting to archaeologists and historians. It was a ceremonial object of iron and bronze ornamented with gilded panels of raised decoration.

Treasures from the Tumuli

Almighty and everlasting God, infuse our service and this object, fashioned by the craft of the heathen, with your supreme power so that ... all corruption removed, it may be used by your faithful people throughout all time in peace and tranquillity.

In the Middle Ages this prayer was supposed to be recited by a priest over any item of treasure found in a pre-Christian burial. Its very existence indicates just how frequent such finds were. Britain (and, indeed, the whole of northern Europe) was studded with tumuli – the circular or long barrows in which ancient civilizations had interred their dead. In the popular imagination every one contained buried gold. Therefore, they were frequently broken into by hopeful treasure-hunters. Such activity was, of course, illegal. The Crown claimed all buried property and excavation was only permitted under royal licence – 'the King's gracious placard'. Such a licence was, for example, granted by Edward II to Sir Robert Beaupel in 1324 to open six barrows in the county of Devon. But no official edict could control natural cupidity. The clandestine opening of tumuli was a common occupation. Its exponents were known as 'hill-diggers'. They were deterred neither by fear of the law nor of the supernatural guardians of popular legend –

> Within the cavern's gloomy round,
> Where hidden lies the treasure hoard,
> By magic arts forever bound
> A demon hound keeps watch and ward.

Sometimes they were caught: in 1312 a certain Alexander of Wotton was apprehended on a charge of finding treasure and was clapped into Bedford jail, where he remained for two years before being brought to trial. Nor was it necessary to find anything in order to be laid open to

The Tomb of St Cuthbert

St Cuthbert, the great Celtic bishop and evangelist of northern England, died at Lindisfarne in 687. He was buried on the island in rich robes, and with his pectoral cross and the sacred vessels of the altar. But a hundred years later the monks fled from the Danes, taking Cuthbert's coffin with them. Thus began three hundred years of almost constant movement for these holy relics. Periodic bouts of persecution obliged the saint's guardians to change his resting place time and again. Not until 1104 did Cuthbert's bones find a permanent resting place in the cathedral abbey at Durham. But their adventures were not over. In 1537 Henry VIII's agents arrived to confiscate the treasures of the monastery. What happened then is not clear. Official records state that the saint's shrine was violated and anything of value removed. Tradition, however, insists that the monks once again moved Cuthbert's relics to safety. In 1827 the tradition was confirmed. Excavations beneath the cathedral located a walled grave containing three coffins, one inside another. They held the bones of the saint, wrapped in embroidered silk robes, a portable silver altar, a comb, the head of St Oswald, and a pectoral cross of gold and garnet. Our pictures show the cross and fragments of the original seventh-century coffin.

Barrows varied in shape and size in Dark Age Britain. Burial traditions and customs also differed from place to place. However, the general principles of barrow construction were the same. A structure of rough stone slabs was built over the remains, which might be placed in one or more 'rooms'. The structure was then covered with earth, often to a considerable depth. Such burials were reserved for important people. The humbler members of society were interred in much simpler graves. Our pictures show the interior and exterior of a Celtic barrow at Bryn-Celli-Ddu, Anglesey.

prosecution: the mere act of searching for buried treasure was indictable. Bringing such a charge falsely was a favourite way of discomfiting one's enemies in medieval times.

Obviously, there is very little record of all the grave looting that went on over the last thousand years. But some finds of more recent times have been documented. In 1815 a Viking shield and a gold torque together with some coins were dug up at Barney, Norfolk. A ninth-century gold and silver cup was found at Great Ormside, Cumbria, in 1823. When a ploughman at Mountfield, Sussex, turned up gold torques and other ornaments in 1863, he thought they were made of brass and sold them to a local dealer for six shillings. The new owner disposed of them at the current scrap metal price – £500 – and they were melted down. So the story continues to our own day, of discoveries made accidentally or by amateur archaeologists. In 1976 a nine-year-old boy found a Viking sword in a river near Richmond, Yorks, which was subsequently bought by a museum for £10,000. In the same year a seventh-century gold necklace was found at Desborough, Northants, in thirty-seven pieces, and was skilfully reassembled at the British Museum.

Professional excavation of tumuli goes on continuously, and though nothing as exciting as Sutton Hoo has come to light in recent years, important finds are frequently made. Sword mounts, harnesses and buckles have been found in sufficient number to enable various styles to be recognized and classified. Fine brooches, glassware and a rock-crystal pendant came from graves at Faversham, Kent. Tumuli at Mucking, Essex, yielded a lovely collection of gold and bead jewellery. And, to revert again to an earlier period, a barrow was opened at Taplow, Bucks, in 1883 and among the wealth of objects within were a silver gilt mounted drinking horn, a Coptic bowl, glass vessels, bone counters and even an embroidered garment. Truly, the past lives on around us.

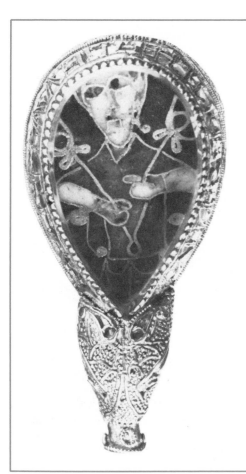

The Alfred Jewel

There is a particular thrill about any object which has definite connections with a famous historical personality. The Alfred Jewel, found near Athelney, Somerset, in 1693, is just such an object. A legend round its edge declares 'Alfred had me made' and there can be no doubt that King Alfred, who used Athelney as a base and founded a monastery there is the person referred to. The front depicts a personification of Sight worked in cloisonné enamel under a dome of rock crystal. The gold back bears a foliage pattern derived from Carolingian tradition. The jewel seems to have been the top of a reading pointer (an *aestal*) given by the king as a present to a church or bishop. This prized possession of the Ashmolean Museum, Oxford is certainly one of the more remarkable and beautiful pieces of Anglo-Saxon jewellery to have survived to the present day.

The Fascination of Gold

The Incorruptible Corrupter

It was over 10,000 years ago that man first became smitten with what Tennyson called 'the narrowing lust of gold'. By 8000 BC neolithic farmers had learned that certain small 'rocks' which they found on the surface of the ground or in riverbeds behaved strangely when hammered with flint cleavers or crushers: they did not split or break; they squashed and bent. They could be made into pleasing or even useful shapes. When their surfaces were smoothed they gleamed attractively. This was especially true of the yellow metal we now call gold.

Surface deposits of gold and silver were fairly widespread, and so for about two thousand years the craftsmen of Stone Age Asia and Europe used simple cold-smithing techniques to hammer out personal ornaments, symbols of wealth and objects of religious devotion. There seems never to have been a time when precious metals were not associated with man's highest material and spiritual aspirations. Several civilizations made the obvious association between gold and the sun god, and silver and the moon god. One such was the Inca civilization, whose ruler was believed to be an incarnation of the sun god. The first Spaniards to visit the Andean empire were staggered at the lengths to which popular devotion and the pursuit of power drove the Incas:

> all the service of the ruler's house, even water jars and kitchen utensils, was of gold and silver: and not only in a single place, but in many, especially the capitals of the provinces, where there were many gold and silversmiths engaged in the manufacture of these objects. In their palaces and lodgings there were bars of these metals, and their garments covered with ornaments of silver, emeralds and turquoise, and other precious stones of great value ... And as they observed and held to that custom of burying treasure with the dead, it is easy to believe ... incredible quantities of it were placed in their graves ... It was a law that none of the gold and silver brought into Cuzco could be removed, under penalty of death.

Stone Age man loved gold but there was another metal he prized even more. Copper was more versatile than gold. Pounding made it harder

This second-century BC bronze shield found in a Lincolnshire river about 1826 was made locally but displays quite distinctive artistic influences from Gaul and Italy. The profusion of continental articles and styles in Britain indicates the vigorous commercial and cultural links between dispersed societies.

In Bronze Age Denmark gold was used for votive offerings such as these boats from a bog at Nors.

A bucket may seem a very humble object but all bronze artefacts were highly valued in Austria in the sixth century BC, for metal was very expensive. The owner certainly wished to take his treasured bucket with him to the next world. It was buried with him in his grave at Hallstatt.

The La Tène culture was an accomplished Iron Age civilization named after an important site on Lake Neuchâtel in Switzerland. Precious bronze was often carried in the form of collars and arm rings. This collar was found at Courtisois in the Marne district of France.

and skilful sharpening could give it a sharp edge. And so the farmers, or rather the blacksmiths of their communities, manufactured the first metal knives and sickles. These tools made many everyday tasks – clearing the ground, harvesting grain, skinning animals, gutting fish – very much easier but they did not revolutionize neolithic life.

The new metals and the artefacts made from them probably had some impact on trade. Tools and ornaments would certainly have been coveted by peoples whose territory yielded no natural gold and copper. In later ages many societies used metal bars or standardized tools as units of currency (for instance the X-shaped copper ingots which were a standard medium of exchange throughout Central Africa *c.* 1350–*c.* 1850 AD) and such a custom may well have existed in late neolithic times in a very rudimentary form. Copper items from the highlands of Turkey and Iran were finding their way to the cities of the Euphrates valley as early as the fifth millennium. Primitive metallurgy also had an influence on warfare. It was only natural that man should fashion weapons as well as tools from metal. Neolithic warriors defended their homes and attacked their neighbours using copper-bladed spears, copper daggers and copper axes. Yet still metallurgy had not become the basis for a new stage in human history.

About 5000 BC smelting began. Neolithic villagers already knew that natural copper and gold could be made much more malleable by heating. They now made the remarkable discovery (probably by accident) that when they put copper ore (malachite) into the fire it broke down, yielding the pure metal in molten form. This led to the production of a whole range of new artefacts: pins, brooches, pipes, musical instruments, rivets, needles, awls, and the first cast figurines. An important development was the creation of alloys. As the demand for metal increased and the supply of surface green malachite diminished, they experimented with other kinds of rock and they tunnelled into the earth in search of it. Thus they discovered the yellow copper sulphide or chalcopyrites (Cu_2S) which, owing to its high level of impurities, had two distinct advantages: it was easier to cast than purer copper and it was harder.

By 3000 BC copper and other metals were known in urban and rural settlements from Spain to the Indus Valley. It was at that time that powerful states began deliberately and massively to exploit supplies of metal. The acquiring of metal was in itself a spur to increased commercial and military activity. Egypt extended its control over the mountainous region fringing the Red Sea in order to mine gold and copper. Ships sailed from Eridu and Ur to the sea and brought home, among other things Egyptian gold. By *c.* 2000 BC Cyprus had emerged as the major source of high-quality copper.

As manufacturers experimented with various metallic 'mixtures' they made the discovery that the hardest alloy of all was produced by adding to molten copper quantities of a still softer metal – tin. Tin was found in surface cassiterite or tinstone and was probably first combined with copper around 3800 BC. The spread of the new alloy was slow, largely because of the scarcity of cassiterite. Indeed, the earliest dated artefact we have is a rod discovered in the pyramid of Maydum, which was built by Pharaoh Sneferu *c.* 2600 BC. Yet the potential of the new material was so great that the revolution it caused, though delayed, was inevitable. The Bronze Age had begun.

Now, men began to fight for metal – and with metal. They killed each other with swords, spears and axes of bronze. Frequently the object of

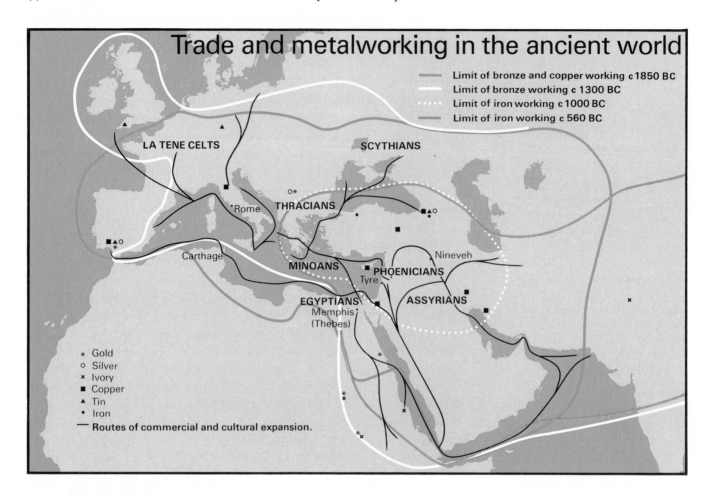

Trade and metalworking in the ancient world

Limit of bronze and copper working c 1850 BC
Limit of bronze working c 1300 BC
Limit of iron working c 1000 BC
Limit of iron working c 560 BC

LA TENE CELTS

SCYTHIANS

Rome

THRACIANS

Carthage

MINOANS

Nineveh

PHOENICIANS

Tyre

EGYPTIANS

ASSYRIANS

Memphis
(Thebes)

* Gold
o Silver
× Ivory
■ Copper
▲ Tin
• Iron
— Routes of commercial and cultural expansion.

A Celtic Princess with a Taste for Greek Art

The Vix Treasure was one of the most spectacular discoveries of postwar European archaeology, both for the richness of the grave goods and the light they cast upon prehistoric trade. Vix was a Celtic hilltop fort in France not far from the modern town of Dijon. There in the late sixth century BC an obviously wealthy and influential woman died. Into her tumulus went her most treasured possessions – brooches, rings, armlets and a diadem of gold, and a beautiful bronze statuette, perhaps of the princess herself. But more intriguing than all these precious objects was an immense bronze crater or wine vessel. It was of Greek manufacture, as were items of pottery found in the tomb. It is larger than any other known piece of ancient Greek bronze and of superb workmanship. It shows that the Celts, no mean metalworkers themselves, admired the craftsmanship of other peoples. One reason why Vix seems to have flourished was its position on the trade route from the Greek colony of Massilia (modern Marseilles) to the north coast and the tin mines of Cornwall. It was Cornish tin that went to make the bronze from which such objects as the Vix crater were fashioned.

An elaborate late Bronze Age gold collar found at Cintra, in Portugal.

The custom of wearing heavy neck-rings, or torcs, of bronze or gold continued for centuries. By the first century BC these torcs provided opportunities for metal workers to apply beautiful, intricate decoration. Several of these torcs have been found. In Britain there have been three major finds of Iron Age hoards, at Ulceby, Lincs; Snettisham, Norfolk; and Ipswich. The examples shown here are from the Snettisham hoard.

The Rillaton Cup is a remarkable example of Bronze Age workmanship in gold. It was discovered in a grave in Cornwall in 1818.

their warlike expeditions was the acquisition of gold and silver. One of the earliest Greek legends, that of Jason and the Golden Fleece, grew out of just such an expedition. The foundation of the story was a raid made c. 1200 BC on Colchis where the people were rich in gold which they panned from rivers – using sheepskins. Gold, silver and copper spurred trade, conquest and colonization throughout the ancient world. Metalworking centres throughout Europe became commercial magnets attracting traders from a wide area.

Ironically, much of this hard-sought metal ended up in the ground from which it had come. This was not only because of objects consigned to the graves of the wealthy; much bronze, gold and silver was buried in hoards in times of danger, or by nomadic societies. Bronze Age hoards are many and varied. In Romania deposits of metal weighing as much as four tons have been found. Hoards of gold and bronze in North Germany consisted almost entirely of broken objects and scrap metal. They must have belonged to smiths and they remind us that it was the intrinsic value of the metal that was important and not the skill and artistry expended upon it.

The Copper Island

The Romans called it Cyprus, after their word *cyprium*, which means copper. It was the abundance of high-grade copper ore which gave the island its importance in ancient times and which led to its conquest and colonization by Assyria, Babylon, Phoenicia, Greece, Egypt, Persia and Rome. A modern authority has said that between 1200 and 1050 BC 'Cyprus passed through strange and terrible years, years of ordeal', and the same verdict could be given on many other periods of Cypriot history, including the Greco–Turkish conflict of recent times. Cyprus was a bridge or stepping-stone, touched upon by all the great Levantine and Mediterranean civilizations, and despite its many upheavals it maintained a high level of cultural achievement. As a result, few places on earth are as rich as Cyprus in buried objects of beauty and value. The streets of the ancient ports, Salamis and Kition, were lined with the shops and ateliers of copper and bronze smiths, ivory workers, jewellers and potters. Their work had a distinctive style and was much in demand along the trade routes of the Levant. Examples have been dug up on archaeological sites in Syria, Turkey and Greece.

But much of the best work was for the home market; for the merchant kings of Cyprus and their pampered families. Among the tombs excavated near Salamis are a series known, for the wealth of their contents, as the 'Royal Tombs'. The entrance passages to these stone-built chambers contained the remains of slaves and horses, consigned to death with their masters. The elaborate chariot and horse harness beloved by the eighth-century overlords was, in some cases, still intact – blinkers, bells, hub-caps, breast plates and pendants all in decorated bronze. We have to thank the fastidiousness of ancient looters for these survivals; they were only interested in objects of gold and silver which could be melted down. Most of the main tomb chambers have been stripped of their more precious contents. But the thieves' crass preoccupation with precious metal has left us a wealth of beautiful work in ivory and terracotta which tell a lot about this civilization. Tomb-robbing has flourished continuously in Cyprus for over three thousand years. Millions of pounds worth of ancient artefacts have left the island. Many have subsequently disappeared or been deliberately broken up. Some that have found their way to museums are now displayed with cards proclaiming 'Provenance Unknown' or 'Bought'. Sadly, much of the value of items of antiquity is lost when the details of their discovery are denied us.

Amazingly, Cyprus is so rich in archaeological sites that important discoveries continue to be made. At Enkomi, late Bronze Age (1625–1050 BC) graves were found in the courtyards of ancient houses. They were obviously carefully tended by the descendants of the dead and thus protected from violation at least in the early centuries of their existence. Excavations over the last hundred years have brought to light intricately inlaid silver bowls, gold necklaces, diadems, rings and pendants. Also the magnificent bronze statuette of the horned god. It was work on this site that revealed the close connection between the copper industry and religion. In one of the temples the Cypriots worshipped an 'ingot god' portrayed as standing upon a copper currency bar. At Kition, also, evidence indicated the priestly control of metal production. There the workshops of the copper and bronze smiths were part of the temple complex. No stronger proof could be found of the importance of metal

This silver bowl found at Enkomi dates from c. 1400–1375 BC and depicts a bull, an object of a sacred cult usually associated with the Minoan civilization of Crete.

Greek influence is very evident in this second century BC statue of the goddess Aphrodite, unearthed at Soloi, north-western Cyprus.

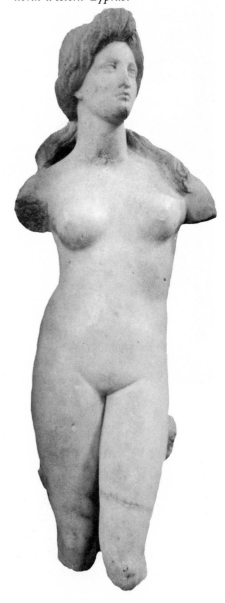

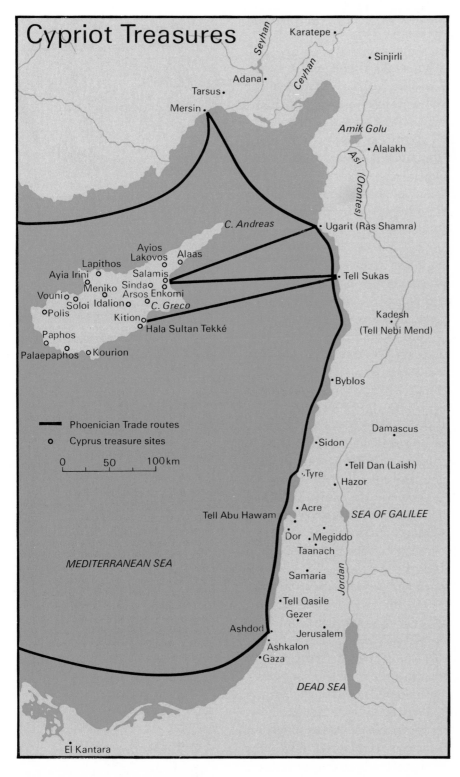

and metal technology to ancient Cyprus. Kition is also an area which has produced a wealth of magnificent grave goods in gold, silver and ivory.

Very different is the Vouni Treasure discovered by Swedish archaeologists. It dates from the fifth century BC, when the island was divided between pro-Greek and pro-Persian factions. A palace was built at Vouni by a king who drew his power from Persia, but it was later occupied by a Hellenistic ruler who surrounded himself with precious objects in the Athenian taste. About 380 BC the palace was destroyed by fire. Before fleeing from the flames someone hid a hoard of silver cups and bowls, coins and gold jewellery beneath a staircase. There it remained for over 2,000 years.

Sometime in the twelfth century BC this remarkable bronze statue of a horned god was made and worshipped in the Cypriot town of Enkomi. It is the finest and most important surviving pre-Classical bronze from the eastern Mediterranean, remarkable for its technical accomplishment, and for the strong expression of peace which it conveys. This unique treasure came from the ruins of a town ravaged more than once by invaders during this period.

Gold of the Centaurs

For centuries wave after wave of wild horsemen thundered over the steppes of central Asia to fall upon the wealthy cities and farmland of Europe and bear away their rich loot. When the conquering chieftains died, their wealth was buried with them.

Among the more remarkable of these warrior hordes was a group of tribes known collectively as the Scythians. Impelled westwards by an upsurge of Chinese militarism and seeking grazing for their horses, they entered southern Russia between 750 and 650 BC and established an empire which survived until the second century AD. From this region groups of Scythians subsequently expanded further westwards. The peoples of the region had never seen mounted warriors before and were amazed at this remarkable phenomenon. When strange tales about the Scythians reached Greece, a new creature was added to Greek mythology – the centaur: half man, half horse. With impunity the conquerors raided their neighbours – Cimmerians, Assyrians, Persians – acquiring great wealth. The powerful chieftains had fine craftsmen among their followers, and their new homeland was rich in gold. Thus they were able to bedeck themselves and their beloved horses in an exotic array of sumptuous decoration. When they died they took their finest possessions with them.

After death a Scythian ruler was embalmed and his body laid in a tent, such as he had used in life but pitched in an excavated hollow. He was adorned with his finest jewellery and clothes and accompanied by his favourite wife, his servants, companions and horses, all richly equipped. Everything needed for the next life was placed in the tomb, including weapons, bronze cauldrons and the equipment necessary for inhaling hemp fumes. Then earth was piled over the grave. In some places water seeping into the barrows froze in the severe temperatures, a natural deep freeze which preserved the contents for over 2,000 years.

In fact very few graves survived intact for so long. For centuries tomb-robbing was a regular pastime among the peasants of southern Russia. Some Siberians took up grave-looting as a profession and were generally known as 'mound men'. In the early eighteenth century Tzar Peter the Great, alarmed at the news that objects of Scythian art were being melted down, ordered officials to acquite the mound men's treasures. Hundreds of gold and silver items poured into St Petersburg became the basis of a national collection. Grave-robbing, however, was not without its hazards. In 1862 the large tumulus of Tchertomlitsk, on the Dnieper, was opened by a team of Russian archaeologists. Within lay the bodies of a king, a queen and a number of their retainers. A fabulous treasure gleamed in the excavators' lamps. But the crowns, jewellery, plates, cups, weapons and horse harness did not lie neatly on and around the forms of their owners: they were piled together in a heap. Puzzled, the archaeologists probed further and soon came upon the macabre answer to the mystery. Beneath a pile of earth and rotton timbers lay another body – that of the thief who had been trapped when the roof caved in.

The rulers of tsarist Russia showed only sporadic interest in ancient burial mounds even though some official forays into the realm of archaeology produced spectacular results. In the mid eighteenth century the government, hearing of vast treasures illicitly removed from barrows

Similar in theme to the portrayal of the monstrous bird and its prey, opposite, is this gold belt mount from a Siberian grave of the fourth or fifth century BC. It portrays a battle between a tiger and a fabulous wolflike animal.

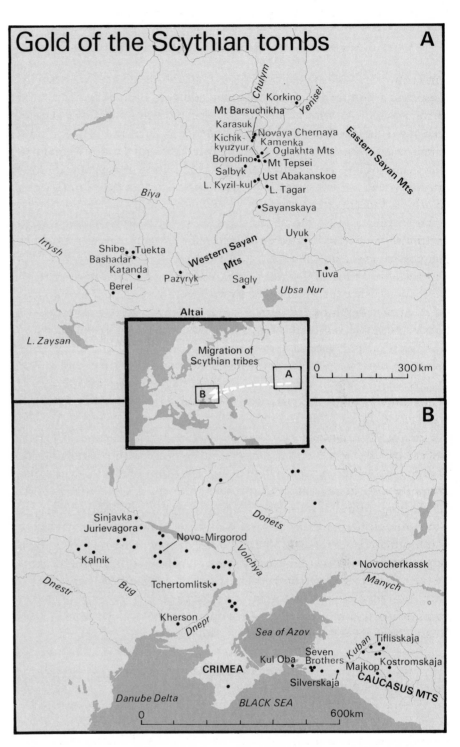

Gold of the Scythian tombs

To these nomadic peoples animals were an important part of everyday life. Stories of wild beasts and fabulous monsters must have featured prominently in the talk around their camp fires. Such creatures were certainly featured in their art. In this gold plaque a gigantic bird of prey carries off a deer.

The Scythians were open to foreign cultural influences. This vase from a barrow at Kul Oba is reminiscent of Persian silverware. It is made of electrum – gold found to be naturally mixed with 20 to 50 per cent silver – and seems to depict someone having a tooth extracted.

This gold quiver mount from the Seven Brothers Barrow, Kuban Region, also suggests Persian influence. Once again the motif is one of mythical winged beasts.

near Tomsk, sent a detachment of troops thither armed with picks and shovels. They tore open a barrow covering the remains of a Scythian chief and his consort. The burial chambers had not been disturbed. The bodies lay each on a sheet of pure gold and each was covered by a similar sheet. There was forty pounds' weight of precious metal in these items alone. The chief was wrapped in a mantle decorated with gold, rubies and emeralds while his wife was adorned with jewelled necklace and bracelets. Alas for the limited knowledge of those times: the centuries-old robes were stunning in their barbaric beauty, but when the discoverers touched them the fabric crumbled to dust.

In the present century excavation has been much more systematic and a wealth of Scythian treasures has come to light, much of which now graces the cases of the Hermitage Museum, Leningrad.

Thracian Gold

Midas was the foolish king who, according to Greek legend, wished that everything he touched would turn to gold and, unfortunately, had his wish granted. As with all myth, this story contains a grain of truth. It explained the dazzling wealth of the northern territories of Macedonia and Thrace whose princes were heavily decked with precious ornaments and whose rivers were rich in alluvial gold. Nowadays the evidence of this glittering age is less immediately obvious, but travellers in Bulgaria, northern Greece and European Turkey can hardly fail to notice the tumuli which are dotted about the lowland regions. It is these burial mounds which have yielded up an incredible amount of treasure – almost enough to make one believe the Midas legend.

For over a thousand years (c. 1300–200 BC) the area known to the Romans as Thracia was inhabited by more or less settled tribes who lived in villages (though by the end of the period they had begun to develop urban life) and lived by herding and agriculture. The Greeks, to whom all other people seemed barbarous, were not complimentary about Thracian customs. They regarded their northern neighbours as warlike peoples who tattooed themselves and sold their children into slavery. A Thracian warrior aspired to ownership of several wives who did all the work at home and in the fields while he waged or prepared for war. Certainly, Thracian society was a violent society. The fortunes of various tribes rose and fell. Confederations and empires were created and disintegrated. Yet the existence of so many fine works of art from the tombs gives the lie to the Greek verdict that the Thracians were mere savages. Their own cultural tradition was vigorous and was influenced freely by contact with their Greek, Persian and Scythian neighbours.

One of the more remarkable early finds, dating from the late Bronze or Iron Age, was not in a tumulus. It was a hoard concealed in the wall of a royal palace at Vulchitrun and consisted of a large bowl and a set of golden, lidded cups. They were obviously made as ritual objects connected with libations or feasting in honour of one of the Thracian gods. Eloquent as these superb objects are they can tell us nothing about the

One of the most exciting Thracian tomb excavations was at Vratsa. The mound covered a complex of three graves, two of which had been ransacked in antiquity. The third contained the remains of a man and a woman. The latter had been buried wearing gold earrings and this elaborate wreath of laurel leaves (left), intricately worked in gold.

The most important find at Vratsa was a silver and gold greave (a piece of leg armour) (above). It is decorated with a riot of figures – a woman's head, lions, snakes, griffins and an eagle. The workmanship is as striking as the imagination which conceived this item of fourth-century BC ceremonial armour.

Impressive in a different way is a Thracian warrior's bronze helmet of the sixth century BC found in a mound tomb at Chelepochene, Bulgaria. It speaks to us of the power and arrogance of the Thracian nobility — men who could command the wealth and splendour of which their tombs bear eloquent testimony.

Very different were the helmets in fashion seven hundred years later. By then Thrace had come under Roman sway and armour was often decorated with scenes from Roman mythology. Some helmets had a face mask attached and the style of these is distinctly Thracian. The custom of burying the wealthy dead with their treasures continued unabated.

Thracian Tomb Treasures

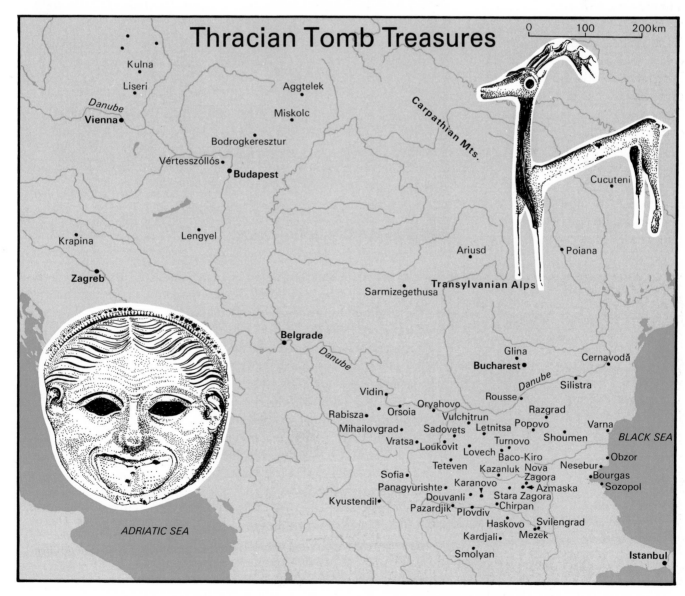

Among the magnificent finds of armour and silver horse harness in a fourth-century BC tomb at Panagyurishté was this heavy elaborate amphora-rhyton designed for two people to drink from simultaneously. The wine gushed from holes in the mouths of Negro heads at the base (which was obviously plugged while the vessel was being filled). The handles are formed by two Centaurs. The figures on the body of the vessel are of naked Thracian warriors.

religious beliefs of their owners. The early Thracians, seemingly, had no written language (they later used Greek characters to put their words in writing) and helpful inscriptions which would tell us more about them are completely lacking on their gilded treasures.

The largest and most magnificent discovery of recent years came from a series of tombs around the village of Douvanli. Unlike most other tumuli, these had not been rifled in earlier ages, and the hundreds of objects found in them would be more than enough to fill a large museum. The tombs of men and of women contained a great variety of ornaments – rings, necklaces, earrings, pectorals, belt clasps and arm rings of silver and gold. There were formidable decorated helmets and breastplates of bronze. There were embossed plaques, bowls, amphorae and beautiful drinking vessels (rhytons).

With the passage of time, workmanship became more elaborate, though not always more attractive. Cups and jars for wine feature prominently in treasures of the fourth and third centuries. They suggest a custom familiar in warrior societies – the sharing of a communal cup as a symbol of fellowship in arms. Some amphorae had two holes out of

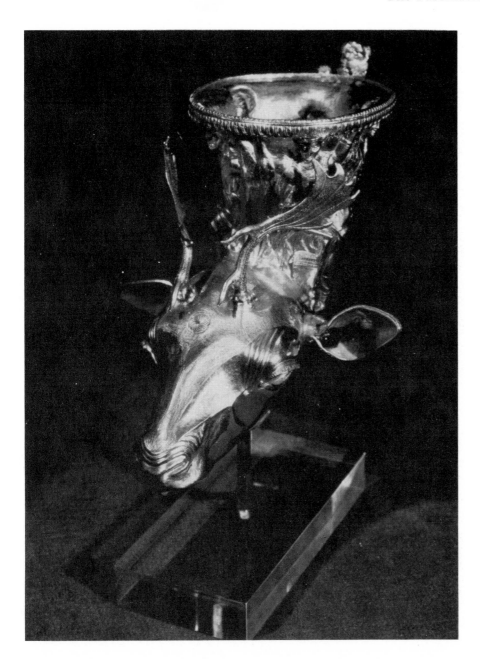

Also found in the Panagyurishté treasure was a pair of solid gold stag's head rhytons. These goblets also dispensed wine from a hole in the base and were richly decorated with mythological scenes.

which the wine poured simultaneously. We can easily picture a pair of young Thracian braves, at the height of some revel, holding such a vessel aloft and gulping the wine down, their heads close together, as the red liquid poured out in twin streams. Decorations from other objects show men on horseback drinking from rhytons and suggest that this was part of the ritual connected with hunting and warfare. Later tumuli are rich in golden horse trappings, statuettes of horses and decorative motifs portraying horses. Some scholars suggest that this shows Scythian influence. More likely, it simply represents the growing skill of the Thracians as horsemen and their increased reliance on their war steeds.

From the mid fourth century Thrace was confronted by a series of powerful opponents. First there was Macedonia, expanding under Philip II and Alexander. Then, from the east, the Celts burst in upon the Balkans. No sooner had they been expelled by the combined forces of Thrace and Macedon than the region was confronted by Roman legions. The tribesmen put up a spirited resistance but, by the time of the birth of Christ, their homeland had become just one among the many provinces of the empire of Augustus.

Graves of the Merchant Kings

There is a fascination, not altogether macabre, about the preservation of bodies from the distant past. That fascination is all the greater when the preservation is unexpected. The success achieved by Egyptian funeral directors, who were specialists in embalming and mummification, is remarkable but scarcely exciting. It is different when the complete, frozen bulk of a woolly mammoth emerges from a Siberian bog or when a Bronze Age grave yields not only the possessions of the occupant but

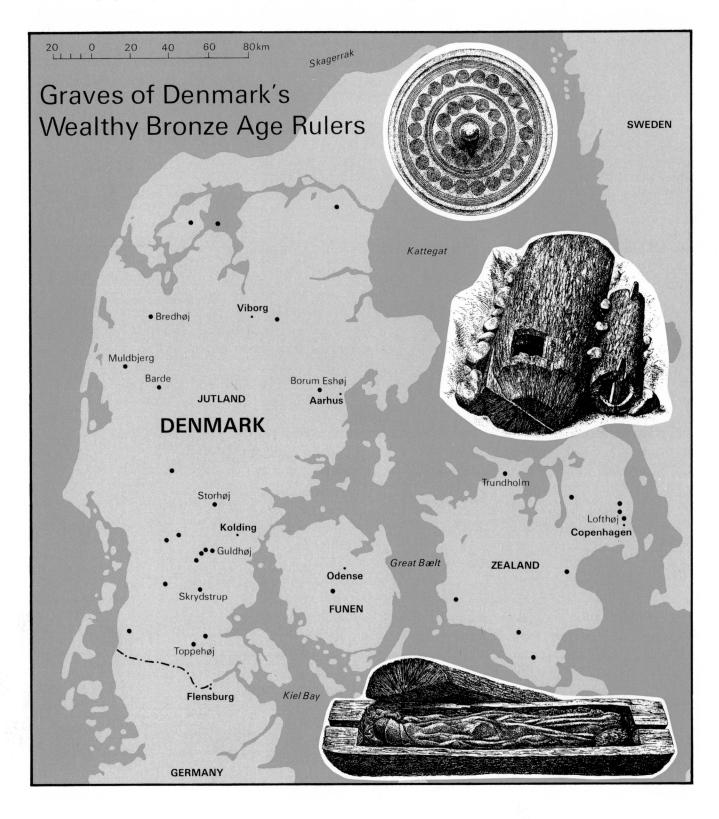

Graves of Denmark's Wealthy Bronze Age Rulers

20 0 20 40 60 80km

Skagerrak

SWEDEN

Kattegat

Bredhøj

Viborg

Muldbjerg

Barde

Borum Eshøj

JUTLAND Aarhus

DENMARK

Storhøj

Trundholm

Lofthøj

Kolding

Copenhagen

Guldhøj

Great Bælt

ZEALAND

Odense

Skrydstrup

FUNEN

Toppehøj

Flensburg *Kiel Bay*

GERMANY

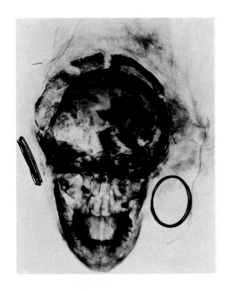

This X-ray of a burial at Skrydstrup shows how the woman was interred wearing her golden earrings. Another lively nature god is shown in the bronze figure of a horned deity found at Grevensvaenge. The bronze, shown below right, of the sun being drawn across the sky, was ploughed up at Trundholm in 1902. It was probably an offering to the sun god.

the occupant himself showing comparatively little sign of decay. Such a discovery – or series of discoveries – has been made in recent years in Denmark.

As the knowledge of metal technology spread westwards through Europe it gave to those people who possessed it a power which enabled them to exert authority over their more primitive neighbours. Ruling dynasties and aristocracies were set up. These élites provided the warriors and the merchants. It was their subjects who tilled the ground and tended the flocks. Splendid in life, they remained splendid in death, and their burial mounds existed to proclaim their power and importance to the living as well as to the spirit world. The rulers of Bronze Age Denmark have become known as the Mound People and, thanks to a chemical accident, several of them have been preserved along with their precious belongings until the present day. The bodies of chieftains and members of their families were placed in coffins made from hollowed oak trunks before being interred, and the tannic acid in the wood and the all-pervasive bog water preserved not only weapons, tools and votive offerings of metal, but also skin, woollen cloth, wood and bone. As a result the treasures of the Mound People are more important than many more spectacular grave treasures discovered elsewhere: they provide us with a much more complete picture of the life and beliefs of these people.

About 1000 BC a twenty-year-old girl was buried at Egtred. She had fair shoulder-length hair, held in place by a black woollen band. She tended her locks with a horn comb and decorated her arms with rings of bronze. She wore a brown tunic and a very short skirt wound round rather like a kilt. Her belt was fastened by a large bronze disc. Those who laid her, sorrowing, in the earth placed with her a container holding wine made from wheat and wild cranberries. They cremated her little serving girl and put her in the grave also. Finally, they laid by the young woman's head a sprig of white yarrow flowers, believed to have healing and magical qualities.

This reveals the other side of Bronze Age life to that demonstrated by the graves of the mighty warriors, men who swaggered in full cloaks and whose strong wrists wielded long bronze swords. They carried their wealth about them in the form of neck rings and arm rings of gold or bronze. They were protected by magic charms held in leather or wool pouches and they sat upon folding stools exactly like those used today for family picnics. They hunted the stag and they worshipped the sun. They made journeys in long rowing boats and their trading contacts extended deep into the European continent. All this and more we know from the Mound People and their treasures.

The Celtic Achievement

Why are some cultures stronger than others? Racial survival is usually associated with geographical stability. How long would a recognizable British, French or Turkish culture remain if the inhabitants of Britain, France and Turkey were driven out and dispersed throughout the world? Some peoples (notably the Jews) have survived by maintaining their racial purity, and this has enabled them to preserve their language, customs and religion. Yet some cultures have gone on living without such a physical host to support them. Predominant among such cultures is that of the Celts.

Bronze Age Greeks gave the epithet 'Celtic' to all peoples living beyond their immediate neighbours to the north-west. Europe was, in fact, more complex racially than that but it is now clear that Celts (or proto-Celts) were living in parts of modern Austria and Germany towards the end of the second millennium BC. From eastern invaders the Celts learned how to smelt iron and ride horses. After that (*c.* 700 BC), Celtic power and influence spread dramatically. Vigorous, expansionist and technically more accomplished than their neighbours, they conquered and raided in all directions; to the Atlantic, the Baltic, the Black

Treasure of the Celts

Whoever fashioned the beautiful silver gilt Gundestrop Bowl, which was carefully placed in a bog in northern Denmark in the first century, clearly had contact with the Mediterranean world. For the high-relief decoration depicts Celtic, Greek and oriental influences. The ceremonial slaying of a bull may also have Mithraic connections. The most likely explanation for this intriguing treasure having been buried in Denmark is that a band of Teutonic invaders attacked Celtic settlements along the Danube far to the south and on returning home placed this particularly good piece of loot in the ground as a votive offering to the gods.

When Celtic culture became fused with Christianity in Ireland the result was a powerful force that showed itself in vivid works of art as well as in a vigorous missionary movement. Of course, the church frequently came into conflict with pagan neighbours and then religious treasures had to be hurriedly buried. This bronze plaque showing the crucified Christ surrounded by angels was found at Athlone.

The Monymusk Reliquary was made to carry a relic of St Columba, the saint who brought Christianity to Scotland in the sixth century. The box is a mere ten centimetres long and is covered with sheets of bronze decorated with silver and enamel.

Sea, the Aegean, the Adriatic and the Mediterranean, and in 387 they sacked Rome and ransomed it. Yet they were never a unified empire, merely tribes and tribal groupings frequently at war among themselves, relying for defence upon the hill forts with which they studded the land. Under pressure from Rome their power wilted: tribe after tribe was ousted from its homeland or absorbed by the Empire. Only in the far north-west, in Ireland and Scotland did they maintain their independence. When the Roman legions at length departed their place was taken not by resurgent Celts but by Teutonic invaders. And yet Celtic culture did not die. Its language survived in a multitude of place names – Thames, Rhine, Danube – and in the tongues spoken in certain regions – Brittany, Cornwall, Ireland, Wales, Scotland. It allied with Christianity to produce a devotional yet muscular version of the faith. And in its visual aspects – work in stone, gold, silver and manuscript illumination – its hauntingly beautiful mingling of interwoven lines and stylized figures produced the finest examples of European art.

Buried Celtic treasure is of three main kinds: grave objects, concealed hoards, and votive offerings. Items in the latter category have usually been found in lakes or bogs. The most striking of all such offerings so far discovered is the silver Gundestrop Bowl. More typical, however, are the finds at Llyn Cerrig Bach: during the first century BC, 150 bronze ornaments were thrown into a lake on the island of Anglesey off the Welsh coast. Presumably such action was intended to propitiate the gods, perhaps at times of crisis for the tribe. Such sites would have been traditional and the deposit of objects built up over several generations. Such an explanation will not, however, fit the beautiful gold and silver communion vessels found in recent years in a bog in Tipperary; for the propitiation of pagan deities, of course, died out with the establishment of Christianity. Perhaps in this case the holy items were hurriedly thrown away at the time of a Viking raid to prevent them falling into profane hands. Pre-Christian graves were well equipped with the usual items which, it was thought, the dead would need. Burial customs varied from place to place and from time to time, the more remarkable being the chariot or cart burials of the Vix type (see above, page 44), though no others have been found which are as rich as that of the Vix princess. More typical is the Newnham Croft burial, excavated in 1903. This Cambridgeshire chariot-grave contained the body of a man accompanied by bronze weapons, brooches, armlets and a pony harness.

Hundreds, perhaps thousands, of buried Celtic hoards have been discovered in Britain and mainland Europe, a fact which we probably owe to the vanity of this people. One Greek writer was scornful of their love of display: 'They wear ornaments of gold, torcs on their necks, and bracelets on their arms and wrists, while people of high rank wear dyed garments besprinkled with gold.' The commonest finds are torcs, for it seems that almost all Celts wore them – gold torcs for the wealthy, torcs of bronze or iron for the other members of society. Groups of gold neck rings, such as the Snettisham and Ipswich hoards (see above, page 45), constitute deliberate burials by rich individuals or families. Yet numerous finds have been made of single torcs often close to the surface of the ground. These suggest hurried concealment when some personal or tribal danger threatened. Wealth was not always in this form, however. In 1927, workmen at Basse-Yutz in the north-west corner of France unearthed two magnificent fifth-century BC wine flagons. They were in such fine condition that experts at the Louvre believed them to be fakes and refused to buy them. Thus these pieces of Celtic art, strongly influenced by Etruscan models, came to the British Museum. Impressive as early examples of Celtic art are, they do not compare with the work produced during the centuries when craftsmen applied their skills in the service of the Christian god. The most famous piece of church plate yet discovered is the Ardagh Chalice, found together with a bronze chalice and some brooches by an Irish boy digging potatoes. This magnificent silver cup is richly decorated with filigree gold and bosses of coloured glass and enamel. Every face of the chalice, even the underside of the foot, is ornamented, a fact which testifies to the skill, exuberance and dedication of the craftsman. Also typical of the later Celtic style are the circle-and-pin brooches, used to fasten cloaks. The best examples, such as the 'Tara' Brooch and the Hunterston Brooch, are among the finest pieces of jewllery ever created, with their strikingly delicate gold filigree and their symmetrical balancing of glass, enamel and amber.

Beginner's Luck

When a party of archaeologists arrived on St Ninian's Isle in the Shetlands in 1958 to excavate the foundations of a medieval church, a local schoolboy with time on his hands and an interest in history offered to help them. And to him fell the honour of finding the stupendous St Ninian's Hoard. Beneath the floor of the church he came upon the remains of a larch-wood box. Inside was a jumble of late Celtic silver: a large hanging bowl, 2 sword chapes, items of sword harness, a spoon, 12 brooches and sundry other items – 28 objects in all. The hoard, probably deposited around 800 AD at a time of Viking invasion, is the finest collection of Celtic metalwork discovered in the British Isles. The pieces are varied in style but represent the highest achievement of Celtic craftsmen in terms of exuberant and imaginative, yet disciplined, decoration.

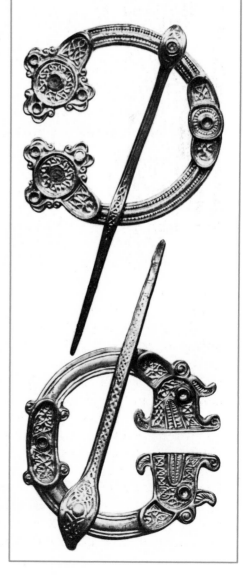

The Second Oldest Profession

Tomb-robbing has been called the second oldest profession. It is as ancient as the custom of burying precious objects with the dead. Respect for the departed, fear of discovery, tombs made as secure as human ingenuity could manage – nothing stood in the way of the greed of determined criminals. In their haste, Egyptian tomb-robbers cut through the outer coverings of mummies with sharp knives and hacked off limbs with axes. Others were more careful: an archaeologist, examining two mummies at Deir el-Bahri, found that amulets and jewels within the wrappings had been replaced with cheap baubles and the folds carefully rearranged. The thieves who broke into the Seventeenth Dynasty tomb of Pharaoh Sekenenre scraped all the gold from his coffin and painted it yellow to conceal their crime.

The pursuit of this particular kind of buried treasure was no task for ill-disciplined gangs of bandits. The problems attached to opening up massive stone mausolea or excavating deep shaft graves, without detection, of removing valuable objects and disposing of them profitably are such as can only be adequately tackled by the cohorts of organized crime. The Egyptian thieves who looted the tombs of the pharaohs had to lay out considerable funds in the bribery of officials, and they needed a large black-market network to sell the magnificent objects of gold, ivory and lapis lazuli they had acquired. A set of papyri dating from the reign of Rameses IX (1142–23 BC) deals with legal proceedings against just such a well-organized gang. Its leader was none other than the mayor of West Thebes, the area in which the great necropolis lay, and his accomplices included police, tomb workers, and probably some of the priests. Such a man was too powerful to be easily brought down: the case against him fizzled out, thanks to some well-greased official palms.

Tomb-robbers were active in ancient Greece, where they were known as *tymborychoi*. We have already seen how Etruscan and Viking graves were systematically plundered over the centuries. The story is repeated almost everywhere. For generations the inhabitants of southern Russia

Tomb-robbing

Every physical obstacle that could be devised was used to protect dead pharaohs and their treasures – traps, false corridors and chambers, great wedges of stone and imitation doors. The areas round the tombs were constantly patrolled by guards. It was all to no avail; robbers invariably found some way of breaking in. They even penetrated the great pyramid of Cheops. They avoided the sealed entrance to the tomb, which was high up on the wall and fully open to view, and tunnelled into the main passage from below. It must have been long, patient labour, removing and concealing tons of debris and working only at night. The corridor leading upwards to the tomb chambers was blocked by stone wedges, so the thieves descended the false corridor, then burrowed upwards from there into the heart of the pyramid, stacking the rubble in the empty underground chamber. They obviously knew the layout and had detailed information from one of the builders or priests.

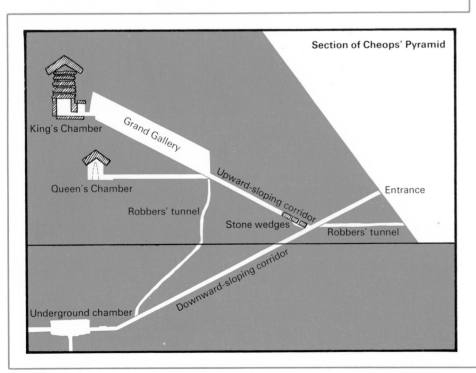

Section of Cheops' Pyramid

King's Chamber

Grand Gallery

Queen's Chamber

Robbers' tunnel

Upward-sloping corridor

Stone wedges

Entrance

Robbers' tunnel

Downward-sloping corridor

Underground chamber

The Vaphio Cups

The highly impressive Minoan civilization flourished on Crete from *c.* 2000 to *c.* 1500 BC, when a volcanic eruption on the island of Thera sent stifling ash and gigantic tidal waves across the sea. The island culture enjoyed a brief revival under Mycenaean leadership in the fourteenth century BC. The once-magnificent palaces of the Knossos, Mallia and Phaistos have been thoroughly excavated and are well known. Of equal importance are the many tombs, especially the *tholos* tombs of the Mesara Plain which, despite centuries of looting, have yielded a wealth of grave goods.

But Minoan cultural influences extended far beyond the island. The Vaphio *tholos* was a once impressive hilltop tomb near Amyclae in southern Greece. Archaeologists who excavated it in 1888 discovered that it had been looted, though very hurriedly – for several rings, seals and other small items littered the floor. To one side of the circular chamber was another grave, sunk in

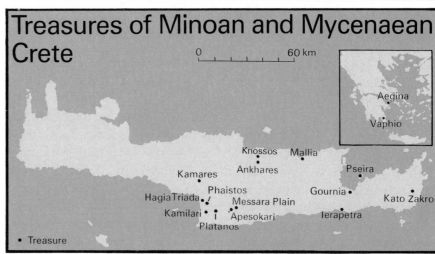

the earth. When the diggers had removed a metre of soil they found a hitherto undisturbed burial. The skeleton was surrounded with rich objects of bronze, silver, clay, alabaster and gold. Most exciting of all were the Vaphio Cups. These exquisite and now famous examples of the ancient goldsmith's art were decorated in relief with scenes of bull hunting, associated with the well-known Cretan game.

augmented their meagre living by haphazard excavations in the burial mounds of the Scythians beside the Don and Dnieper rivers. There is evidence that this activity was common as early as 1437. In that year a Venetian merchant, Josafa Barbaro, resident in the port of Azof at the mouth of the Don, engaged with certain colleagues to dig a tunnel to the centre of a tumulus near Bagaevskaja where a fabulous treasure was reputed to lie concealed. Their first expedition was thwarted by the Russian winter which had frozen the ground to a depth of several feet. Undaunted, they returned in the spring and set an army of labourers to work with picks and shovels. After twenty-two days they had driven a tunnel sixty paces into the mound – and found nothing. However, they now dug through the floor of their shaft and soon found themselves in the burial chamber. There stood the funerary urns containing the ashes of the dead. There were beads and other trinkets offered to the Scythian gods. But of items of intrinsic value all the merchants found was a fragment of a silver ewer. Other excavators had clearly been there before.

We cannot know the scale of the treasures discovered over the years by Russian peasants, but in 1864 a hoard of stolen grave goods came to light. The banks of a reservoir had collapsed during heavy rain and a gang of workmen was sent to effect repairs. Near by stood a conveniently large mound of earth, the tumulus of Khokhlatsh. The labourers did not hesitate to dig into the ancient grave. Very soon their tools laid bare objects of gold set with jewels. There was a third-century diadem studded with garnets, amethysts and pearls, and a golden collar decorated with coral and topaz. There were bracelets, cups, clasps, jars, vases of gold and silver, and a magnificent lion fashioned of agate and gold. All these items had been removed from the tumulus, then hastily concealed beneath a thin covering of loam, safe but accessible. As we shall see shortly, the second oldest profession is still in a healthy state.

Diplomatic Plunder

One of your duties as consular agent for France is to purchase any antiquities of value which are found on Melos ... It is important to remember that the Fine Arts are also a source of prestige for the country you serve and you must always attend to acquiring any archaeological pieces of value ... in the utmost secrecy.

Such was the directive received early in the nineteenth century by one of France's diplomats. Such a licence – nay, order – to plunder may strike us as shocking. A hundred or more years ago few people would have questioned it. The acquisition of ancient treasures had, for centuries, been the hobby of wealthy dilettanti and amateur scholars – essentially an individual pursuit. There had always been enough collectors around to encourage peasants and adventurers to seek out and rifle sites and tombs. It was in the era following the Napoleonic Wars, however, that the building up of important collections became a matter of national prestige and the trade in antiquities became an industry. A few great museums, notably the British Museum (1753), had been founded in the eighteenth century but it was the French Revolutionaries who gave real impetus to the idea of art for the people when they turned the Louvre into a museum and stuffed it with curios taken from royal and aristocratic houses. Thus official representatives were sent to seek out treasures and ship them home before the agents of rival governments could find them. Such men could easily persuade themselves that they were performing a valuable service for the world of art. Most of the countries richest in ancient artefacts were controlled by governments which were either indifferent to their heritage or too poor to preserve it. Therefore, looting could easily be renamed 'rescuing'.

Lord Elgin certainly interpreted his actions in that way. Newly appointed as British ambassador to the Ottoman Empire, he arrived in Athens, at that time under Turkish rule, in 1800 and was appalled by the neglected state of many of the buildings and monuments on the Acropolis. He sought permission to have them removed. The Islamic government had little interest in 'infidel' relics and allowed Elgin to dismantle parts of the Parthenon, the Temple of Victory and other structures. The work occupied three hundred men for nearly four years, by which time the Scottish peer had amassed hundreds of marble sculptures and pieces of carved stone. These were dispatched home in several consignments aboard royal naval ships. One such vessel was the brig *Mentor* which set out in September 1802. Sitting low in the water, she wallowed slowly southwards. Some hundred and twenty miles brought her into the lee of Kythera, an island notorious for the rocks and reefs which lurked beneath an innocent blue sea. The *Mentor* was holed close by the entrance to St Nicholas Bay and sank in ten fathoms. Elgin was horrified at the thought that his precious marbles, saved from certain neglect and decay, should now be lost for ever. He employed a team of local sponge divers. For two years these incredible swimmers descended into the Aegean without any kind of breathing apparatus, to locate Elgin's crates and attach lines to them. Most of the cargo was thus recovered. Elgin, it must be said, intended the statues, not for a national collection, but to grace his new house in Scotland, but a series of reverses brought him close to ruin and obliged him to offer the collection to the

Buried Beauty
The Venus (or Aphrodite) of Melos, better known as the Venus de Milo, was fashioned by an unknown Greek sculptor in the very highest classical tradition, in about 100 BC. It adorned the goddess's temple on the island of Melos. But later Aphrodite's temple was destroyed and the statue damaged. But devoted worshippers managed to conceal it from further profanation in an underground chamber. It was discovered there in 1820 by a local peasant. He knew that foreign diplomats were paying good money for old works of art and he made sure that news of his discovery reached the Marquis de Rivière, French ambassador at Constantinople. De Rivière bought the Venus and had her repaired, though her arms remained missing. De Rivière subsequently presented her to King Louis *XVIII*, and now she is the most famous of all the treasures in the Louvre.

British Museum, which acquired its most famous – and controversial –
set of exhibits for £35,000.

Lord Elgin was the most celebrated diplomat-plunderer of the modern
world but he was very far from being the only one. Indeed, down to our
own day important antiquities continue to be smuggled abroad in diplomatic bags. The growth of national consciousness, however, has
forced the trade in ancient treasures underground. There is no longer
scope for consular representatives to indulge in such amateur excavations
as that of Charles Champoiseau. He was French consul at Adrianople and
in 1862 he visited Samothrace. He was struck by the possibilities of the
ruined Cabiri shrine and began excavations there the following year. He
discovered over two hundred marble fragments which, when reassembled, made up the superb statue of a goddess. It is now known as the
Winged Victory of Samothrace, one of the Louvre's greatest treasures.

*The celebrated Parthenon Sculptures
brought back by the Earl of Elgin.*

Cohorts of Purple and Gold

The Assyrian came down like the wolf on the fold
And his cohorts were gleaming in purple and gold ...

So the poet Byron pictured the might of the great Assyrian Empire at its height, an empire long since vanished without trace beneath the sands of Mesopotamia. Vanished, that is, until Austin Henry Layard came on the scene.

In 1839 this young English lawyer of French extraction decided to throw down his pen and follow his dream:

I now felt an irresistible desire to penetrate to the regions beyond the Euphrates ... and to explore those lands which are separated on the map from the confines of Syria by a vast blank stretching over Assyria, Babylonia and Chaldea ... great nations and great cities dimly shadowed forth in history; mighty ruins in the midst of deserts.

With one companion and virtually no funds, Layard wandered through Turkey and Syria examining every deserted tell (or mound) and sand-choked ruin he could find. On the banks of the Tigris near Mosul he came across a large, grass-covered mound with, here and there, carved columns and brick walls laid bare by the winter rains. And instinctively he 'knew' its identity. So steeped was he in the history and mythology of the ancients that he felt sure he was looking at Nimrud, one-time capital of the mighty Assyrian Empire.

In 1845 he returned to the spot. With a small sum of money donated by the British consul in Constantinople (much of which was spent bribing Turkish officials) he began to excavate. Immediately, he struck lucky. In two places he located what turned out to be palace walls, covered in magnificent decoration in low relief. Every day brought fresh encouragements and fresh problems. The Pasha became suspicious and put a stop to Layard's work. Protests availed nothing. Weeks of frustrating inactivity followed. Then the unprincipled official was toppled in a power struggle and the digging continued. No gold or jewels were brought to light. Instead, an amazing architectural treasure emerged. It was a palace whose size and warlike decorative motifs testified to the might of Assurnasirpal II, the warrior king who lived within its walls. The most impressive finds were thirteen pairs of massive winged lions and bulls carved in alabaster.

Layard determined to rescue them from the desert. More bribes and diplomatic pressure were needed to get the necessary permission for their removal. Then began the incredible task of detaching the figures and moving them, undamaged, on carts across the uneven ground to the river Tigris, and thence by raft to the Persian Gulf for shipping onward to England.

In 1854 Londoners and visitors to the capital were able to gaze for the first time on the treasures Layard had brought home. A special exhibition was staged in the Crystal Palace; the walls and gateways of the palace of Nimrud were faithfully recreated. The hunting and battle scenes in bas-relief and the proud winged creatures – all were there, just as, two and a half thousand years before, they had appeared to men and women who approached the court of Assurnasirpal.

Austin Henry Layard, here depicted as staid, respectable Victorian, was, in reality, a man of immense vigour and enthusiasm. He was only twenty-two when he forsook the security of the legal profession and, with scant funds, embarked on several years of travel and archaeological exploration in the Middle East.

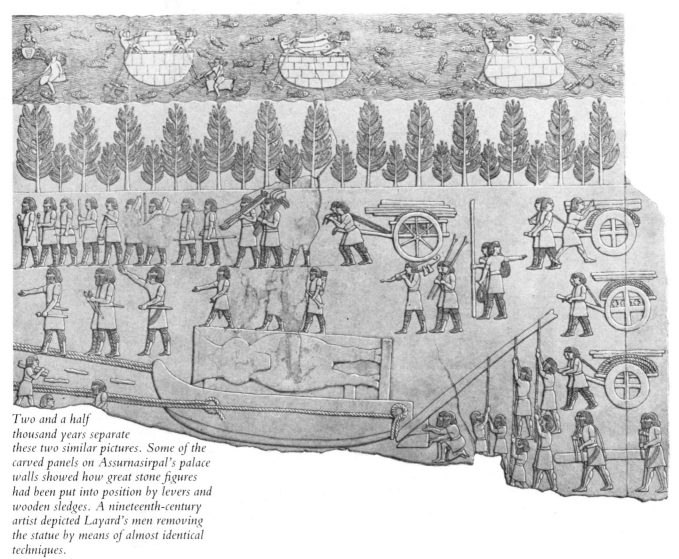

*Two and a half
thousand years separate
these two similar pictures. Some of the
carved panels on Assurnasirpal's palace
walls showed how great stone figures
had been put into position by levers and
wooden sledges. A nineteenth-century
artist depicted Layard's men removing
the statue by means of almost identical
techniques.*

General Cesnola and the Cyprus Campaign

Emmanuele Pietro Paolo Maria Luigi Palma di Cesnola arrived in the USA in 1858. Like many other Italian immigrants, he owned little but the clothes he stood in. However, unlike most of his compatriots, he was of noble stock and had already, at the age of twenty-six, distinguished himself as a recklessly brave cavalry officer. His tumble into penury and disgrace had been the result of a scandal – probably a madcap love affair – which had outraged Piedmontese high society. He enlisted in the Union army during the American Civil War with the rank of colonel. He served with bravery, was taken prisoner, and emerged replete with honours – although the title of 'General' he now assumed had almost certainly not been bestowed upon him, as he claimed, by the late President Lincoln. A grateful government appointed him US consul in Cyprus in 1865.

He spent eleven years on the Turkish island and used his position to make a fortune. After exploring various commercial possibilities he turned his attention to the plundering of ancient graves and other sites. During his term of office, he removed from Cyprus no less than 35,573 objects of antiquity. He was quite indiscriminate – everything from the Bronze Age to the classical period was welcome to his collection: coins, pottery, Roman glass, statuary, votive offerings of gold and silver – all had a market value and could supplement his consular salary. It was a highly profitable business. Local peasant labour employed on the digs was cheap. Since Cesnola did not trouble himself with the niceties of archaeological excavation, he needed to devote only the minimum of time to research and supervision of the work. The market for curiosities was brisk and resulted not only in ready cash: Cesnola was always seeking promotion and, on one occasion, wrote to a superior suggesting that a few antiquities might be appreciated by 'some of your influential friends and would make them work with more activity for our cause'.

Yet the US consul was not oblivious to what was happening in the archaeological world. He realized that a growing number of new museums were on the lookout for large collections to fill their display cases. He therefore kept the bulk of his loot and opened negotiations with the Louvre, the British Museum, the Berlin Museum and the Leningrad Hermitage for bulk purchases. In 1870 he offered the remainder of his haul to leading museums. After two years of negotiations it was acquired for $50,000 by the Metropolitan Museum, New York. Cesnola was now a wealthy man but still unsatisfied. He craved the fame acquired by other archaeologists and resolved, therefore, to make a find which would rival those of the great Schliemann. He chose for his excavations the royal Phoenician capital of Kourion at the west end of the island. The account of the dig which Cesnola subsequently published described in detail how he explored graves cut into the hillside and accumulated an incredible treasure of gold and silver objects. There were diadems, arm bands, rings set with amethyst, earrings, statuettes and an abundance of objects delicately carved with animal and floral motifs. The find made Cesnola famous overnight. The collection was soon on its way to the Metropolitan and, in 1879, he was appointed director of the museum. But the 'Treasure of Kourion' never existed – not as a single hoard. Cesnola acquired some of the pieces from various sites and bought others from

Italian nobleman, soldier, diplomat, dealer in antiquities, museum curator: in his long and eventful life General Cesnola played many roles. He never did anything by half measures. During his years as US consul in Cyprus he acquired precious objects by the thousand. Among them was this elaborate fourth-century BC gold and silver ornament, a fine example of Greek craftsmanship, once worn by a stylish lady, probaby a prominent member of society in one of the colonies on Cyprus.

Cypriot peasants. To this day some of his 'finds' remain, undisplayed, in the museum's vaults.

Cyprus is now perhaps the most plundered of all Mediterranean countries. The political upheavals of recent years have made it difficult for the authorities to exercise control, and the large number of tourists to the island has for generations ensured that local people have rifled the ancient sites for objects of value. An entire Mycenaean city near Sinda was destroyed by grave-robbers in the 1960s.

Tomboroli and Huaqueros

'It is the most beautiful thing in life, finding these things. Until the end of the world I will do this, because it is so beautiful.' These words of an unabashed Italian tomb-robber, from an interview given willingly to a researcher only a few years ago, take us to the heart of the problem. As well as greed, the plunderer is possessed by a sense of adventure. There is, for him, the thrill of possible detection and the still greater thrill of bringing to light, for the first time in centuries, objects of great beauty and value. For this man and his confrères, who are called *tomboroli* in Italy, looting ancient sites is a way of life. Few of them grow rich from it. Some spend spells in prison. But they cannot rid themselves of the obsession.

In some countries economic circumstances virtually force people to turn to tomb-robbing. Costa Rica is a poor country of 1½ million people. It has few natural resources. But it is rich in pre-Columbian sites. There are approximately 5,000 'professional' *huaqueros* (tomb-robbers) in the country and thousands more who are involved in the antiquities trade. The government winks at it. Police and officials take their cut. Until recently the National Museum issued permits to *huaqueros*. The average wage is £20 a month. One looter found gold worth £6,000 in a single day. In many countries compliant or overworked police do not give the protection of tombs a very high priority and the existence of inadequate treasure trove laws does not encourage honesty. An Italian farmer who handed over to the authorities an Etruscan bronze received a reward of £250. A local dealer had already offered him £8,000.

A jade mask from Los Soldados, Veracruz.

A Royal Treasure – Found and Lost

Are there circumstances which justify, even demand, the removal of tomb treasures? In 1774 some members of the Society of Antiquaries got permission to open the tomb of King Edward I in Westminster Abbey. When the coffin was opened the body was discovered to be in a good state of preservation and wrapped in a waxed linen cloth. The king certainly merited his nickname 'Longshanks'; the body measured 6 ft 2 in, very tall by medieval standards. The scholars made their examination and noted what they saw. Edward was dressed in a robe of red damask, a white stole sewn with pearls and gold thread and a red mantle fastened with a gold and jewelled clasp. In one hand he held a copper gilt sceptre. In the other was a gilded rod decorated with green enamelled oak-leaves and topped by a dove in white enamel. On the king's head was a plain gold crown. All these pieces comprise the only medieval English regalia still in existence. Having seen all they wished, the antiquaries resealed the tomb with all its contents intact. Were they right to do so? Many people at the time and since have believed that they were not. The contemporary author Horace Walpole commented: 'There would surely have been as much piety in preserving them in [the Abbey] treasury as in consigning them again to decay. I did not know that the salvation of robes and crowns depended on receiving Christian burial.'

While archaeologists fume about the unscientific plunder of ancient sites the value of antiquities soars, the clandestine art market flourishes, poor countries earn valuable foreign exchange by allowing their heritage to be sold, and more people than ever before engage in tomb-robbery. They have developed skills akin to those of the archaeologist: they know how to take earth samples and how to locate burial sites by observing the mixture of soil strata; they know how to care for fragile objects, how to clean and repair them. Behind them is a network of dealers, agents, smugglers, corrupt customs officials, collectors and even museum authorities.

For many respectable curators of public collections find themselves with little alternative than to encourage this criminal subculture by buying looted grave goods and other items exported illegally from their countries of origin. In 1913 a Berlin museum acquired the celebrated limestone bust of Queen Nefertiti. It was not put on display for ten years.

The authorities either knew or suspected that its transfer from Egypt to Germany had not been above board. When it was, at last, shown to the public there was an immediate outcry from Cairo but the bust remained in Berlin. As recently as 1970 a similar case occurred involving the Metropolitan Museum, New York. A press revelation declared that the museum's vault contained a collection of silver looted from tombs in the Hermus valley, Turkey. When pressed, the authorities stated that they had bought 219 articles from an American dealer but that they were unable to give details of the original provenance of the articles.

Such stories are by no means rare. Officially, the world of scholarship condemns the illegal traffic in antiquities. At the very time that the issue

The plunder of tombs and temple sites has reached alarming proportions in Central America. Peasants living near Los Soldados, Veracruz discovered a group of Olmec tombs and took from them jade masks (like those pictured here), figurines, mirrors and other jade items. When news of the finds reached Mexico City there was a rush of dealers eager to buy and museum authorities anxious to protect the site. The result was a compromise: the national museum acquired some of the pieces while others changed hands on the international market at astronomical figures. One jade mask realized $110,000 in 1970. It is not only small, easily transportable treasures that are open to looting. In 1968 a dealer came across a Maya temple hidden deep in the Mexican jungle. He spent $80,000 having part of its façade shipped to New York where it was offered to a museum for $400,000. The offer was declined and the massive sculpture was donated to the Mexican Museum.

The Boston Treasure

The problems of museum curators are well illustrated by the story of the Boston Treasure. In 1968, 137 pieces of gold that had adorned a beautiful woman four and a half thousand years ago were illegally excavated from a grave in Turkey and smuggled abroad. The dealer handling the gold eventually sold it to the Boston Museum for a six-figure sum. When the collection was put on display the storm broke. The museum was 'exposed' in the international press. The Turkish government angrily demanded the return of the treasure. Scholars complained that without fully documented evidence of the collection's origin it was worthless from a historical point of view. The museum authorities not only rejected these criticisms; they claimed they were performing a public service. Was it their fault the tomb had been plundered? What should they have done – haughtily rejected it? What would have happened then? It would have been peddled around wealthy private collectors, dispersed, and would have disappeared from public view, perhaps for ever. At least the Boston Museum could claim to have preserved it intact.

of the Turkish treasure was brought to light an article in the *American Journal of Archaeology* stated:

> If we, as archaeologists, are truly interested in artefacts as evidence for ancient history, rather than as possessions to be selfishly prized because of their rarity, it is time to take a firm stand. The clandestine excavator and antiquities smuggler are criminals to be abhorred.

Yet what curator can decline the offer of an important collection of dubious origins when by so doing he is only ensuring that it goes to a rival museum, a private collector, or – worst of all – that it is broken up and disposed of piecemeal?

And every successful sale is monitored by the tomb-robbers. In their humble dwellings in Puerto Rico or Florence the professionals scan their newspapers and auction catalogues. They explore the ancient sites with renewed vigour for whatever articles appear to be in fashion – and they put up their prices. In 1972 a magnificent Greek painted vase was sold for a record $1 million. Almost certainly it was looted from an Etruscan tomb. A few months later a newspaper reporter declared, 'Even small shacks around this ancient town [Cerveteri] bear television aerials, and shepherds talk knowingly about Euphronius [a great Greek vase-painter] since they saw a picture of his vase on the screen ... Something like an archaeological gold rush is on in Cerveteri ' *Tomboroli*, like dealers and museum curators, are part of a movement that is gathering momentum all the time. It is difficult to see what can stop it.

The Legacy of Fear

The Grandeur that was Rome

When Alaric the Visigoth pillaged Rome in 410 AD he was the first invader to set foot in the Eternal City for almost eight hundred years. Yet for many decades the world's greatest empire had been collapsing as barbarians from the North and East pressed upon its over-extended frontiers. In province after province civilized urban life and the luxurious ease of country villas were disrupted by plundering savages or the internal warfare that results from political chaos. Wealthy citizens fled their homes, taking only necessities with them. Their treasures of gold, silver, ivory and jewels they buried, hoping to return for them in better times. But better times never came and those hoards which were not discovered by the looters remained concealed for centuries.

Kaiseraugst was a substantial fortress near Basle on the Rhine–Danube frontier. About 350 AD the allegiance of the garrison was divided by the claims of rival emperors. In the resulting conflict one extremely import-ant Roman crammed his precious possessions into a chest and buried them – 187 silver coins and medallions, silver ingots, a large set of silver and gilt tableware and a beautiful statuette of Venus. So valuable is the hoard (accidentally unearthed by a bulldozer in 1961) and so exquisite the decorative work on the dishes that some historians have suggested that the Kaiseraugst Treasure belonged to the Emperor Julian.

There is no doubt about who owned the Carthage Treasure, for one of the silver gilt dishes bears an inscription in praise of the Cresconii, a leading family which provided consuls and other officials for the prov-ince of Africa. This cache of beautiful silver plate was probably hidden in 439 when Gaiseric, King of the Vandals, captured Carthage.

Most discovered treasures cannot be so easily identified and this opens the door wide to romantic speculation. In 1868 a detachment of Hanoverian soldiers was building a rifle range near the picturesque old town of Hildesheim when one of the soldiers turned up some fragments of blackened metal. As soon as he realized that this was no mere rusted scrap he reported to an officer and the find was examined carefully. Though heavily oxidized and much damaged, what eventually came to light was a collection of silver dishes, cups, spoons, ladles and a magnifi-cent candelabrum. Scholars were soon describing this as the personal treasure of Quintilius Varus, a Roman general who suffered a serious defeat in the Hildesheim area. A more prosaic evaluation of the hoard suggests that it was the stock in trade of a provincial jeweller.

More fanciful yet is the claim made for the Antioch Chalice. This was part of a cache of Christian relics and precious objects discovered by Arab workmen, digging a well near the Syrian town in 1910. All the objects are of sixth-century origin except the chalice. Or, rather, chalices; for within a silver gilt cup decorated with representations of Christ and ten Apostles is another of plain silver. Could this be the Holy Grail, the cup used at the

The craftsmen of Rome's eastern enemy, Persia, had a vigorous style of their own, as articles from buried hoards along the fluctuating frontier prove. This parcel gilt ewer (c. 600 AD) shows dancing girls, frequently employed to entertain at banquets.

The magnificent silver Achilles Dish from the Kaiseraugst Treasure is 53 cm across and displays scenes from the life of the Homeric hero. The centrepiece portrays Odysseus discovering Achilles, disguised as a daughter of Lycomedes because of a prophecy that he would die fighting at Troy.

The intriguing chalice from the Antioch Treasure.

Last Supper? Antioch was an important Christian centre at a very early date (it was from here that St Paul set out on his missionary journeys). Most scholars would not support such an early date for the inner vessel but there is no positive evidence for or against the legend.

The eastern (Byzantine) empire survived the fall of Rome by a thousand years but was under constant pressure from barbarians, Sassanians and Muslim Arabs. The island of Cyprus and its wealthy Byzantine settlements were overrun by Arabs in 653–4 and it was then that a magnificent treasure was concealed beneath the floor and in the walls of a house at Lambousa. Most remarkable element in the treasure is the set of six 'David Plates' decorated with events in the life of the Old Testament hero and believed to commemorate a great victory by the Emperor Heraclius over the Persians in 627.

Most treasures buried during the declining years of the Empire consisted largely of coins, the portable wealth of moderately well-to-do citizens. But the not uncommon finds of embossed and engraved gold and silver testify to the cultural wealth of Rome. Most of them now enrich leading European museums but, undoubtedly, further treasures still await discovery.

The Traprain Law Treasure

Barbarian invaders who ransacked Roman towns had, it seems, little appreciation of the intrinsic worth of what they found. Embossed ewers and dishes, graceful statuettes, delicate personal jewellery were merely valued by weight as bullion. In Roman times part of the Scottish Lowlands was occupied by the Votadini whose principal settlement was a hill fort on Traprain Law. After the First World War the site was excavated by the Society of Antiquaries of Scotland. What they discovered was a shock in more ways than one. In a shallow burial they uncovered a slimy, purple mess that smelled abominably. When the stench had dissipated the find was examined carefully. It turned out to be a miscellaneous hoard of silver, badly corroded by sulphur in the soil. Tableware, personal ornaments, Christian and pagan religious objects – all were jumbled together in a heap. And almost all were deliberately damaged – squashed, bent or hacked into pieces in readiness for the melting pot. In all there were fragments of over a hundred items, dating from the fourth century. The treasure may have been the profits of honest trading, for such 'hack silver' was often used as currency. More probably, though, it was a hoard of loot seized by the Votadini in raids across Hadrian's Wall. Before the silver could be melted down and turned into ingots the Votadini themselves came under pressure. Either there was a Roman reprisal expedition or an attack by Picts from the North. The hoard had to be quickly concealed while the warriors armed themselves and went forth to battle. No one returned to reclaim it.

The Traprain Law Treasure is not a unique find of its kind. Similar hoards of hack silver have been found outside the frontiers of the Empire at Coleraine and Balline in Ireland, Høstentorp in Denmark and Gross Bodungen in West Germany. Silver fragments sometimes found with coins may support this theory.

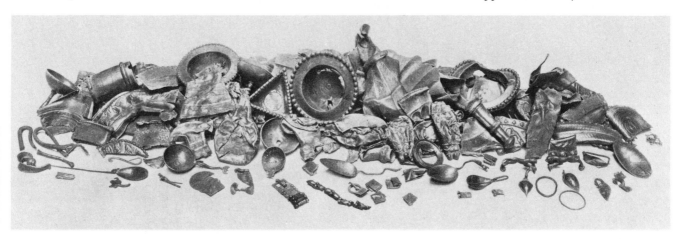

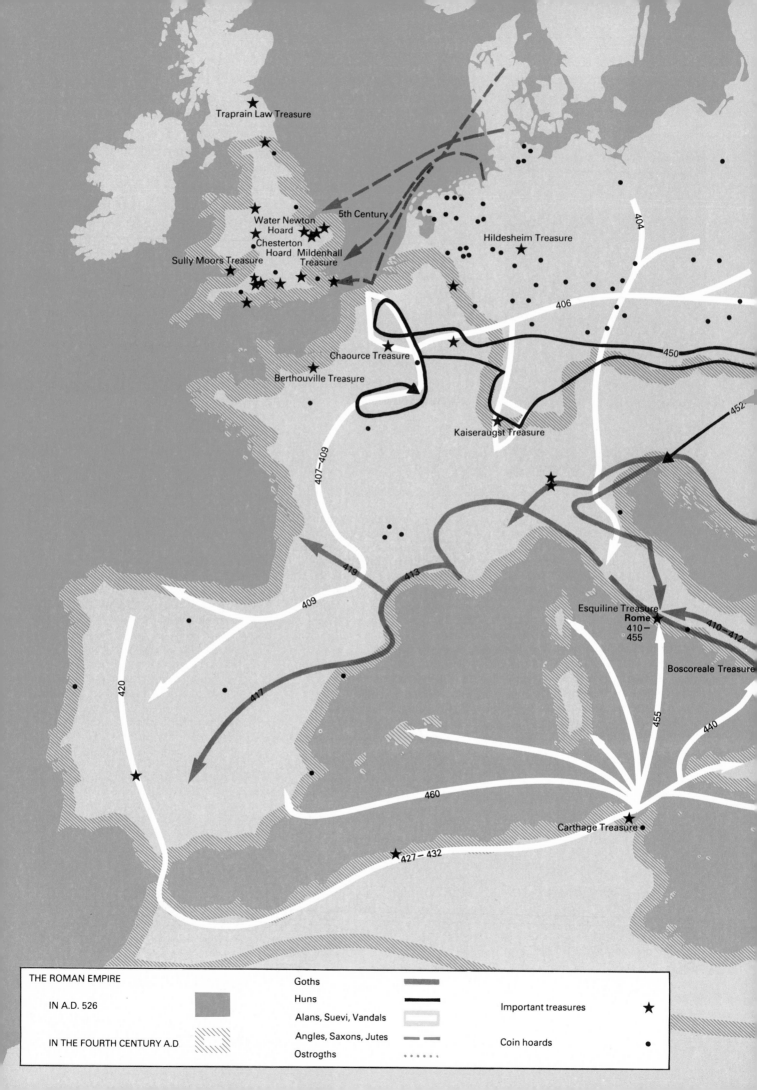

Traprain Law Treasure

Water Newton
Hoard
Chesterton
Hoard Mildenhall
Treasure
Sully Moors Treasure

5th Century

Hildesheim Treasure

404

406

450

452

Chasource Treasure

Berthouville Treasure

Kaiseraugst Treasure

407–409

419

413

409

420

417

Esquiline Treasure
Rome
410–
455

410–412

Boscoreale Treasure

455

440

460

Carthage Treasure

427–432

THE ROMAN EMPIRE

IN A.D. 526

IN THE FOURTH CENTURY A.D

Goths

Huns

Alans, Suevi, Vandals

Angles, Saxons, Jutes

Ostrogths

Important treasures ★

Coin hoards •

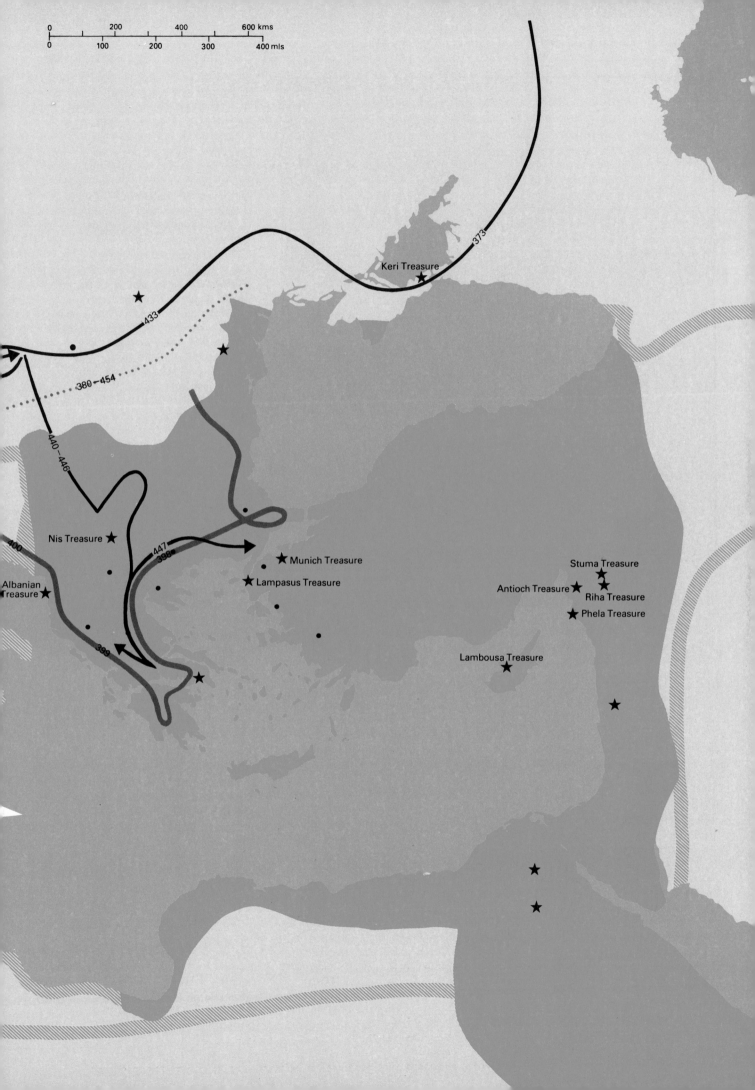

Keri Treasure

373

433

380 — 454

440 — 446

400

Nis Treasure

447
398

Albanian
Treasure

399

Munich Treasure

Lampasus Treasure

Stuma Treasure

Antioch Treasure

Riha Treasure

Phela Treasure

Lambousa Treasure

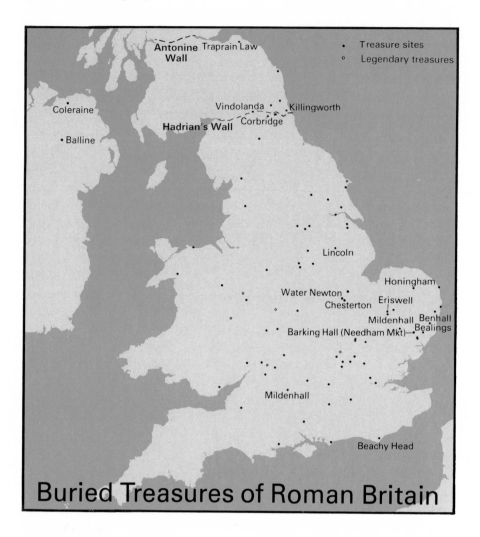

Buried Treasures of Roman Britain

Boudicca and Roman Britain
The Roman conquest of Britain was begun by the Emperor Claudius in 43 AD. Imperial power was at its height around 200. Between 408 and 410 colonists and Romanized Britons rejected rule by a distant government which could no longer protect them from marauding Angles and Saxons. Within fifty years all vestiges of classical culture and administration had vanished. But material evidence of the Roman period remained in plenty – flagged highways, walled towns, farmsteads, forts – and hundreds of hoards of treasure buried at times of crisis.

Most of these deposits date, as we would expect, from the fourth century, the period of the slow decline of Roman power. Important discoveries of earlier date have, however, been made. Among the more interesting British archaeological excavations of recent years is that of Vindolanda, a Roman fortress on Hadrian's Wall. Both the military and civilian quarters yielded finds of personal jewellery, implements, pottery, statuary and even leather and textiles which helped to date Vindolanda's periods of occupation. Then, as the excavators were concluding their 1976 season, they suddenly came upon a cache of more than one hundred silver and bronze coins of 260–70 AD. The disconcerting point about this find was that earlier work had led the archaeologists to conclude that the period 245–70 was one when Vindolanda was unoccupied.

Many other finds made in the region of Hadrian's Wall testify to the troubled life of the frontier. In the winter of 1812, a group of workmen unearthed a hoard of Roman gold and silver objects near Killingworth, Northumberland. As well as coins, the treasure included chains, rings, spoons and a harp-shaped brooch. It dates from the mid-second century, the brief period when lowland Scotland was occupied under the orders of the Emperor Antonimus Pius and a new wall built from the Firth of Forth to the Firth of Clyde. Perhaps it represents the loot from a successful raid upon an advancing Roman column or even upon the nearby fortress at Newcastle. The Killingworth Hoard could very easily have been lost to posterity for its finders secretly disposed of it to a local goldsmith. He in turn sold the pieces to a collector. Only on the latter's death in 1850 did the treasure come, by bequest, to the British Museum.

Not so fortunate was the Corbridge Treasure. Corbridge was an important garrison town just south of the wall on the main road to the North. In 1731 a young girl found a silver basin in the bank of the River Tyne, and sold it for ninepence. Over the next few years other discoveries were made in the vicinity by various people. All were turned into ready cash by their finders. Only one dish, the Corbridge Lanx, has survived.

Peace did not always reign south of the wall. In 60 AD Boudicca's Iceni spearheaded a revolt that engulfed East Anglia and much of central England. This and the subsequent reprisals doubtless account for the 327 silver Iceni and Roman coins found at Erswell, Suffolk, in 1972 and, perhaps, for the bronze figure of the Emperor Nero at Barking Hall in the same county. East Anglia is particularly rich in Roman remains, thanks largely to its vulnerability to barbarian attack.

A farmer with land on Beachy Head, Sussex, benefited considerably from Roman occupation of the region centuries earlier. The rulers of the late fourth century increased their coastal fortifications in the face of mounting pressure from Jutland. The limited success of these measures is suggested by the fact that three separate hoards were found on Mr Edgar Williams' land between 1961 and 1973. In all more than 13,500 coins were discovered and, under the law of treasure trove, Mr Williams received a substantial share of their market value.

Even this find pales into insignificance beside a more recent one made by two amateur treasure-hunters at Mildenhall, Suffolk. Working with metal detectors in October 1978, they located a cache of 60,000 third-century coins, enough to pay the wages of a Roman legion for a year.

The Defeat of Boudicca

The Emperor Claudius came in person to begin the conquest of Britain. After a succession of easy victories, he entered Colchester in triumph and ordered a temple to be constructed there where he could be worshipped. The impressive building with Claudius' statue before it soon stood at the heart of a bustling Roman town. From it the local Trinovantes and their neighbours the Iceni were gradually pacified and Romanized. When Suetonius Paulinus arrived to begin his governorship in 58 AD, he believed he could safely turn his back on the South and East while he subjugated Wales. He reckoned without Boudicca, Queen of the Iceni. Her people had already been goaded to the point of revolt by being disarmed and heavily taxed, but fear of the legions held them back. In 59 their king died. Not only did the Romans refuse to accept Boudicca, his wife, as their new ruler, they treated her and her family with contempt. She was bound and beaten and her daughters raped. Suetonius and his countrymen paid dearly for their folly. At the head of 100,000 Iceni and Trinovantes, and soon joined by other tribes, Boudicca fell upon Colchester, killing, burning and plundering. The remnant of the garrison made a last stand in the very temple of Claudius. London and Verulamium (St Albans) next experienced Boudicca's wrath. For a while it seemed to the victory-crazed Britons that their conquerors might be driven from the land. But superior Roman discipline and strategy at length told. The British host were defeated in one last battle. The Queen died, perhaps by her own hand. The slaughter which followed was the worst ever perpetrated on British soil. The Iceni and their allies were annihilated. A few had time to conceal their treasured possessions. At Honingham near Norwich an Iceni family buried their little fortune. And at Benhall, in Suffolk, a warrior concealed his most prized piece of booty, the proud head of Claudius hacked from the statue in Colchester.

The Casket of Projecta

When the Lady Projecta was married to the wealthy patrician Turcius Secundus, she received some magnificent wedding presents. To grace her table there were silver dishes and flagons, some bearing her monogram. There were gifts of a more personal nature, including a little silver box for oils, perfumes and other cosmetics. But it was the marriage casket which took pride of place; a beautiful, exuberantly embossed silver box, about the size of a small suitcase, with the portraits of the happy couple on the lid and the legend *Secunde et Projecta Vivatis in Christo* ('Secundus and Projecta, may you live in Christ'). Like all leading Romans since the establishment of Christianity as the official religion of the Empire (in 363), the newlyweds were adherents of the new faith. Indeed, when Projecta died some years later, her epitaph was written by the pope himself. Projecta's casket and other prized possessions were bequeathed to another, probably Projecta's daughter. Two or three

The Casket of Projecta, among the most magnificent examples of fourth-century Roman silverware, is enriched with wedding scenes and portraits of the bride and groom. The beautiful domed toilet casket still contains the pots for oils and perfumes.

generations of the family enjoyed a position of privilege and luxury while their civilization collapsed around them. The end came in 410, when Alaric's hordes swept through the city. Secretly the Turcii treasures were interred in the grounds of their house on the Esquiline Hill, close to the church of S. Martino ai Monti where Projecta herself lay buried. Then the family fled. Perhaps they left it too late, for none of them returned to dig up the Esquiline Treasure.

It was found in 1793. This was the era of the great private collector. Classical antiquities were fashionable among the European nobility. Many fine houses boasted their own galleries and museums. Ambassadors like Lord Elgin, who shipped the celebrated Elgin Marbles from Athens to England, and Sir William Hamilton, who amassed a personal collection of Greek pottery, were among the many travellers and officials who toured the Mediterranean lands in search of the interesting, the curious or the beautiful. The Esquiline Treasure was bought by Baron von Schellesheim and later passed into the collection of the Duc de Blacas. Not until 1866 was most of it acquired for a public museum.

This magnificent treasure consists of table silver, horse trappings and personal items of the highest standard of workmanship. But all of them are dwarfed by Projecta's marriage casket and her toilet box. The latter has a chain for carrying and is decorated with figures of the Muses. Within, marvellously preserved, are the lidded silver jars which used to contain the lady's cosmetics. The domed box, or one very like it, is actually shown on the marriage casket. One of the panels of the casket is devoted to a scene showing a bride being conducted to her wedding, and one of her attendants carries the toilet box. All the casket's panels depict scenes connected with the nuptial ceremonies, including the bathing and dressing of the bride. So, as well as being one of the finest pieces of silver to survive from the ancient world, the Casket of Projecta allows us some fascinating glimpses of the life of wealthy society in fourth-century Rome.

The treasure was found upon the Esquiline, one of Rome's seven hills, in the centre foreground of this picture.

The Silver in the Furrow

'Dig for Victory' – that was the propaganda slogan used during the Second World War to urge the British people to self-sufficiency. Whether or not it urged one farm labourer to greater efforts we do not know, but it was while ploughing for his employer at West Row, near Mildenhall, Suffolk, that he discovered the most spectacular cache of Roman silver yet found in Britain. For beauty and historical interest the Mildenhall Treasure is quite unsurpassed.

It consists of thirty-four pieces of tableware – dishes, bowls, spoons, ladles and goblets, most of them richly decorated and all dating from the fourth century. The centrepiece is the famous Great Dish of Mildenhall, an exuberantly embossed platter, half a metre in diameter and weighing over eight kilos. Around a mask of Oceanus, nereids and fantastic marine creatures cavort. The outer circle of the dish is occupied by

The Great Dish of the Mildenhall Treasure, shown with one of its matching smaller plates, a bowl decorated with leaves, flowers, grapes, birds and rabbits, a spoon and a goblet which, when inverted, also served as a platter.

The small, peaceful town of Mildenhall as it was in 1940 when the treasure was discovered. Its tranquillity was soon shattered by the drone of war planes.

revellers at a Bacchanalia – gods and heroes dancing and tippling merrily together. The subject is a fitting one for the object's use: we can imagine it piled with fruit or other delicacies on the low table at a Roman banquet. Other pieces in the collection also draw their inspiration from pagan festivals and courtly luxury. Some items, however, strike a very different note. There are slender spoons which bear the early Christian *chi-rho* symbol. Whoever owned this treasure did not mind displaying at the same board items commemorating both the old religion and the new religion of Rome. There must have been many such men in the upper ranks of imperial society but mixed hoards like that at Mildenhall are rare. The only comparable treasures of a similarly late date, such as the Water Newton Hoard and the Chesterton Hoard are specifically Christian.

According to one theory, the owner of the magnificent tableware found at Mildenhall may have been Lupicinus, a general sent to Britain in 360 to repel the Picts and Scots who were harrying the northern parts of the province. This he apparently achieved within a few months. During that time another military leader, Julian, was raised to the purple. Julian was a pagan and later tried to restore the old religion. Lupicinus was a Christian. The new emperor seems to have regarded Lupicinus as a possible rival and hastened to recall him to Gaul, where he was arrested. May the successful general not have had some inkling of the political situation and concealed his treasure before obeying the imperial summons? Perhaps he cherished some hope of returning to Britain and using it as a power base against the champions of an alien faith. Certainly the sumptuous Mildenhall Treasure must have belonged to a Roman of the very highest rank.

Whatever the treasure's earlier adventures, there were more to come in the twentieth century. The labourer who discovered it reported the find to his employer who carefully collected the pieces and locked them away in his farmhouse. And there they remained for the duration of the war. Considering the large number of British and American air bases in the area – prime targets for enemy attack – it was hardly the safest depository for a collection of such enormous historical importance. Nor was its concealment a wise move on the part of the farmer. The British law of treasure trove clearly states that any object made wholly or in part of gold or silver, or an alloy of either, must immediately be reported to the local coroner. Had the farmer complied with the law he would eventually have received the full market value of the treasure – perhaps half a million pounds. In fact, when the discovery did come to the attention of the authorities, in 1946, it was decided that the hoard had been illegally concealed. As a result the farmer and his employee only received token payments – £1,000 each.

If there were no regulations many important sites would be crudely plundered and items of value offered to the highest bidder, as they were in previous centuries and as they still are today in some parts of the world. The advantages of keeping within the law are illustrated by two Lincoln families who took up treasure hunting as a hobby. Patient research aroused their interest in a particular piece of land. With the owners' permission they explored and after nine months found 2,932 Roman coins in an earthenware pot. They reported their discovery. The British Museum was able to examine the hoard and select items of particular interest. And the finders were eventually richer by about £25,000.

In this detail of the Great Dish the rich decoration can be seen. The sea god is shown with dolphins in his hair and mythical marine creatures dancing within a circle of sea shells.

Merchants and Heroes

NORTH SEA

NORSEMEN! The word struck terror into the hearts of men and women from Ireland to Russia, from the Baltic to the Mediterranean. The Scandinavians were forced because their lands were mountainous and covered with forest to travel mainly by water, and they became the finest seaborne warriors of their age. Taking advantage of the anarchy and the scantily defended kingdoms left by the collapse of Roman rule in Europe between AD 700 and 1000, the Vikings ventured far and wide in their longboats – terrorizing, plundering, exacting tribute, sometimes settling but more often taking their spoils home.

And many – perhaps all – of them buried their wealth. Norway, Sweden and Denmark have already yielded about nine hundred hoards of silver and gold, quite apart from precious objects placed in human burials. The most fabulous of all is the great hoard of Hon, Norway – 2,548 grams of gold and precious stones. It is a veritable magpie's nest of widely differing objects. There are rings, one with an inscription in Greek. There are coins from Europe and the Levant, all fitted with gold links for ease of transport. A magnificently intricate Carolingian trefoil brooch was found side by side with a gold and garnet pendant that must have been at least a hundred and fifty years old when the hoard was concealed (*c.* 860). There are armlets, bead necklaces and ornamented gold discs.

The metal for locally made objects came largely from gold coins looted from the towns and cities of the crumbling Roman Empire. Viking goldsmiths achieved the highest standards of technical skill, producing items of barbaric splendour and also great intricacy. They could draw silver and gold threads to a tenth of a millimetre and work them into 'ropes' for fashioning heavy collars or armlets. Two examples of their craftsmanship must, unfortunately, be catalogued among the great lost treasures of the world. At Gallehus, Denmark, two magnificent golden horns were discovered. They carried both engraved and applied decoration, one bearing the proud legend, 'I Laegaest, son of Holte made this horn'. Together they weighed about seven and a half kilos and were over seventy centimetres long. For many years after their separate discoveries (in 1639 and 1734) they were in the royal collection. Luckily, drawings and copies were made of them, for in 1802 they were stolen and melted down. Another interesting gold hoard was found at Kitnaes, Denmark. As well as gem-studded jewellery it contained a large number of 'bracteates', small pendants which copied late Roman coins.

Silver, however, is much more common than gold in these northern hoards. A cache found in 1903 at Asarve on the Baltic island of Gotland consisted of sixty-six arm rings or ring fragments, which originated far to the south-east beyond the Volga, and nineteen ingots, weighing altogether 7,060 grams. At Birka, Sweden, a trove of Arabic coins, armlets and brooches of local manufacture was unearthed. A similar hoard was discovered as far away as Skaill in the Orkneys. Many finds consist largely or wholly of hack silver (objects deliberately broken or crushed). At Botels, Gotland, a cache was hidden in two clay vessels and a birch-bark box. It comprised Arabic, German and Byzantine coins and a few arm rings. Everything else was in fragments – bits of brooches, armlets, and tableware – proving that the silver was only important to its owner as bullion.

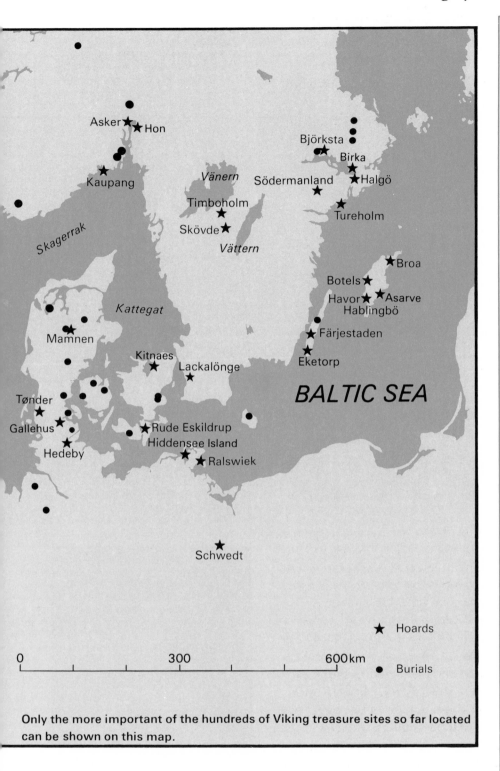

Asker ★★ Hon

Björksta
Birka
Vänern Södermanland ★ Halgö

Kaupang ★

Timboholm ★
Skövde ★
Vättern

Tureholm ★

Skagerrak

★ Broa
Botels ★
Havor ★ ★ Asarve
Hablingbö

Kattegat

Mamnen

Färjestaden ★

Kitnaes
Lackalönge ★

Eketorp ★

BALTIC SEA

Tønder
Gallehus
Hedeby

Rude Eskildrup ★
Hiddensee Island
Ralswiek ★

Schwedt ★

★ Hoards

| 0 | 300 | 600km |

● Burials

Only the more important of the hundreds of Viking treasure sites so far located can be shown on this map.

Gotland

On the island of Gotland, which lies in the Baltic Sea almost midway between Sweden and Russia, no less than 525 finds of buried Dark Ages silver have been made. Most of the items were in the form of currency – spiral arm rings, rectangular ingots, coins from all over eastern Europe, western Asia and the Levant. In 1936 two schoolboys stumbled on a cache of 2,673 coins in a quarry. Every one came from Arabia. In date they spanned two centuries and fifty-five caliphates (Muhammadan reigns). They must have been hidden about AD 910 by a Scandinavian merchant recently returned from a successful journey via the Dnieper and Kiev to Constantinople and Baghdad. At Asarve, another hoard consisting almost entirely of arm rings and silver bars from beyond the commercial centre of Bolgar on the middle Volga was found.

The island was clearly a very important entrepôt where businessmen from the lands fringing the Baltic met to deal in goods culled from northern seas and forests. The wealth of its inhabitants must have made it a frequent prey to Viking raiders.

Sometime in the eleventh century a stone memorial was erected to the memory of Ailikin, a queen of this wealthy troubled island. The decoration is similar to that on the work of contemporary goldsmiths.

These anonymous treasures do not necessarily point to a time of raiding and insecurity. One evening in the year 990 the aged Norse poet Egil Skallagrimson rode from his homestead carrying a chestful of silver and accompanied by two slaves. In the morning he returned alone and empty handed. He died a few months later, having told no one where his treasure and the bodies of his servants lay. Such behaviour seems perverse in the extreme until we probe the afterlife beliefs of the Dark Ages. In Viking lands it was widely held that warriors could enjoy in Valhalla the treasure they had personally buried. If Egil held that conviction he certainly would not want slaves or inquisitive neighbours impoverishing his eternity by digging up his silver.

Objects from far and wide have been found in Viking hoards and burials. The silver beaker from Thyra's mound, Jellinge, was of Scandinavian workmanship but the metal which went into it came from coins or other objects brought home as plunder. The arm rings are part of a large hoard of silver coins and jewellery which came to Assarve, Gotland, from western Russia. The belt mount, found in Sweden, is of Frankish origin as is the gold disc brooch from the Hornelund hoard. Most surprising of all, however, is the bronze Buddha with inlaid silver eyes. By what adventures did it come from north India to its final resting place at Helgo, Sweden?

Over 80,000 Arabic coins have been found in Scandinavian treasure hoards; coins that were minted for sultans living 2,000 miles and more from the lands of the Norsemen. The adventurousness of the Vikings showed itself as much in legitimate trade as in warfare and pillage. By the middle of the eighth century they had established bases on the southern shore of the Baltic. From there they travelled along the Volga, the Dvina and the Vistula, reaching the warmer lands of the South by means of the Dnieper and the Don. They settled in and even founded some of the great mercantile centres along the way – Novgorod, Staraja Ladoga, Kiev, Smolensk. They took furs, white slaves, ropes, honey and walrus ivory to the caliphate of Baghdad. From the fabulous land of Sinbad and the *1001 Nights*, whose ruler possessed 1,200 tons of silver annually, mined from the mountains of Afghanistan, they brought home spices, silks, wine and precious metal. And more exotic items yet found their way back to Scandinavia. A bronze Buddha from north India was discovered in a hoard at Helgö, Sweden. Many craftsmen had their workshops in this major trade centre and there they turned foreign gold into jewellery.

Most silver was carried in the form of currency, either coins or armlets and ingots of standard weights. The Vikings lived simply and they liked to have their wealth in an easily portable form. Coins were often pierced or had rings attached, so that they could be threaded on wires or strings. Armlets were tied in bundles. And this is just how they have been found in the majority of buried hoards both in Scandinavia and along the trade routes. Interestingly, a cache of ring bundles and ingots found at Skövde was identical in form to the majority, but was entirely of gold, and

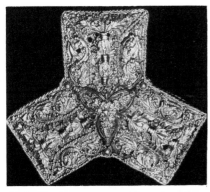

Probably the most magnificent hoard found in Scandinavia is the collection of gold and jewellery buried in a grave at Hon, near Oslo, about 860. One of the finer objects in the collection is this three-tongued, intricately-worked mounting from a sword belt. It came from the Carolingian empire far to the south.

The Vikings were a unique blend of ferocity and sensitivity. Nothing captures this almost paradoxical fusion of elements better than the wooden post of unknown use found at Oseberg, Norway. The evil, grimacing lion's head is decorated in intricate detail. This one piece tells us more than volumes of words about a truly remarkable people.

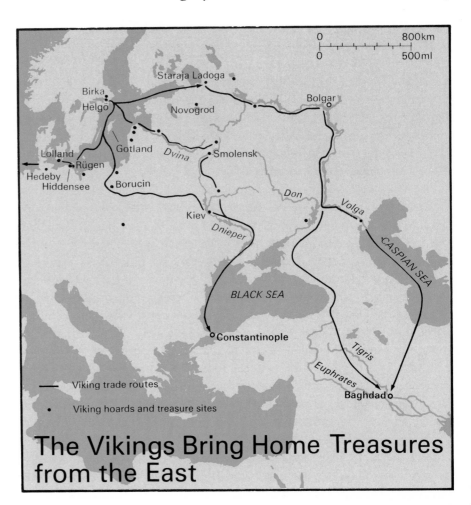

The Vikings Bring Home Treasures from the East

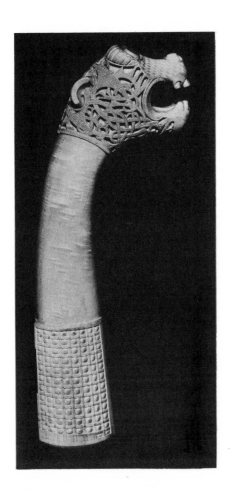

weighed over seven kilos. But some sites yield unexpectedly beautiful treasures. At Borucin in modern Poland was found a pot containing, among other items, a Viking silver chain with pendent animal heads, a Russian necklace of heavy, ornate silver beads and a delicate silver casket of oriental workmanship. At Hiddensee, off the Baltic coast of East Germany, a small but magnificent collection of Viking jewellery was unearthed. It contained pendants and a brooch of the highest standard of filigree work. The adjacent, larger island of Rügen was the site of one of the largest coin finds – 2,270 items, mainly Arabic and Asian. The hoard at Birka, Sweden, contained a unique set of oriental glass chessmen. Of an earlier period were the Roman bronzes discovered at Hablingbo, Gotland, and the beautiful silver cups on the Danish island of Lolland, which date from Augustan Rome – between 30 BC and 14 AD. For a thousand years some of the world's finest treasures found their way to the lands of the remarkable Norsemen.

All this portable wealth was, in times of crisis, easily concealed. Some hoards were lowered into peat bogs or buried beside trees, boundaries, large stones. Occasionally an owner would divide his treasure in two before hiding it, in the hope that a searcher finding one would believe he had found all. Some caches were buried with talismans, to guard them against evil. Nine hundred of these hoards have been found. It is a staggering number but it represents only a fraction of the treasures originally concealed and, perhaps, only a fraction of those still awaiting discovery.

The Richest Treasure in All England?

According to ancient legend anyone standing upon Walton Hill, Lancashire, who turned his eyes towards Ribchester was looking over the richest treasure in England. Such stories abound probably in every country of the world and always have to be treated with great caution but the story of the Cuerdale Hoard indicates that it is unwise to dismiss out of hand the folklore of buried treasure.

The M6 motorway now cleaves the park of Cuerdale Hall as it by-passes Preston and cuts across the meandering Ribble. The scene was considerably more peaceful in the spring of 1840 when a gang of labourers worked in a leisurely fashion to repair winter damage to the banks of the river where it passed close to the hall. They were carrying soil from a spot some forty metres distant when one of the men noticed some greyish discs in the disturbed earth. When he looked more closely and discovered them to be silver coins he let out a yell which brought his colleagues running. The ensuing hubbub attracted Mr Richardson, steward of Cuerdale, to the scene and he ordered the treasure to be disinterred carefully and carried up to the house. The work must have taken several hours, for when the hoard was laid out on the sitting-room floor, the astonished Richardson counted over 8,000 coins and a large quantity of hack silver. It was eventually known to be the largest Viking hoard discovered in the whole of Europe.

Once the cache had been claimed as treasure trove and examined by experts it was seen to comprise coins of Alfred the Great, Edward the Elder, kings of Wessex, as well as other English and continental pieces. These placed it in the early tenth century. Was there any recorded event of that period which might account for the burial and subsequent loss of such a large and miscellaneous collection? The *Anglo Saxon Chronicle*

In 1840 Preston was a quiet market-town on the river Ribble. Cuerdale Hall lay two miles upstream across open meadows and parkland. There were few signs of the industrial and communications development which was to swamp the area in factories, houses and trunk roads. It was upon this peaceful community that the news broke that 'the richest treasure in all England' had, at last, been found.

The Cuerdale Hoard may certainly claim to be in the running for the title of richest treasure in all England. It is certainly the largest Viking hoard so far discovered in northern Europe. This fact alone suggests that it represents much more than the wealth of one man or one community. It comprises 8,000 coins, mostly of Northumbrian origin, and several kilograms of hack silver. All this suggests that the hoard must have belonged to an army that had been marauding in the north of England for some time.

reports that in 911 a Danish army was harrying the northern parts of England at will. When King Edward learned of this he sent his own army and summoned his allies from Mercia, 'and they came up with the rear of the enemy as he was on his way homeward, and there fought with him and put him to flight, and slew many thousands of his men'. This unlocated conflict, it is suggested, holds the key to the Cuerdale Hoard. The retreating Danes hurriedly concealed their war chest – the result of three years' plundering in Northumbria – before offering battle to Edward's army. Some historians have preferred to connect the treasure with an even more celebrated victory, that of Athelstan over the Danes at 'Brunanburg' in 937.

Whatever the truth, some such conflict surely accounts for both the size of the treasure and the persistence of the legend. Or does it? Lancashire tradition still asserts that the 'greatest treasure in all England' has yet to be discovered and that the Cuerdale Hoard was not the one referred to in the old saying. Perhaps the real treasure is lost for all time beneath layers of concrete and the pounding tyres of the juggernauts.

Crown and Cross

The greatest treasure houses of the Middle Ages in Europe were the leading Christian abbeys and cathedrals, where the clergy prayed constantly for the souls of their benefactors and kept the shrines and relics of the saints. Devout pilgrims came to offer gifts to the churches for the adornment of their worship, so that within their dim, incense-laden interiors, fabulous treasures were accumulated, protected as much by superstitious dread as by locks and iron grilles. But there was no protection against determined men who did not fear the Christian God.

In the eleventh century Byzantine Asia Minor fell under the sway of the Seljuk Turks. Churches were sacked and pillaged by the advancing Muslims. Before leaving their monastery, the monks of Holy Sion, Kumluca (near Antalya), buried their collection of silver communion plate, gilded crosses, jewelled censers, candlesticks, illuminated books with ornamental metalwork covers and gold-framed icons – over a hundred pieces of magnificent Byzantine craftsmanship – in a field near the abbey.

There it lay until 1962 when a local peasant woman dreamed that a great treasure lay at the foot of a nearby tree – or so the story goes. The next day she set her menfolk digging, and soon the entire hoard lay spread out on the ground. News of the find brought officials and dealers flocking to Kumluca. The latter, the scavengers of the international art

The Château of Carcassonne in the South of France, one of the Templar castles where a fortune is reputed to be hidden.

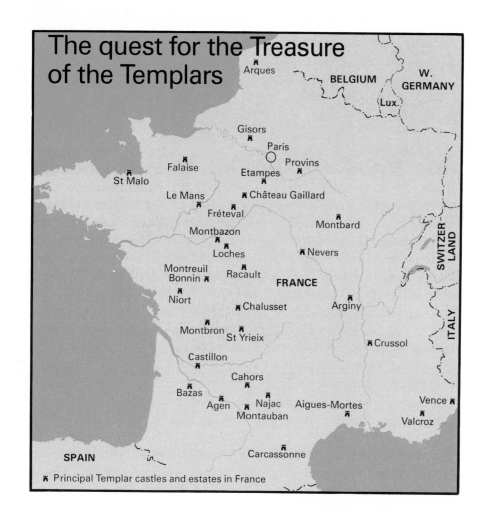

*Rare fifth-century chalice and dish
found by a peasant girl at Gourdon,
southern France.*

*The Castle of Gisors in Normandy is
one of the many possible sites of buried
Templar treasure. During excavations
there in 1962 a French newspaper
reporter went to investigate, only to
find himself trapped for two hours when
part of the diggings caved in.*

and antiquities market, were on the spot first with their large sums of
ready cash. By the time the museum authorities from Antalya arrived,
certain pieces had already disappeared. The peasants readily turned over
to their own countrymen enough of the treasure to keep them happy.
Most of the finer pieces went to the highest private bidder. They now
form part of the Byzantine collection at Dumbarton Oaks, Washington,
DC.

This story has similarities with the discovery of the Treasure of
Gourdon. One day in 1845 a peasant girl noticed a tile marked with a
cross set in the earth of a field near the little French town of Gourdon.
Beneath it she discovered an exquisite chalice and patten of gold set with
garnets and turquoises. They dated from the fifth century and must have
been part of a church treasure concealed when the Franks overran
Burgundy in 524.

No group of medieval Christians was richer or more powerful than
the Knights Templar, one of the three military orders founded to protect
pilgrims to the Holy Land. By 1300 the Templars owned over 8,000
castles spread throughout Christendom, had gained enormous wealth
from donations and war with the Muslims and had added the role of
international financiers to their other occupations. King Philip IV of
France was jealous of their power and their wealth. With the connivance
of the Inquisition he arrested their leaders on spurious charges of heresy.
The order was suppressed in 1312 and some of their valuable goods
seized by Philip and his fellow monarchs. But the Templars had had
plenty of time to conceal much of their wealth, and many people believe
that fabulous hoards are still hidden deep within their castles, churches
and tombs, and the locations are indicated by cryptic signs which they
carved on walls.

Treasures of 1000-1700 AD Found in Britain

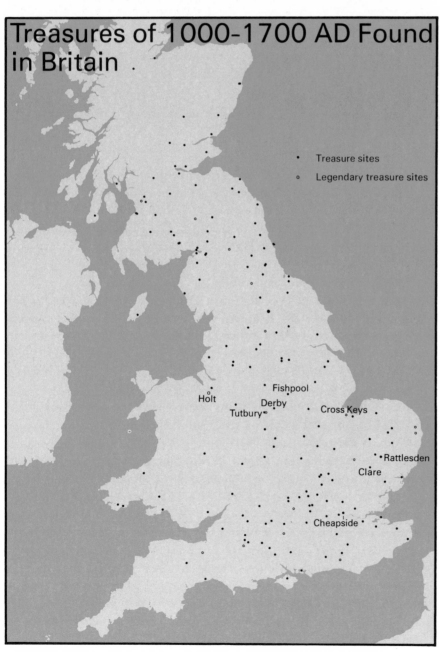

- • Treasure sites
- ○ Legendary treasure sites

Holt
Fishpool
Derby
Tutbury
Cross Keys
Rattlesden
Clare
Cheapside

It was a nineteenth-century historian who first made the joke about King John losing his clothes in the Wash. The loss of the unfortunate monarch's treasure makes a good, dramatic story and one which appealed to Victorian artists. It also appealed to schoolmasters and the writers of history books. This must largely explain the persistence of a legend which has so little factual basis.

The outline of the Wash was very different in the thirteenth century, long before extensive land reclamation took place. King John's baggage train had to cross a wide expanse of tide-washed sand.

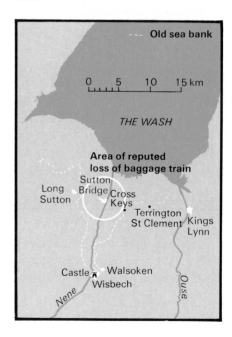

--- Old sea bank

0 5 10 15 km

THE WASH

Area of reputed loss of baggage train

Long Sutton
Sutton Bridge
Cross Keys
Terrington St Clement
Kings Lynn
Castle
Walsoken
Wisbech
Nene
Ouse

King John's Treasure

It may be no more than the misreading of a medieval text that lies at the root of the legend of King John's treasure. In October 1216 a terrible disaster certainly overtook part of the King's entourage. The previous year John had been forced by his barons to agree to Magna Carta but he had no intention of accepting any loss of power, and as soon as opportunity arose he launched a vigorous campaign, travelling rapidly around the country. On 10 October 1216, he left King's Lynn in Norfolk to circuit the wide estuary of the Wash. What is now rich farmland was then a treacherous stretch of tide-washed sand, quicksand and marsh. John travelled by way of Wisbech and Spalding with his army but for greater speed he sent his slow-moving baggage by the hazardous, direct route.

While they were crossing the wide Nene estuary, carts, horses and men were overwhelmed by an abnormally early tide. There were no survivors. News of the tragedy shook the King, already ill and suffering from fatigue. He died a week later at Newark. Those are the facts. But what was in the lost wagons? The chronicler Roger of Wendover tells us that it was the *regium apparatum*, a somewhat ambiguous phrase. It may simply mean the royal baggage – clothes, furniture, tents, weapons, utensils. Or it may mean, as legend prefers to believe, the royal regalia – crown, sceptre, treasure chests and the rich trappings of the King's chapel. The answer to this ancient riddle lies somewhere beneath the Norfolk–Lincolnshire border.

The medieval conflicts between king, church and nobility in England have resulted in an abundance of buried treasure hoards. Thomas, Earl of Lancaster raised the standard of revolt against his cousin, Edward II, in 1321. In February 1322 he and his adherents were surprised by the royal army at Burton-on-Trent and forced to flee northwards. While hurriedly crossing the Dove at Tutbury, Derbyshire, he lost his war chest. Shortly afterwards the Earl was captured and executed. None of his followers, apparently, tried to recover Lancaster's fortune and it was not discovered until 1831 when some labourers were deepening the river. Over 20,000 silver pennies were scooped out of the swirling waters.

In the next century rival Yorkist and Lancastrian factions struggled for the crown. An important battle was fought at Hexham in 1464 and just before or just after it, someone, perhaps the monks of nearby Newstead Abbey, buried at Fishpool 1,237 gold coins and ten pieces of jewellery to protect them from being plundered. This hoard, worth at least £250,000, was discovered in 1966 by workmen on a building site.

Hundreds of other finds are of anonymous origin. In 1937 634 coins were found at Derby, probably concealed at the time of the Black Death. A bronze statue of St John was ploughed up at Rattlesden, Suffolk, in 1973. The finder thought so little of it that he gave it to his young son who swapped it for a toy car. However, the father had second thoughts and must have been glad he did: the statue made £37,000 at auction. He fared rather better than another Suffolk labourer a century before who unearthed an exquisite fourteenth-century gold crucifix studded with pearls in the castle bailey at Clare. This priceless relic may have originally belonged to Edward III and was claimed by Queen Victoria for the royal collection. She graciously rewarded the finder – with three sovereigns.

The London Museum houses this beautiful collection of sixteenth-century and earlier rings, pendants, crucifixes, chains, watches, unmounted stones, flagons, a pomander and a crystal salt-cellar. It was found in 1912 below the foundations of a house in Cheapside where it must have been hidden about 1600. But why or by whom it was hidden remains a mystery.

In 1344 Holt Castle, Clwyd, belonged to Earl John de Warenne and, so the contemporary chronicler reports, in that year he slew a dragon living in a nearby cave and possessed himself of the creature's treasures. This story is typical of many medieval legends which link treasure-seeking with the black arts, demonology and mythology. Some, at least, of these tales do have a basis in fact. John de Warenne, like many other landowners, may indeed have found treasure on his property.

The Dissolution of the Monasteries

In 1536 there were over 800 monasteries, nunneries and friaries in England and Wales, most of them richly endowed and adorned. Four years later there were none; their buildings, lands and treasures had been appropriated by Henry VIII. The royal haul was gigantic. The shrine of Thomas à Becket at Canterbury alone yielded two large chests of jewels and twenty-four wagon-loads of gold and silver. But though the King and his agent, Thomas Cromwell, were very thorough, the monks had plenty of time to hide some of their possessions. Those at Glastonbury concealed 'as much plate and adornments as would have begun a new abbey'. Under torture and threat they revealed the hiding places, but legends persist that some treasures escaped. One chalice, perhaps the Holy Grail, is now believed to be hidden in South Wales. In the middle of the nineteenth century a fisherman after eels on Whittlesea Mere, Huntingdonshire, brought up from the slimy bottom a silver Gothic censer, an incense boat, a chandelier and some pewter dishes. These came from either Ramsey Abbey or Peterborough. Twenty years later a fifteenth-century silvered reliquary was prised from the Thames mud at Wapping. It had once belonged to nearby New Abbey. A similar casket was discovered recently in the ruins of Reading Abbey. When the old vicarage at Ormesby, Yorkshire, was repaired in 1838 a box was found built into one of the walls. It contained a hoard of fifteenth- and sixteenth-century gold coins, perhaps removed from Guisborough Priory, to which the vicarage belonged. These proven treasures were all disposed of hurriedly with the minimum of elaboration. They contrast strangely with those colourful hoards of legend, concealed in secret passages and underground chambers.

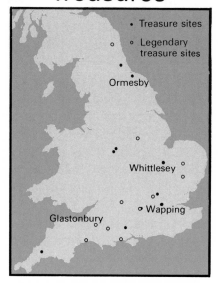

England's Monastic Treasures

Very little English medieval, ecclesiastical plate survives. Most of it was confiscated and melted down at the Reformation. This fact enhances the value of the few remaining pieces. The Ramsey Censer and Incense Boat are excellent examples of fourteenth-century craftsmanship in silver gilt. The appearance of a ram's head and undulating decoration on the incense boat suggested a punning reference to their origin: ram, sea. It was, therefore, generally accepted that the items came from Ramsey Abbey. However, other items found with the two shown seemed to have come from Peterborough, and between 1353 and 1361 the latter monastery was ruled by Abbot Robert of Ramsey. Here is yet another example of buried treasure remaining rich in mystery.

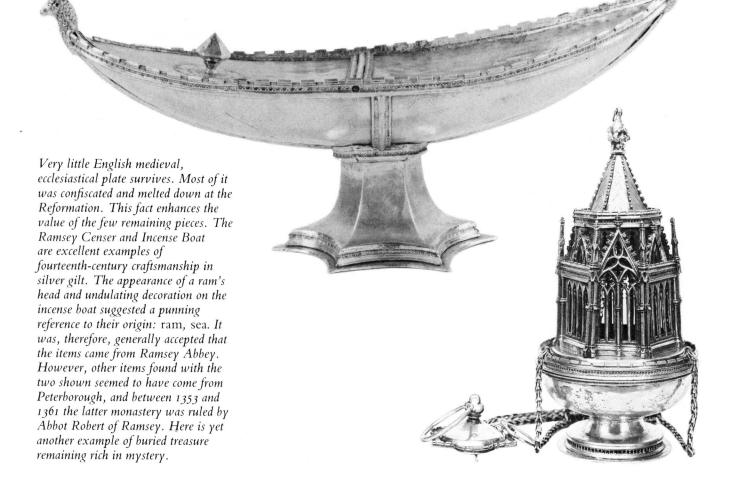

The Roundheads destroyed Corfe Castle after its capture in 1646. It had held out against them for eight weeks, and Lady Mary Bankes threw her treasure down the well to prevent it falling into enemy hands.

Siege Silver

At the outbreak of the Civil War in 1642 most of South-west England was Royalist. But there were exceptions. One was the town of Taunton, defended by its ancient castle – and that was rather unfortunate for the people of Taunton. Sir Ralph Hopton brought an army up from Cornwall and captured the town for the King in 1643. Within months the Parliamentarians had retaken it.

In 1645 the Royalists were back, their cannon trained on the town's defences. For three months they battered away at the walls until the appearance of a relieving force under Sir Thomas Fairfax obliged them to withdraw.

Sometime during these troubles a well-to-do citizen buried his life savings in an earthenware pot. He was never able to return for it, so there it remained until June 1980. Then men digging some foundations broke the pot, and out cascaded a stream of silver shillings, crowns and half-crowns.

The English Civil War

A hundred years after the Dissolution, England was engulfed in the Civil War, and this too has produced a rich crop of treasure legends. Corfe Castle, Dorset, was held for the King by Lady Mary Bankes against a besieging Parliamentary force. After eight weeks, surrender became inevitable but the redoubtable lady vowed that the Roundheads should gain nothing from their success. She threw her jewels and plate down the castle well and followed this with a keg of powder and a lighted fuse. To this day the well remains blocked with tons of rubble. A similar treasure is supposedly concealed somewhere in Heskin Hall, Lancashire, which also fell to Oliver Cromwell's men. A previous owner was so certain of the legend that she called in a team of Royal Engineers to search, without success. Sir Nicholas Stuart, lord of the manor of Hartley, Hampshire, buried his personal fortune to prevent it falling to the enemies of the crown. Part of it was discovered in the eighteenth century but some 800 coins remain buried. Smaller Civil War hoards have been found at Winterslow, Wiltshire, Nuneaton, Catford, Tunstall, Kent, and many other places.

During this war many gentlemen changed sides as opportunity and advantage served. One such was Sir Edward Littleton, who in 1643 was entrusted with £17,500 to raise Parliamentary forces in Staffordshire. Littleton then declared for the King but his treachery was discovered and he was forced to leave his house, Pillaton Hall, hurriedly. He concealed the money in two caches behind panelling in different rooms. When the royalist cause was lost, Littleton was captured and though he avoided serious punishment he was kept under surveillance in London, and was still there when he died in 1658. The hoards therefore remained hidden. Not until a century later, when another Littleton stripped the panelling out, did they come to light.

England's Civil War Treasures

• Treasure sites
○ Legendary treasure sites

Heskin Hall
Pillaton Hall
Nuneaton
Messing
Hartley
Tunstall
Winterslow
Catford
Taunton
Corfe Castle

Treasures of the French Revolution

Madame du Barry was still beautiful when she went to the guillotine and, if legend is correct, she proudly carried with her the secret of her treasure. For five years she had been the mistress of Louis XV, who had showered on her jewels, lands and precious trinkets. She retired to her estates on the death of her royal lover but when the French Revolution broke out in 1789 she did all she could to succour her old friends among the court aristocracy. For this she was arrested, tried and executed (7 December 1793). In the last days of her liberty she concealed the remainder of her money and jewels in and around her château at Sceaux. Some, but not all, of these hoards were discovered by the sansculottes.

There is scarcely a region of France which does not have its stories of wealth hidden by aristocrats and *émigrés*. Over 17,000 'enemies of the people' perished on the guillotine and thousands more fled abroad. Fear and contempt for the new regime inspired many of them to hide their treasures, and while some of these hoards were discovered by local people or government agents, or ultimately reclaimed by their owners, others undoubtedly remained concealed. An oxhide full of silver and gold coins still lies buried near Moissac, the property of a nobleman who fled to Spain and died there. Somewhere in the Château de Bourdeilles in the Dordogne one and a half million gold *livres* are hidden. The forests of the Vendée, south of Nantes, were a royalist stronghold where General Charette, aided by English gold, long resisted the revolutionaries. When at last he was forced to retreat he sank his war chest in the bottom of a

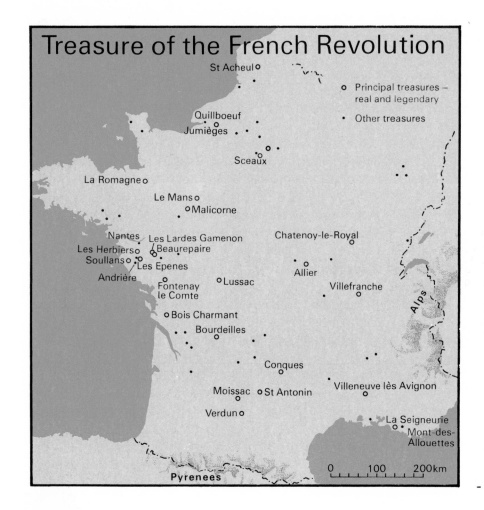

The remains of the priory at Villeneuve-lès-Avignon where a mystic inscription indicates the whereabouts of a great monastic treasure.

Madame du Barry, one-time mistress of Louis XV, was fifty when she went to the guillotine without revealing the hiding place of her money, plate and jewels. This rich hoard lies somewhere in the grounds of the beautiful Château de Sceaux.

deep well. This legendary well has never been located, and probably now never will be.

Many tales are told of Louis XVI's treasures and it is known that he made careful provision for an escape which never materialized. One of the more reliable stories concerns the brig *Telémaque*, which tried to reach England disguised as a merchant ship carrying timber and pitch. Hidden aboard was royal gold, Marie Antoinette's diamonds, and the possessions of several *émigrés* and wealthy abbeys. The ship was anchored in the Seine estuary near Quilleboeuf when she was caught by a winter storm, torn from her moorings and sunk in nine fathoms. Salvage attempts in 1830, 1850 and 1939 all failed to penetrate the thick silt covering the wreck.

In 1792 the government stretched out its hands to grasp the treasure of the monasteries. Many abbots and prioresses took care to prevent sacred objects falling into profane hands. The Carthusians of Villeneuve-lès-Avignon buried enough gold, 'to rebuild the priory three times over', as one of them boasted in exile. The coin, plate, gold reliquaries and jewelled chalices had been concealed in various deposits marked by boundary stones. The secret of the stones was passed on by word of mouth from generation to generation; as recently as 1957 information brought to the custodian of the ruined monastery caused him to remove some panelling from one of the rooms. Engraved in the wall behind was a plan with figures and symbols. Unfortunately neither he nor anyone else has yet been able to decipher the inscription.

Redcoat Treasure

Major General Edward Braddock was, according to Benjamin Franklin, a leader who 'had too much self-confidence'. When he arrived in North America in 1755 to assume command of an expedition against French and Indian forces menacing England's colonies, his military principles were few and simple: soldiers only responded to harsh discipline; the tactics of European warfare were fully valid in New England; a rabble of 'frogs' and 'savages' was no match for his redcoats. Thus motivated, he set out from Fort Cumberland on the Potomac to storm the enemy stronghold, Fort Duquesne (modern Pittsburg). The march took several weeks and one of the overnight camps was on high ground above what is now the town of Frederick, Maryland. It was at this point that the General decided he should leave the large army payroll he was carrying. His men were entering hostile territory and it seemed unwise to burden them with an extra load. Furthermore, should the money fall into enemy

'We shall know better how to deal with them next time' – reputedly Edward Braddock's last words before dying of wounds received at the Battle of Monongahela River. On the campaign of 1755 he lost many men and also the army pay chest.

The coins used to pay King George's armies were probably mainly silver crowns similar to the type shown at the top. Few British soldiers earned sufficient wages to be paid in gold. It is from later hoards that the magnificent coins such as the George III sovereign (bottom) are found.

hands his own troops would immediately be impoverished, and the enemy enriched. He therefore went out at night with one trusted soldier, and together they buried the pay chest. Braddock was in no doubt that he would shortly be returning victorious and able to repossess himself of the money for his majesty's army.

A few days later his force was cut to pieces by devastating enemy gunfire at the rout of Monongahela River. Braddock himself was fatally wounded and died on the retreat. To the end he was faithful to his principles. The remnants of the army trudged back to safety. The payroll – wages enough for 1,200 men for several months – remained behind. Presumably it is still there, beneath the neat rows of suburban houses known as Braddock Heights.

Three years later the boot was on the other foot. Another British expedition was launched against Fort Duquesne. An eyewitness describes what happened:

A detail of 10 men and 16 pack horses were selected to carry the French Army's gold and silver away from the fort ... Three days and a forenoon later, Northwest of West from the fort, while on the Tuscarawas Trail our advance guard returned to our little column and reported British soldiers advancing on us. The officer in charge of our detail ordered us to stop in our tracks and dig a hole in the ground. He posted a few guards while the rest dug. The gold was unloaded from the horses and placed in the hole. Then the silver was lowered into the hole. On top of this we shovelled the dirt and covered it with branches.

The British started firing at this time ... Eight were killed, only Henry Muselle and myself were spared. The English had not noticed where we hid. We made the following marks on the area before we fled. The gold was buried in the centre of a sort of square formed by four springs. About one half-mile to the west of the hole where the gold was buried Muselle jammed a rock into the fork of a tree so that it would stay. 600 steps to the North of the hole, the shovels we hid under a log. As we left by the east I carved a deer into a tree which I judged to be about one mile east of the hole.

The colonial and Indian wars produced many similar stories of lost treasures – Indian silver hoards and buried loot, lost payrolls, the concealed savings of early traders and trappers, etc. Most have never been found but there are exceptions. In 1965–6 a team of divers located $700,000 worth of French coins in a wreck off Cape Breton. It was *Le Chameau*, a French ship which went down in 1725 carrying pay for Louis XV's troops in Canada. Not far away lie the remains of HMS *Faversham*, a British warship involved in the war with France. Many rare and valuable coins have been recovered from this wreck. In 1787 the loss off Delaware Bay of the British (ex-Dutch) sloop *De Braak* was reported. She was carrying 'an immense amount of treasure, consisting of gold and silver bars and precious stones, and also £80,000 in English gold'. She has defied many attempts at salvage over the last two hundred years.

Returning to the mainland, one of the more reliable stories concerns the silver of the Shawnees. The Indians mined the metal near the shore of Lake Erie. This naturally attracted the colonists who advanced steadily deeper into Indian territory. Rather than let this wealth fall into enemy hands Chief Black Hoof ordered all silver objects to be gathered up and thrown into a nearby swamp. Then the Shawnee set their villages on fire and fled.

The Lawless Frontier

Gold! The discovery in California in 1848 turned the steady westward flow of migrants into a stampede. Many fortunes were won and lost in the following half-century before the Wild West was tamed. The relics of this turbulent era are ghost towns, abandoned workings and a wealth of stories about lost mines, prospectors' hoards, and bandits' buried loot.

Among the first prospectors to make a lucky strike in Montana, after the original gold rush area had become overcrowded, was Almenzo Yerdon. He made a great deal of money very quickly, lived well and was soon engaged to one of the beauties of Diamond City. At the last moment she turned him down. The jilted Yerdon became a recluse from that day. He bought a small homestead, turned all his ore into gold coins and retired to a cabin in the Big Belt Mountains, only venturing into town for essential supplies. So he lived for half a century. In 1918 a visitor found Yerdon's scorched body in the burned ruins of his cabin. The

In 1848 James Marshall picked a gold nugget from the American River, near Coloma, California. A year later 80,000 prospectors ('forty-niners') had arrived in the area, most of them equipped with only a few tools and unlimited optimism. When the surface workings had run dry the hopefuls drifted northwards along the Rockies. Strikes were made in Nevada, Oregon, Colorado, Idaho, Montana, S. Dakota, Washington and British Columbia. Camps were isolated – the miners worked in secrecy, alone or in small groups. Often they were attacked by Indians who resented the intrusion on their territory. Always there were criminals, ready to kill prospectors for their precious dust and nuggets. Prudent miners hid their gold until such time as they could take it into town and bank it. David Weaver found a rich lode at Emigrant Peak in Crow country but after working it for a few months was warned off by Indians; burying what gold he could not carry, he returned east, with enough money to set himself up in business. Joseph Knoles made a fortune in the Bannack gold rush and retired to Dillon. He became a recluse after the death of his Indian wife. When he knew that he was dying he wrote to relatives asking them to come so that he could tell them where his gold was hidden. They arrived too late. Such are the stories that abound in the old frontier districts.

CANADA

Columbia

WASHINGTON

Spokane

Snake

Portland

R

Malta

Choteau

Augusta

Missouri

MONTANA

Big Belt Mts

Deer Lodge
Basin

O

Three Forks

Sheridan
Dillon
Bannack

Virginia City

C

Yellowstone

Hardin

Busby

Powder

Big Horn Mts

OREGON

IDAHO

WYOMING

Jackson Hole

K

Wind River
Indian Reserve

Glenrock

Fort Laramie

Rock River

Sacramento

Y

Salt Lake City

Denver

NEVADA

UTAH

COLORADO

Sacramento

M

San Francisco

Colorado

CALIFORNIA

T

COLORADO

PLATEAUS

S

NEW MEXICO

ARIZONA

Los Angeles

PACIFIC OCEAN

Phoenix

Gila

Pecos

El Paso

Rio Grande

Gulf of California

MEXICO

• Treasure sites

Treasures of the Wild West

belief that the old prospector's hoard was buried there brought a crowd of would-be purchasers to the auction of the homestead which was knocked down for five times its current market value. But the successful buyer found no gold, so Yerdon's treasure, now worth more than a million dollars, presumably still awaits discovery.

Probably the most persistent and best authenticated rumour about rich gold workings is that concerning the Lost Cabin Mine in the Big Horn Mountains of Wyoming. Three prospectors, apparently, stumbled across an exceedingly rich vein of ore, deep in Sioux and Shoshone country, in 1863. They worked it for nearly a year, accumulating several hundred dollars' worth of gold daily. Then two of them were murdered in an Indian raid. The survivor, Allen Hulbert, hurriedly buried all the gold he could not carry and made the long, arduous journey back to white man's land. When he returned, months later, he could not find his way back to the Lost Cabin Mine. But another group of prospectors did find it. They worked it for a further season before succumbing to the same fate as their predecessors. The lone survivor of this enterprise gathered a group of adventurers at Fort Laramie and returned to the Big Horn Mountains in 1866. None of them was ever seen again. Another man who did see the mine and lived to tell the tale was Father Jean de Smet, a Jesuit missionary. But he died in 1872 without revealing the location of the Lost Cabin, because he had promised the Indians that he would keep their secret and not encourage palefaces to overrun the land. A century of growth on the wooded slopes of the Big Horn Mountains has now made it much more difficult for anyone to find the lost mine and its buried prospector hoards.

There seems to be a breed (and by no means a dying breed) of compulsive American treasure-hunters who devote themselves to tracking down legendary frontier hoards. Yet, in all probability, most discoveries are made by accident. In 1884 four young Texans were hunting across the Red River in Indian Territory (now Oklahoma) when their dog disappeared into a hole in the rocks. The men removed boulders and found themselves in a complex of caves. There were obvious signs of human occupation – tools, charred wood, animal bones – though, quite clearly, no one had been there in decades. Then, venturing further in, they saw six boxes. And in one of the boxes there lay 'two bushels of Spanish money and bullion' – silver dollars and ingots and two gold crucifixes. The finders emerged from that cave rich men, for the treasure of some long dead Spanish prospectors brought them $25,000.

Indian Territory was a favourite haunt of another breed of frontiersman, the outlaw. Here, where no state or federal law could touch them, notorious criminals such as the James Brothers and the Dalton Gang had their hideouts and sometimes buried their loot. Yet the richer pickings were further west, where small banks stored the prospectors' gold and stagecoach and train carried it across desolate country. Most criminals had a short career and came to a bloody end. Few escaped justice and lived to enjoy the proceeds of villainy and this fact has given rise to hundreds, perhaps thousands, of stories of concealed bandit caches. After a hundred years and more it is impossible to sift fact from fiction.

Take, for example, the case of Henry Plummer. Having been run out of California, Nevada, Idaho and Washington, this scoundrel arrived in Bannack in 1862, at the time of the Montana gold rush. He contrived to have himself elected sheriff, a position which enabled him to protect an unsavoury miscellany of villains and profit handsomely from their

Despite his distinguished appearance, Henry Plummer was a vicious and ruthless villain. He used his position as sheriff of Bannack, Montana, to organize and brilliantly execute a series of stagecoach hold-ups along the trails leading from the gold fields. When he was eventually captured by vigilantes he grovelled and pleaded for mercy, attempting to buy his life with stolen money.

The Deadwood Stage

The hold-up of the Deadwood Stage on 26 September 1878 caused a sensation throughout the Midwest; part of the loot was never recovered. Gold was discovered in the Black Hills of South Dakota in 1876 and Deadwood gained an evil reputation as a lawless mining town (Wild Bill Hickok was killed in a saloon gunfight here). The Cheyenne and Black Hills Stage Line transported gold to the Wyoming capital, whence it was railroaded east for the US Mint. They used an armoured coach called the Monitor and they were very proud of their unbroken record of successful delivery. Charles Carey, who had fought in the Indian Wars under General Custer, was not daunted by the difficulty of the task and he was attracted by the $400,000 in bullion which the Monitor usually carried.

On that September day he prepared an ambush at Canyon Springs stage post. He and his men locked the stable hand in the grain store and took up positions in the timbered barns and stables. About three o'clock, the Monitor trundled into Canyon Springs and, as usual, stopped to change the team of six horses. It immediately came under heavy fire. Two of the guards were wounded and a telegraph operator travelling in the coach was killed. The fighting was fierce, however, and the CBH employees accounted for two of the gang, before being forced to surrender. The bandits' task was still only half done: they now had to break open the heavy, securely locked, iron and steel chest containing the gold. This took them two hours of sweating work with sledgehammers and chisels. At last they were successful. Their haul was 700 lb of gold dust and bars, $3,500 in currency and a quantity of diamonds and jewellery. Now they had to move quickly; the stable hand and one of the guards had escaped and would soon be back with a posse from Deadwood. Some of the heavy gold had to be buried near by and a further cache was deposited at Pino Springs.

Enormous rewards were offered for information about the criminals and their loot, and one by one the crooks were tracked down; Carey was hanged by vigilantes at Jenny Stockade. About three-fifths of the stolen valuables was recovered but no record exists of the Canyon Springs cache having been found.

The war against the Sioux and Cheyenne came to a head in 1876 when government troops moved into Big Horn country. On 25 June, Captain Grant Marsh anchored the *Far West*, a requisitioned Missouri River steamer carrying army supplies, at the junction of the Big Horn and Little Big Horn rivers. He was nervous and kept a constant watch for the local Cheyenne and their Chief, Two Moons. (In fact, Two Moons was preoccupied with the massacre of General Custer's force at the Battle of the Little Big Horn.) Suddenly white men appeared on the bank with two wagons. They were taking $800,000 worth of raw gold from the Rockies to Bismarck, N. Dakota. They were afraid to travel further and urged Marsh to convey the bullion for them. Reluctantly the captain agreed. Next day Indian activity forced him to retreat downriver. Fearing that the gold might provoke an attack, he had it unloaded and buried. Then he returned to rendezvous with the US army. Soon he was fully occupied conveying wounded soldiers to safety and the gold was forgotten. As far as is known, it was never collected.

Fort Laramie, Wyoming (above opposite) in hostile Sioux country was the last outpost of civilization for many westbound settlers. Ahead lay a thousand miles of mountain and desert. Even here people and goods were not always safe; almost within sight of the fort a stagecoach was held up and $40,000 stolen. The outlaw buried his loot near by. Days later he was captured and summarily shot.

The Dalton Gang operated mainly in Kansas between 1890 and 1892. Their violent career came to an end at a shoot-out in Coffeyville when they tried to rob two banks simultaneously. The only survivor spent fifteen years in gaol. Their hidden loot remained uncollected.

activities. Gold from the mining town of Virginia City, high in the Rockies, had to travel the mountainous ninety-mile route to Bannack by stagecoach. The consignments were completely at the mercy of Plummer and his gang. During little more than a year of plundering along this and other stage routes the robbers murdered 203 people and made off with untold millions in raw gold and specie. At last the locals were goaded into retaliation. Vigilante bands were set up. Many of the sheriff's colleagues were captured or killed in shoot-outs, and Plummer himself was arrested. Pleading for his life, the villain revealed the whereabouts of some of his loot. Even on the gallows he made a last desperate bid for a reprieve. 'Let me go, and I will tell you where $300,000 more is buried.' He was hanged, without trial, on 10 January 1864. And immediately the legends of his buried hoards began. Scores of deposits are said to exist over an area of a hundred and fifty miles' radius from Helena, Montana: $400,000 buried beside the Rocky Hill stage road north of Bannack; $150,000 at the base of a tree in Centennial Valley; $300,000 under the floor of a cabin at Haystack Butte, near Augusta; $300,000 at 'Pete Daly's corale', between Sheridan and Twin Bridges; $150,000 on the pioneer road near Haugan; $100,000 on the shores of Rainy Lake; $200,000 on an island in Missoula River, etc.

Full Fathom Five

Beneath the Wine-Dark Sea

The ocean floor beneath the sea lanes of the world is littered with the remains of thousands of wrecked ships and their spilled cargoes. Until recent years most of these sites were inaccessible to treasure-hunters and archaeologists, but the development of deep-sea salvage apparatus and the growth of skin diving as a popular and relatively inexpensive hobby have opened up 'Davy Jones' Locker' to all and sundry. The scramble for treasure on the sea bed is now intense. It generates as much greed, competition, anger and ineffective effort at official control as the plundering of ancient burial mounds ashore.

Man first went out on the sea in ships about five and a half thousand years ago. It was probably around 3500 BC that small, coast-hugging vessels propelled by oars and/or sails made their way around the fringes of the Mediterranean and the Indian Ocean. Gradually the early mariners learned to harness wind and current; learned to take the short, direct routes that linked their countries with their trading partners; learned, too, the treachery of the elements that could send merchants, sailors and precious cargoes to the sea bed.

The earliest vessel so far located is a merchant ship which foundered in ten fathoms in the Gulf of Hydra, south of Athens, about 2500 BC. A team of divers in 1975 brought up a number of pottery sherds from the wreck but were able to discover little about the vessel itself. Marine archaeologists had more success with a later ship which sank off Cape Gelidonya in Turkey 3,200 years ago. She was carrying copper ingots from Cyprus packed in baskets made in Syria.

Though such a vessel and its cargo were new, and of great interest to the archaeological world, it was not unique to the professional divers of the eastern Mediterranean. The sponge fishermen of the Aegean have for centuries been familiar with many of the wrecks littering the shallow coastal waters. They are a clannish people who pass on the secrets of their craft from father to son and they are accustomed to thinking of the sea as their domain and everything in it as their lawful possession. They have always supplemented their income from sponges by selling items salvaged from old wrecks. Copper ingots and lead from ancient anchors have considerable scrap metal value. Amphorae can be offered to tourists. And occasionally there are more exciting finds.

Between the west end of Crete and the lip of mainland Greece runs a reef that occasionally thrusts itself above the surface of the sea in the form of rocks and tiny islands. It has always been a marine hazard and the skeletons of many ships lie, coral-encrusted, beneath the waves. In 1900 Dimitrios Kondos and his crew were moored near the barren outline of Andikithera, diving for sponges. They used helmeted suits filled with air from a compressor and took it in turns to go down. Elias Stadiatis went over the side to try his luck on a new location. He had been down no

For thousands of years – from the Bronze Age to the Renaissance – the Mediterranean was the world's most important theatre of maritime commerce. The sea bed is littered with the wrecks of ships which never reached port. The commonest cargo in classical times was amphorae, used for storing and transporting oil, wine and other commodities. Thousands of these jars have been found but few collections are in such good condition as those located in this first-century BC wreck off Giens, southern France.

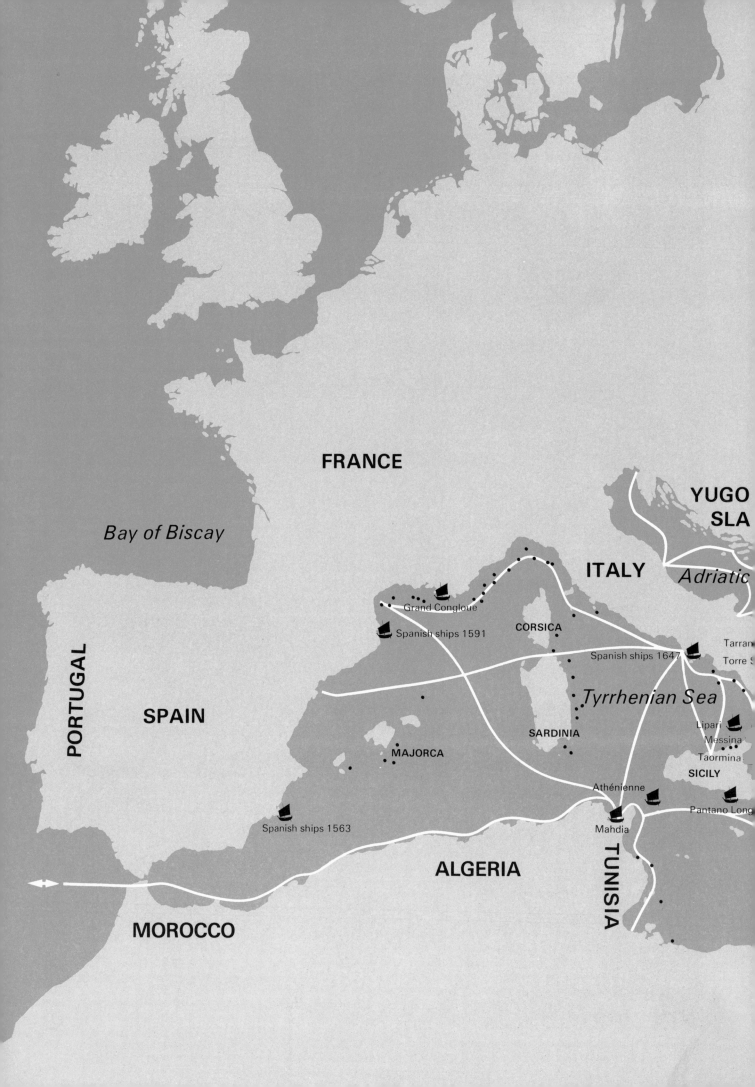

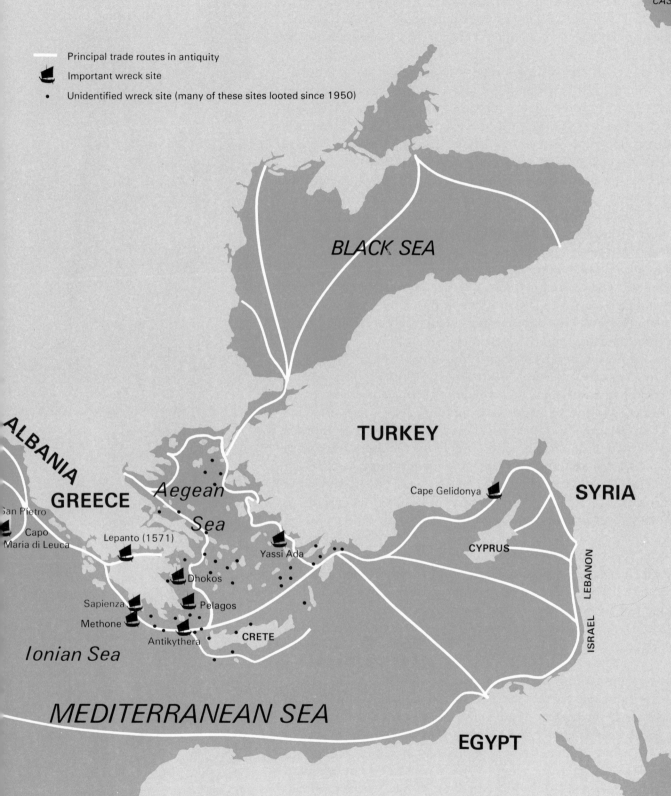

Sunken treasures of the Mediterranean Sea

Principal trade routes in antiquity

Important wreck site

Unidentified wreck site (many of these sites looted since 1950)

CASPIAN SEA

BLACK SEA

TURKEY

ALBANIA

GREECE

Aegean Sea

San Pietro

Capo Maria di Leuca

Lepanto (1571)

Dhokos

Sapienza

Methone

Pelagos

Antikythera

Ionian Sea

CRETE

Cape Gelidonya

SYRIA

CYPRUS

ISRAEL

LEBANON

Yassi Ada

MEDITERRANEAN SEA

EGYPT

Gulf of Sirte

LIBYA

more than a few minutes when he rushed back to the surface. Something was wrong. Quickly his colleagues hauled him aboard and wrenched off his helmet.

'Horses! Women! Naked women!' Stadiatis was babbling ludicrously. He said he had seen a whole city of dead animals and people. Nothing would persuade him to dive again on that spot. It was the captain who donned his suit and went down to try to make some sense of Stadiatis' discovery. He took one end of a rope with him. On the bottom he attached it to something, then surfaced and ordered his crew to haul in his find. It was a human hand – made of bronze. They had found a classical wreck, full of statues. How much Kondos and his men took for private sale we do not know but on their return home they reported the wreck to the authorities. Over the next few months a government-backed expedition raised the bulk of the Andikithera Treasure. It took decades for experts to examine the statues – and even longer to agree about them. There were fourth-century BC bronzes and marble statues which were copies of earlier models. The ship had sunk in the first century BC and was probably a Roman cargo vessel taking Greek loot home to Italy.

Many similar finds – some of greater importance – have been made during the twentieth century in the Mediterranean. In 1927 a trawler net was fouled. When skin divers went down to free it they saw a life-size bronze statue. It turned out to be a representation of Poseidon or Zeus, and one of the finest examples of classical craftsmanship. It is now one of the more prized exhibits in the National Museum in Athens. Nowadays all ancient artefacts are valuable. Museums and private collectors will pay high prices for rare antiquities regardless of their intrinsic or artistic worth. Rumours of any significant new find always arouse interest and rivalry. This was certainly so in 1970 when it was known that the remains of a large Byzantine ship had been discovered off the Aegean island of Pelagos and that items of cargo had been brought up almost intact from a depth of eighteen fathoms. In fact over 1,500 pieces of pottery were salvaged, including large amphorae, and plates colourfully decorated with animal and geometrical motifs. So rare are such objects, which originally were the commonplaces of daily life, that they now have considerable value. Ironically, it is the tragedy of shipwreck which has preserved them. Had the Byzantine cargo been safely landed and dispersed through the normal channels of trade the chances of a single piece being preserved for posterity would have been remote.

Such a find is unusual: coins, pots, statuary – these are the commonplaces of Mediterranean submarine archaeology. Not all finds, of course, are catalogued and end up in public museums. As well as native divers, a whole army of modern adventurers constantly scours the sea bottom for treasure. It is estimated that there are five million scuba divers in Western Europe and the United States. Many of them have tried their luck in the Mediterranean at some time. It wants only the suggestion that an ancient wreck has been located for amateur and professional treasure-hunters to rush to the site. The international art world is constantly buzzing with stories of objects looted from the sea bed, to be subsequently offered discreetly on the market. Only a few years ago, it is said, some Italian divers working off the coast of Sicily retrieved a statue, later attributed to the great Athenian sculptor Praxiteles, which was sold in Germany for half a million pounds.

Two of the more dramatic treasures to be found under Mediterranean waters are the above bust of a philosopher and the winged god below which were in the wreck of a Roman ship off Mahdia on the Tunisian coast. The wreck was full of Greek works of art on their way to wealthy colonial patrons in North Africa.

One of the more charming pieces of classical statuary is the jockey of Artemesion. Behind it lies a fascinating story of marine salvage. It was in the 1950s that a sunken ship was located off Artemesion, and among the consignment of statues aboard was the figure of a young jockey (right). Many years later among the bronze fragments coming up from the wreck archaeologists recognized the sections of a horse. Much patient work had to be done reassembling the animal, but at last horse and rider were reunited after 2,200 years (below).

Apart from goggles to protect their eyes and aid visibility, Greek sponge divers had no equipment. Yet they could achieve prodigious diving feats. The record duration for a skin dive in modern times is 5 minutes 40 seconds. Almost certainly this was exceeded frequently by sponge divers in the centuries before breathing apparatus was invented.

The Aegina Treasure Mystery

In 1891 the British Museum was offered for £6,000 a beautiful hoard of Bronze Age Greek gold. This figure – a large one by the standards of the day – was demanded by the vendor because of 'the personal risks he has run' in acquiring a treasure, 'of higher importance than that found by Dr Schliemann at Mycenae'. What the museum authorities did not realize was that they were buying a mystery which would take almost ninety years to unravel. The owner of the treasure, a Mr Brown who dealt in sponges bought from Greek divers, was very reticent. He would only say that the hundred or so pieces of exquisite jewellery were from a twelfth-century BC Mycenaean tomb on the island of Aegina. Even that was suspect, for close examination of the pieces proved them to be at least 500 years older and to have been of Minoan origin. Had the treasure, in fact, been found on the sea bed by Mr Brown's sponge divers? No; patient research over several years by Dr Reynold Higgins of the museum's staff revealed that the treasure had indeed come from a Mycenaean grave. The likelihood is that some time between 900 and 1150 BC a grave-robber looted several Minoan artefacts, probably from a Cretan settlement on Aegina. He concealed them in another tomb he had previously stripped. Then, nemesis or justice caught up with him and he was unable to return for his plunder. Thus it remained in the 'wrong grave' till its accidental discovery by a vineyard workman three thousand years later.

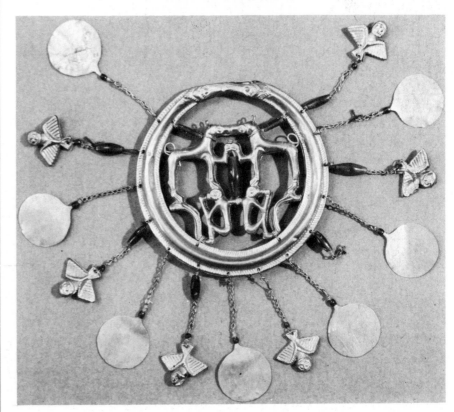

Scuba divers off the Italian coast probe the wreck of a Roman merchant ship, seeking objects of archaeological interest.

A Hero's Treasure

In 1754 Robert Clive was not yet thirty years of age, but his meteoric career in India had won him a personal fortune, the approval of the East India Company and the adulation of the British public. By his brilliant leadership he had enabled the company and its allies among the princes to resist French pressure, and had laid the foundation for his country's domination of the entire subcontinent. Having enjoyed a short spell of home leave in 1754 Clive was recalled to India. He set out the following spring for a second tour of duty, during which he would achieve even greater fame and honour.

A small fleet of five ships was assembled to carry not only Clive, his wife and their belongings, but also fresh troops, provisions and bullion for the company's garrisons. Clive sailed in the *Stretham*, a vessel chartered by the company. Most of his personal property was with him, but a chest containing £3,000 in gold was stowed aboard a sister ship, the *Dodington*, together with 30,522 ounces of silver bullion and £14,496 worth of company cargo. The fleet weighed anchor from the Downs off Dover on 22 April. The *Dodington* was as trim a craft as any afloat and soon proved herself faster than her companions. Long before the Cape of Good Hope was reached, she had lost touch with them. In the second week of July she rounded the southern tip of Africa and headed into the Indian Ocean, where according to the official log she encountered 'Dirty Squally Weather with the Wind from SSW to SSE and a Very Large Sea'. Crossing the wide expanse of Algoa Bay, the *Dodington* ran head-on into a low, uncharted island, now known as Bird Island. Twenty-three survivors out of a complement of 270 struggled ashore. They salvaged several items from the wreck, including some of the treasure. Here the reports and rumours diverge widely. How much bullion came ashore and what happened to it is not clear. Certainly some silver and plate was found and the castaways squabbled over it. Certainly the officers recovered some and delivered it to company officials when, after seven months, the survivors escaped from Bird Island. Beyond that all is mystery. There were stories of hidden caches on the mainland opposite the island and of unofficial salvage attempts but there were no hard facts to support them.

Then, in 1977, two South African scuba divers, David Allen and Gerry van Niekerk, made a scientific search for the *Dodington*. They had already done a dramatic salvage job on the *Sacramento*, a seventeenth-century Portuguese vessel carrying a cargo of new bronze cannon. Now they followed up careful archival research with a detailed survey of the area. So meticulous were their preparations that Allen found the ship on his first dive. Somehow they managed for a while to work the site with the knowledge of the museum authorities at Port Elizabeth but otherwise in complete secrecy. They found a variety of articles – scissors, knives, clay pipes, glass beads for trading with Indian merchants, combs, mirrors, some superb bronze cannon and, financially the most important discovery, twenty tons of copper ingots.

But what of Clive's treasure? The salvage work goes on but, though Allen and van Niekerk have found large quantities of silver coin, no gold has appeared so far. Perhaps it is still on the ocean floor, or perhaps some of the survivors really did find it and bury it on the deserted African coast.

A Mystery Find
The Great Basses Ridge is a reef off the south coast of Ceylon and a vicious death-trap for sailing ships, especially those running helplessly before a fierce monsoon. In 1961 a small group of people arrived there to make an underwater film, choosing the few weeks in March–April when the sea was calm enough to be safe. Two young members of the crew spent a free morning snorkeling over the reef. Suddenly one of them saw a small bronze cannon. Passing over the

Treasure in an underwater valley

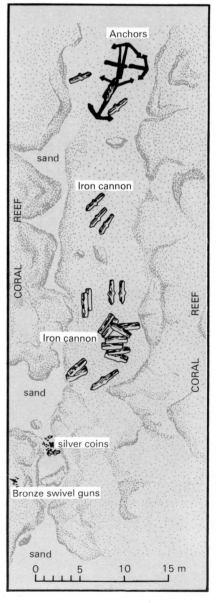

spine of rock and coral, he came upon another similar gun. Two such finds must mean that there were more waiting and it was with great excitement that the boys returned to the spot later in the day. Beyond the first ridge they found themselves in a coral valley and there the dramatic story of an ancient shipwreck lay vividly illustrated. No timber survived, but there was a pile of immense rusting anchors, more cannon in batches along the gully and, where the stern would have been, a mound of objects, some of which gleamed in the filtered sunlight. Silver! Everywhere the divers looked there were coins – eighteenth-century silver rupees. They brought up bagfuls but made little impression on the total treasure. Two years later, the leader of the film crew returned with proper equipment, expert advice and the permission of the Ceylon government to excavate. Eventually 15,000 rupees were salvaged, plus cannon and other artefacts. Yet nothing came up which revealed the identity of the hapless ship. Was she a Moorish vessel? An East Indiaman? Why was she carrying a cargo of newly minted Indian coins? The search goes on – not for treasure, but for truth.

Among the many wrecks lying in South African waters is that of the Dutch East Indiaman Merestijn, *which sank off Jutten Island, near Cape Town, in 1702. It was located by local salvage operator David Allen who is a leading South African expert and archaeology adviser to the South African Underwater Council. Among the usual discoveries of coin, cannon, etc. there were touching mementoes of the men who perished in the marine tragedy – such as these ornate gold buttons from a long-perished coat or waistcoat.*

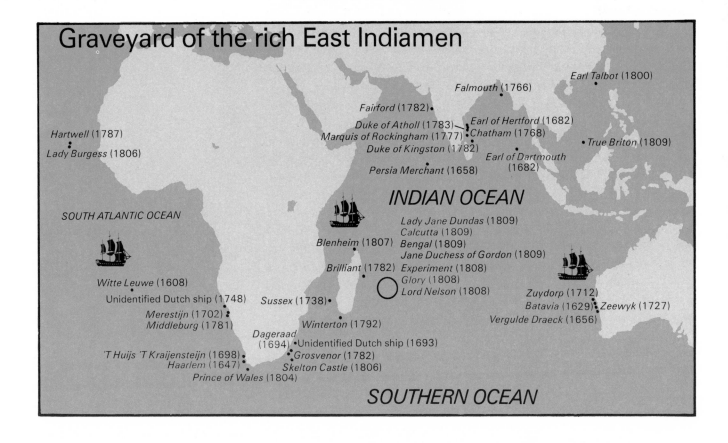

Graveyard of the rich East Indiamen

Earl Talbot (1800)

Falmouth (1766)

Fairford (1782)

Duke of Atholl (1783)
Marquis of Rockingham (1777)
Duke of Kingston (1782)

Earl of Hertford (1682)
Chatham (1768)

Hartwell (1787)

Lady Burgess (1806)

• True Briton (1809)

Earl of Dartmouth (1682)

Persia Merchant (1658)

INDIAN OCEAN

SOUTH ATLANTIC OCEAN

Lady Jane Dundas (1809)
Calcutta (1809)
Blenheim (1807) Bengal (1809)
Jane Duchess of Gordon (1809)
Brilliant (1782) Experiment (1808)
Glory (1808)
Lord Nelson (1808)

Witte Leeuwe (1608)

Unidentified Dutch ship (1748)   Sussex (1738)

Zuydorp (1712)
Batavia (1629) Zeewyk (1727)
Vergulde Draeck (1656)

Merestijn (1702)
Middleburg (1781)

Winterton (1792)

Dageraad (1694) Unidentified Dutch ship (1693)

'T Huijs 'T Kraijensteijn (1698)   Grosvenor (1782)
Haarlem (1647)   Skelton Castle (1806)
Prince of Wales (1804)

SOUTHERN OCEAN

The Silver Fleets

To most people the words 'sunken treasure' probably mean pieces of eight and Spanish gold, and there is no doubt that the area of the sea bed richest in rich wrecks is that beneath the route taken by the Spanish bullion fleets of the sixteenth and seventeenth centuries. Not only were these argosies laden with gold, silver, pearls, porcelain and jewels for the Spanish king, and the precious belongings of rich citizens, they were also a prey to particularly severe hazards. They had to negotiate narrow channels through reefs and jagged coral. Their route lay across a stretch of sea beset by the world's worst hurricanes. Pirates perpetually lay in wait for them. To make matters worse, the fleets were often indifferently captained, manned by criminals and supervised by a government too niggardly to spend adequate funds on new ships and equipment. It is not surprising that only a fraction of the cargoes came in safely.

It was by about 1530 that Spain had gained control of a large part of Central and South America and begun to exploit the silver deposits of Peru and Mexico. But it was not only silver nor, indeed, only the produce of the New World that Spain's ships carried. The output of the Potosi silver mines was brought by ship to Panama and carried by pack animals across the isthmus to Puerto Belo. There it was collected once a year by a fleet sent from Seville, the *flota de tierra firme*, which also called at Cartagena to load gold, emeralds and pearls. While this was taking place another fleet, the *flota de Nueva España*, arrived at Vera Cruz to take on board not only the silver and gold of New Spain but also the proceeds of trading ventures across the Pacific. Here were warehouses full of spices, porcelain and oriental silks brought from China and the Moluccas. After wintering in the colonies, the two fleets crossed the Caribbean to rendezvous at Havana on the island of Cuba. The objective was to start the transatlantic journey in June accompanied by an escort of warships. In fact, departure was almost always delayed until July or August – the height of the hurricane season. During the two and a half centuries that the Spanish bullion trade lasted, thousands of craft came to grief, most of them off the notorious Florida Keys, the 150 mile crescent of reefs and sandbanks that sweeps from Miami into the Gulf of Mexico.

The sad story of the 1622 treasure fleet provides a good example of the fate which befell many of the silver ships. It was commanded by the Marqués de Cadereita, an able and experienced admiral but also a cautious politician who knew how easily an established reputation could be broken by officials ensconced in the comfort of government offices in Madrid. Cadereita had twenty-eight vessels to see safely across the Atlantic. He was delayed by rumours of Dutch pirates and by a stream of often contradictory dispatches arriving from Spain. It was early August before he reached Havana and later before all his ships were assembled. Cadereita consulted his captains, and the merchants and leading men of Cuba as to the best sailing date – 4 September was considered to be auspicious, for the sun and moon would then be in conjunction. Accordingly, the fleet set sail from Havana on that day into a calm Caribbean.

Within twenty-four hours the galleons were hit by a hurricane of enormous ferocity. They were scattered over a wide area, their sails torn clean away, many of their masts snapped off, hundreds of seamen and passengers swept overboard. The captains had no alternative but to run before the storm and wait for it to blow itself out. For five or six days the

The proud galleons crossed the Atlantic to bring back to Spain not only the gold and silver of the Americas but also the treasures of the Orient which came back by way of Panama. The picture here is deceptive. The ships used were often inadequate, badly in need of repair and manned by unskilled, unwilling crews.

One of the more valuable Spanish coins was the golden doubloon, which corresponded in value to about two pounds in the English currency of the day. This was at the time when average wages in England were between six and fourteen pence per day (2½p–6p).

horror of shrieking wind and lashing water persisted. When at last they abated, the surviving vessels headed back for Havana. Of the twenty-eight ships, nine or ten did not return. Most of the missing craft were warships but three prime galleons laden with treasure had also foundered, the *Nuestra Señora de Rosario*, the *Santa Margarita* and the *Nuestra Señora de Atocha*.

Immediately a search was launched, which was initially completely successful. The *Rosario* was discovered, aground on one of the Tortugas islands at the extreme end of the Keys. All its crew and passengers were safe and its cargo was successfully salvaged over the next few weeks. Further to the east the Spaniards saw the partially submerged wreck of the *Margarita* and learned from survivors that the *Atocha* had foundered near by. Unfortunately, fresh storms sprang up before the wreck sites could be located, and when the salvors returned to the area there was no trace of either vessel. But there was far too much at stake for the treasure ships to be abandoned. According to official records, the *Atocha* was carrying forty-seven tons of treasure in the form of silver ingots, coin and gold items, and the *Margarita* perhaps about half that quantity. But in addition each vessel was loaded with large amounts of unregistered contraband bullion being smuggled back to Europe by merchants, colonists and corrupt officials. It was a fortune by seventeenth-century standards. In terms of modern value it represents hundreds of millions of pounds worth of treasure. Little wonder, then, that the government and other interested parties commissioned 'experts' and adventurers prepared to risk life and capital in quest of the lost ships. In 1626 one of these searchers found the wreck of the *Margarita*, and over the next four years part of her cargo was brought up. It consisted of 350 silver bars, 64,750 coins, 109 copper plates, 17 silver artefacts, as well as cannon, muskets, swords, spoons, dishes and other items. The operation was an enormous achievement, considering the primitive salvage equipment available at the time. The amazing fact is not that the Spaniards were unable to complete their task but that they succeeded in recovering, perhaps, two-thirds of the *Margarita*'s treasure. However, the rest remained on the sea bed, together with the far greater *Atocha* treasure.

Silver Fleets

Treasure

The wreck of the Nuestra Señora de la Concepción *1641 (1)*
The Admiral disagreed with the pilot, but had to abide by his calculations as to the ship's whereabouts. After a week at sea completely becalmed, the wind began to blow on 30 October 1641 and the Concepción started to move. At 8.30 on the evening of 31 October she slid on to a reef and was stuck fast. It was All Souls' Day.

USA

TO SPAIN

NORTH   ATLANTIC

MEXICO

GULF OF MEXICO

At Veracruz the *Novo España* fleet loaded Mexican silver and oriental merchandise

The two fleets attempted to rendezvous at Havana and cross the Atlantic together

Concepción (1641)

GREATER ANTILLES

CUBA

DOMINICAN REP.

HAITI

PUERTO RICO

Galleons brought to Acapulco the jewels, silks and porcelain of the East for transport across the Isthmus to Veracruz

CARIBBEAN SEA • *Nuestra Señora del Carmen* (1730)

GUATEMALA

San Felipe (1572) •

Santiago (1660) •

Pedro Serrano (1524)

NEW SPAIN FLEET

Spaniards used slave labour to obtain pearls from around Margarita Is.

NICARAGUA

Capitana (1504)

TERRA FIRMA

VENEZUELA

FLEET

COSTA RICA

San José (1708)

PANAMA

Almiranta (1631)

COLOMBIA

PACIFIC OCEAN

San Rosario (c. 1610)

At Cartegna the *Terra Firma* fleet load gold, emeralds and pearls from New Grenada

Peruvian silver was brought to Panama, carried across the Isthmus and loaded on to ships at Portobello

SOUTH AMERICA

The Concepción *(2)*
On the third day that the ship spent stuck on to the reef the weather began to get worse and worse and by midnight had developed into a full-scale thunderstorm. Suddenly the ship lurched forward and plunged much deeper into the water.

Many other Spanish bullion ships went missing in mid ocean. Their locations remain unknown.

Ships in need of repairs and revictualling could put in at the Azores. This became a favourite spot for pirates to lie in wait

British Isles

EUROPE

Cadiz (?)
Almiranta (1593)

Treasure fleet (1627)

The Vigo Bay treasure (1702)

Capitana (1596)
AZORES
14 Galleons (1591)
Las Cinque Chagas (1593)
Capitana (1554)
La Madalena (1593)

Two ships (1606)
San Pedro Alcantara (1786)

SPAIN

Two ships (1656)

Mercedes (1804)

OCEAN

MADEIRA
San Josefe (1635)

Cantabria (1802)

Treasure fleet sunk (1657)

AFRICA

FROM SPAIN

CAPE VERDE ISLANDS

Concepción (1624)

Two fleets left Spain annually, the *Terra Firma* fleet and the *Novo España* fleet

The Concepción *(3)*
Eventually the stern broke loose and was carried off in the storm, to become wedged in coral heads 150 yards away.

SOUTH ATLANTIC OCEAN

The Perilous Keys

Serious exploration of the wrecks along the Florida Keys began shortly before the Second World War. The first major operator, sometimes called 'the father of Florida treasure-hunters', was Arthur McKee Jr. He was a professional diver, trained in the use of diving suits, and was employed on various engineering projects until he turned full-time treasure-hunter in the 1950s. This pioneer located many ancient wrecks of all kinds – galleons, slavers, British and American men-o'-war, etc. His most exciting find was the remains of the 1733 silver fleet wrecked off Plantation Key. From the *Capitana El Rui* and her sister vessels McKee and his colleagues brought up thousands of silver and gold coins, silver statues, plate, jewellery, pewter, pistols, cannon, swords, nautical instruments, pottery and glass. Many of these items went on display in his treasure museum, the first of its kind. McKee started this and other tourist attractions to help finance his excavations. They also attracted modern 'pirates', aqualung divers who raid wrecks discovered by other explorers. McKee tells of one nasty incident when he was surrounded on the ocean bed by a ring of pirates armed with knives. Fortunately he had with him a home-made underwater shot gun used for scaring off sharks. When they failed to respond to a warning, McKee let the weapon off with a roar. When the 'fog' of air bubbles and sand had subsided all that could be seen of his assailants was a row of flippers, headed for the surface.

The fortunes of another excavator working a 1733 site illustrate the fact that the treasure-hunter's lot is not always a happy one. By the time that Tom Gurr located the wreck of the *San José* in 1967 the Florida state legislature had begun to take an interest in the hectic activity of divers off its shores. They took Gurr to court in an attempt to force him to hand over his finds. In this celebrated case, precedent was found for extending state control over all the sea as far as the outer reefs. Gurr was obliged to agree to a contract dividing his treasure with the government. His excavations continued but after five years he had still not received his share of the salvage money. By December 1973 his patience was at an end. He removed from the bank all the treasure still in his possession – gold rings, silver plates, coins, etc. – took it out to the wreck site, and dumped it overboard.

Hundreds of divers have worked the Florida Keys over the years and millions of pounds' worth of treasure have been recovered, but all excavators now have to work closely with state officials, who are concerned to stop the subaquatic free-for-all of the 1950s and 1960s.

Men whose life is devoted to the search for sunken treasure – many hopefuls dwell along the Florida coast making a precarious living from fishing, teaching scuba diving, taking tourists out to gaze at wreck sites through the clear waters, and going on treasure-hunting expeditions. The 'big names' along the keys are those of the few men who have struck lucky, men like Art McKee, Kip Wagner and Tom Gurr. (Left) McKee's divers using suction pumps on the El Capitana *site.*

The Spaniards took careful security precautions when transporting coins across the Atlantic. They stored their wealth in multiple-locked iron chests like the one shown below. But in the event of shipwreck these heavy coffers were difficult to salvage. They sank well into the debris, and even if a line could be got around them they were cumbersome to raise. Often they remained on the ocean bed, slowly corroding away. Arthur McKee, some of whose salvaged coins are shown here, sometimes found square clumps of silver discs – the contents of chests which had long since disintegrated.

Recovering what is left of the silver fleets' bullion is a task fraught with difficulties and frustrations. However, enough gold and silver still lies beneath the waves to excite the cupidity of generations of treasure-hunters to come.

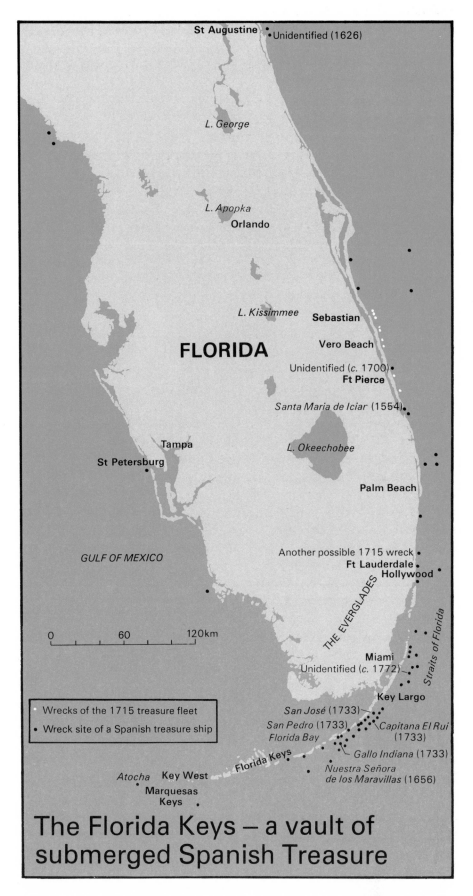

The Florida Keys – a vault of submerged Spanish Treasure

A Labyrinth of Islands

A Spanish king grumbled that the only reason Englishmen settled in Bermuda was to rob his treasure galleons. Two 'nets' of islands and reefs were spread in the path of the homeward-bound treasure fleets. The Bahamas extended 950 kilometres from Florida to Hispaniola, and 1,300 kilometres beyond them lay the smaller 'net' of the Bermudas, three hundred islets and sandbanks occupying thirty kilometres of ocean. Scarcely a year passed between 1550 and 1880 when these 'nets' did not catch some ships. And local people certainly benefited greatly from these wrecks. Bermuda was colonized at the beginning of the seventeenth

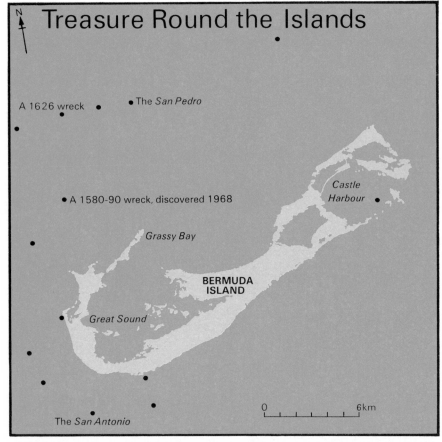

Treasure Round the Islands

N

- A 1626 wreck
- The *San Pedro*
- A 1580-90 wreck, discovered 1968
- *Castle Harbour*
- *Grassy Bay*

BERMUDA ISLAND

- *Great Sound*

0 _____ 6km

- The *San Antonio*

The reefs and shallows of the Bahamas are rich in sunken wrecks, many of them Spanish bullion ships. In 1965 John Klinner, an American diver, found just one such wreck and brought out some of her thousands of gold and silver coins. Like Teddy Tucker, pictured below, Klinner also became a 'treasure addict'.

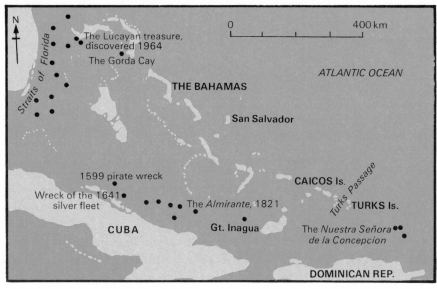

N

Straits of Florida

- The Lucayan treasure, discovered 1964
- The Gorda Cay

0 _____ 400 km

THE BAHAMAS

ATLANTIC OCEAN

San Salvador

- 1599 pirate wreck
- Wreck of the 1641 silver fleet
- The *Almirante*, 1821

CAICOS Is.

Turks Passage

TURKS Is.

CUBA

Gt. Inagua

The *Nuestra Señora de la Concepcion*

DOMINICAN REP.

Piracy was always a major source of worry for the captains of Spain's treasure fleets. The most audacious pirate raid ever carried out on the Main was the work of the Dutch privateer Piet Hayn. In 1628 he sailed his squadron into Havana where the entire combined fleet lay at anchor. He took plunder and prizes to the value of 15,000,000 guilders, but part of his fleet was lost in storms on the homeward voyage.

Part of Teddy Tucker's Bermuda Treasure is laid out on the sand for the photographers. Ingots of gold and silver, coins and Renaissance jewellery still gleam in the sunlight after 360 years on the ocean bottom. Pride of place is given to the magnificent 'Bishop's Cross' with its seven South American emeralds. Tucker sold his collection to the Bermuda government so that it could be put on permanent display.

century, and one of the prime sources of wealth for islanders was the stripping of survivors and their broken ships. But there was usually some treasure that eluded them; sometimes vessels broke up too quickly to allow salvage, or sank in deep water out of unaided diving range. Then there were the scores of pre-1600 wrecks whose whereabouts were unknown.

It was one of these that Teddy Tucker located by accident in 1950. Tucker is an inhabitant of Bermuda and served as a wartime diver in the Royal Navy. After the Second World War he started a small salvage business, and it was while out over the reef in his boat that he spotted three cannon sticking out of the sand. Later in the year he returned to the spot and lifted cannon, some lead shot and an anchor. It was not a remarkable haul and Tucker did not bother to return to the site for five years. It was when he and his partner paid a second visit that the excitement began. Sifting the loose sand covering the wreck, they discovered first a bronze apothecary's mortar in perfect condition and dated 1561. Then came blackened silver coins. Then, something that shone from the sand. It was a cube of solid gold cut from an ingot and, as Tucker later said, 'it was as clean and bright as jewellery in a Fifth Avenue store'. The two men paid many subsequent visits, combing the area thoroughly (although they lacked the sophisticated equipment that treasure-seekers were later to develop for underwater work). The final total of discoveries amounted to the greatest haul from an ancient wreck of the postwar era up to that time. As well as the items already mentioned, Tucker salvaged muskets, copper buckets, pottery, pewter plates, a steel breastplate, navigational instruments and bronze grenades. But there was also 'treasure' in the popular sense of the word – 2,000 silver coins, four gold ingots, thirteen pearls, six pearl-studded gold buttons and, most impressive of all, a gold pectoral cross set with seven large, cabochon-cut Colombian emeralds. This priceless piece of jewellery is known as the 'Bishop's Cross' and is undoubtedly the most important and valuable single find to come from the floor of the Atlantic.

But who did it belong to, and what ill-fated ship carried its owner on his last journey? The evidence of material taken from the wreck has established that the vessel was Spanish and went down between 1592 and 1600. Combing the records of lost galleons, Tucker and his associates satisfied themselves that their ship was the *San Pedro*, part of the *flota de tierra firme* of 1595. And that is probably all that can ever be said about the great Bermuda Treasure.

Man out of his Element

Underwater treasure-hunting is no new phenomenon. Homer and Aristotle are among ancient writers who mention professional divers who retrieved valuable cargo from ships that had foundered on rocks and sandbanks and settled in shallow water. Experts such as the sponge fishers of the Greek islands and the pearl divers of Japan and South America passed on their skill from generation to generation. With no breathing apparatus but with lungs made large and strong by years of practice, such divers achieved prodigious feats of endurance. Natives of the Aegean island of Syme reached depths of more than two hundred feet. They did this by leaping in head-first while clutching a flat, heavy stone which took them swiftly to the bottom. Beyond about sixty feet the pressure of the water cancelled out the natural buoyancy of the diver's body so that, after a carefully measured period of time, he had to be hauled to the surface by a rope. Incredible claims have been made about the duration of dives. Sixteenth-century Spanish salvors claimed that their men could stay down for fifteen minutes. Their operatives were slaves working in fear of vicious taskmasters. Their lives were expendable and many were driven beyond the limits of human endurance. It is possible that occasionally a wretched Negro or Indian diver may, under such pressure, have survived for an incredible time underwater. It is more likely that the salvors tried to impress officials in Seville with exaggerated accounts of their activities. The normal maximum for work on the sea bed must have been about five minutes. This was enough for scooping up silver bars and handfuls of coins or for attaching ropes to chests but not for opening hatches or removing coffers from pitch-black holds. Determined salvage operators therefore had to invent new, sophisticated equipment.

Francisco Nuñez Melian was the man who obtained from the Spanish government the concession to seek and raise the bullion from the lost ships of the 1622 silver fleet. He set out on his quest four years after the disaster when all trace of the ships was lost. But he had with him the very latest in detector equipment. It was a large bronze cone fitted with windows. Air was trapped inside the device and a diver used this to breathe while standing on a platform slung below the cone and looking through the windows for signs of wreckage. Not surprisingly, Melian's

The problem of enabling man to survive for long periods underwater was one which always exercised inventors, as this sixteenth-century woodcut shows.

One of the bas-relief panels brought back by Layard from Nimrud shows Assyrians swimming underwater with the aid of goatskins filled with air which they breathe through short tubes. Over three thousand years ago man sought to emulate the fishes.

Diving Bells

The idea of trapping a bubble of air underwater so that a diver could live in it had been obvious to the ancient Greeks. Alexander the Great is reputed to have been lowered into the Bosphorus in just such a device. Experiments continued over the years, and by the seventeenth century various kinds of bells were in use. It was the astronomer Edmund Halley who made the first major improvements to the basic equipment. He perfected methods of renewing the air inside the bell and also of conveying the air to divers working on the sea bed. Fresh air was lowered in weighted barrels and brought into the bell by flexible tubes. Similar tubes connected the divers to the bell and they breathed by means of head coverings called 'caps of maintenance'. Halley took out his patent in 1690 and claimed that his apparatus would support five men at a depth of nine or ten fathoms. It was an instant success and was used by the Royal Navy in many salvage operations.

There was keen rivalry in the nineteenth century to invent a really reliable diving suit. Inventors knew that salvage companies would pay highly for equipment that enabled them to operate safely at greater depth. Augustus Siebe, in the 1820s, established the principles which governed the manufacture of all later helmeted diving gear.

M. SIEBE'S IMPROVED PUMP AND DIVING-DRESS.

men were not enthusiastic about entrusting their lives to this ungainly looking contraption, but he overcame their objections by promising freedom to the slave who sighted the first lost galleon. The lucky man was an Indian called Juan Bañon. He it was who, from Melian's primitive diving bell, saw the remains of the *Margarita* in June 1626.

Other inventors of the period experimented with primitive diving suits. They wanted to provide the diver with more freedom of manoeuvre. In the opening years of the eighteenth century John Lethbridge, a Devon man, perfected a leather barrel which encased the upper part of a man's body. It had sleeves and it fitted tightly around wrists and thighs. The wearer lived on the air trapped inside the suit and looked out through windows fitted at face level. Thus equipped, Lethbridge, who was reckoned as England's leading salvage expert, is supposed to have dived successfully on to several wrecks and to have made himself rich by profits from his work and from marketing his apparatus. But the equipment did not always work. Indeed, its defects were obvious: the supply of air inside the costume was very limited; the diver's movements could only be cumbersome; working at any great depth was impossible since water forced its way into the suit.

Experimentation went on. By 1830 Augustus Siebe had developed the helmeted suit supplied with air by means of a surface pump. This brought deep-sea diving within the range of salvage experts. It also brought new dangers. Changes of pressure, rapid descent and ascent, breathing compressed air for long periods – all these can take their toll of a man's body and they can kill. The disorder known as the bends, caused by absorbing nitrogen into the tissues, can induce intolerable pain, paralysis or heart failure. When the sponge divers of Syme enthusiastically went over to helmet diving in the 1860s half of them died in the first season. Used properly, however, the new equipment revolutionized the search for underwater treasures.

Yet diving suits and other sophisticated equipment did not create a sub-oceanic 'gold rush', for many reasons. The equipment was expensive and was used almost exclusively by national navies and professional salvage companies. It called for skilled divers, and there were many hazards to be faced. More important than these deterrents was the difficulty of locating wrecks. The sites of most ancient sunken ships are known only vaguely from documents. A diver working on the dim-lit ocean floor looking for fragments of timber covered by mud, sand or coral might search in vain for years yet pass within metres of his prize. Only the development of sonic detection equipment and magnetometers has brought greater precision to the task of pinpointing treasure ships.

The change that came over subaquatic treasure-hunting in the years following the Second World War can only be called revolutionary. The development of the aqualung brought diving within the reach of virtually everyone. A reasonably fit man or woman could master the basic techniques after only a few hours' instruction. Thousands of enthusiasts found that their newly acquired skills opened up for them the fascinating world of underwater archaeology. For them the silent world beneath the waves where man appeared as an alien, constantly at risk, was the last remaining place on the planet where there was scope for adventure and freedom from interference by 'civilization'. When, in 1968, Sydney Wignall was advertising for volunteers to help in his search in Blasket Sound for the Armada ship, *Santa Maria de lá Rosa*, he did not mince his words:

> This is not a treasure-hunting expedition. If there is any treasure, and we find it, then that will be an added bonus ... Blasket Sound is not a place for the inexperienced. Participants must be in sound health, and have no history of heart or respiratory complaints. Discipline for obvious reasons will be tough. Everyone will have a job to do and will be told to do it, or pack up and go. The expedition officers will have the authority to dismiss at a moment's notice any member who is either not pulling his weight, or who by his actions is deemed an unproductive or disruptive person ... If you want a 'jolly time' by the seaside at our expense, do not apply. If you like hard work, don't mind being soaked to the skin and frozen, cut and bloodied, fed up to the teeth with the word 'Armada', and tired but still determined to soldier on with a smile, then you are probably just the chap we are looking for ...

One hundred and sixteen men replied.

Individual divers and subaqua clubs now assist with archaeological reconnaissance and exploration, but others are not ashamed to admit that it is the lure of sunken treasure which beckons them.

Marine archaeology consists of painstaking work using every modern device available. The commonest tool employed to locate a wreck is the magnetometer whose printout must be expertly scanned for indications of metal on the sea bed. When the site is being worked, finds must be accurately plotted in order to achieve a clear picture of the whole wreck.

Some of the elaborate devices used for salvage are shown opposite. The television search (top left) can be used in depths up to 500 metres. The anchored camera will probe the wreck and focus on objects for the tongs to retrieve. The side-scanning sonar (top right) is drawn in sweeps above the sea bed and locates objects in its path. The jet rake (centre) softens the sea bed to a depth of 1½ metres with its jets of water. The electrically operated reticulated arm can move items on the sea bed, and the 'duster' is a propeller which directs a downward jet of water to remove sand.

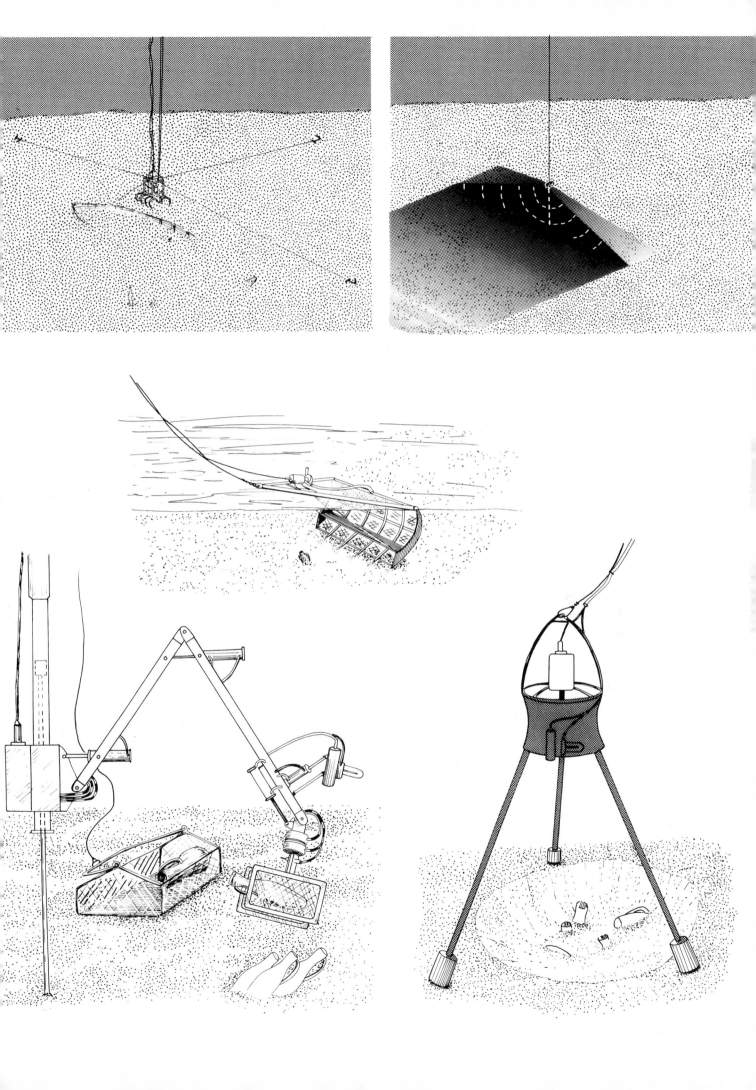

The Brotherhood of the Keys

The end of the Second World War released upon the western world thousands of ex-servicemen ill-equipped for unexciting, peaceful obscurity. Many of those who sought adventure, danger and thrills turned to underwater treasure-hunting. They had learned how to use aqualung equipment while on active service and some were familiar with new techniques developed for military purposes – underwater photography, sonic detection of submerged objects, submarine explosives. They knew all the old legends of sunken treasures. They reckoned that the wealth beckoning from the ocean floor was limitless, belonged to no one, and required nothing but courage and a modicum of luck to retrieve. In the 1940s and 1950s hundreds of diving consortiums were set up. They operated all over the world, but the area which attracted the greatest concentration of interest was the stretch of ocean which tumbled about the reefs and banks off Florida and the West Indies, where so many Spanish galleons were known to have foundered.

The pioneer treasure-divers were a strange breed – tough men, dropouts, loners. Many of them threw up good jobs, sold their possessions and mortgaged their homes to follow the will-o'-the-wisp of ocean gold. They ran up enormous debts in buying boats and expensive equipment and were so obligated to their backers that success became desperately important. In these circumstances a kind of 'Wild West' atmosphere was created. In remote areas of ocean, where few laws applied and none could be enforced, rival gangs clashed, boats were sabotaged, feuds and vendettas were pursued, recovered treasures were stolen, and beneath the waves desperadoes fought to the death with knives instead of six-guns.

Some operators struck it rich. Arthur McKee located the 1733 bullion fleet wreck and brought up the first silver ingots to be found. Kip Wagner and his colleagues raised almost four thousand coins in a single day. But these were among the lucky few. The majority experienced the disappointment and failure that attended Wagner's first undertaking in 1949:

> By the end of August it was obvious that we had failed. The selfish sea had not yielded a single coin. After three months of backbreaking work – work you couldn't have gotten any of us to do on a regular job for less than $4 or $5 an hour, if for that – we went broke.
>
> Not counting our time, just the equipment as supplies and what little living costs were incurred, we had dropped $12,000 ... We were utterly fatigued, disillusioned, disheartened, and in total despair ... Our wives, who had been so patient and hopeful at first, would barely speak to us, and our friends, most of whom were sceptical of such a folly from the start, would only wag their heads and say, 'I told you so but you wouldn't listen' ... We dissolved our little group ... and everyone went his separate way.

A profound change came over the treasure-hunting community of the Keys in 1958. That was the year the Florida state legislature began to take a hand. Alarmed at the unscientific disturbance of underwater sites, the removal of artefacts and the loss of potential revenue, they extended state authority over coastal waters, obliged diving companies to buy leases covering specified areas and demanded surety bonds. This removed many less secure operators from the scene and also took much of the

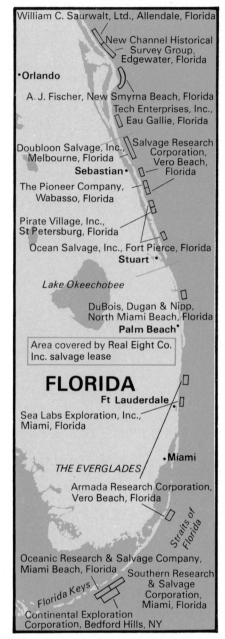

William C. Saurwalt, Ltd., Allendale, Florida

New Channel Historical Survey Group, Edgewater, Florida

•Orlando

A. J. Fischer, New Smyrna Beach, Florida

Tech Enterprises, Inc., Eau Gallie, Florida

Doubloon Salvage, Inc., Melbourne, Florida

Salvage Research Corporation, Vero Beach, Florida

Sebastian•

The Pioneer Company, Wabasso, Florida

Pirate Village, Inc., St Petersburg, Florida

Ocean Salvage, Inc., Fort Pierce, Florida

Stuart •

Lake Okeechobee

DuBois, Dugan & Nipp, North Miami Beach, Florida

Palm Beach•

Area covered by Real Eight Co. Inc. salvage lease

FLORIDA

Ft Lauderdale

Sea Labs Exploration, Inc., Miami, Florida

•Miami

THE EVERGLADES

Armada Research Corporation, Vero Beach, Florida

Straits of Florida

Oceanic Research & Salvage Company, Miami Beach, Florida

Southern Research & Salvage Corporation, Miami, Florida

Florida Keys

Continental Exploration Corporation, Bedford Hills, NY

Joseph Salvo happily displays some of the treasures belonging to the Real Eight Co., of which he is a member. They are on permanent exhibition in the First National Bank at Satellite Beach, where they attract on average three hundred visitors a day, each of whom pays $1 to see the Spanish gold and silver found by Kip Wagner and his colleagues.

Art McKee, a pioneer among Florida treasure-hunters, had an imitation castle built to house his collection of coins, cannon and sixteenth- and seventeenth-century artefacts retrieved from Spanish wrecks. Many visitors come to see the exhibits.

The great treasure-hunters of the Florida Keys rely on tourism for some of their regular income. Mel Fisher displays some of his finds and relics in the Golden Doubloon *(below), a painted replica of a Spanish galleon.*

cut-throat element out of the competition. It helped to create a new camaraderie along the Keys for it gave the diving outfits a new 'enemy'; as well as the sea they now had the government to fight. Official control over the divers' activities was gradually extended, encouraged by such organizations as the Council of Underwater Archaeology, formed to ensure the cataloguing of sites, the establishment of codes of conduct, the training of marine archaeologists and the achievement of cooperation between archaeologists and salvors. There was increasing 'interference' with salvage activities, and ownership of finds was sometimes disputed in the courts.

The treasure-seekers are now part of the tourist attractions of Florida. Along the coast they show off their finds in little museums. Old stagers in the favourite divers' bars are always ready to regale visitors with gilded tales of staggering finds and near-finds. For a few dollars they will take people out to old wreck sites and allow them to enjoy vicariously the thrill of discovery by snorkeling over the reef or gazing down through glass panels in the bottom of the boat. The Keys still act as a magnet drawing hopeful scuba divers longing to find employment with one of the larger companies and, perhaps, longing just as much to belong to the select association of friends and rivals who live – or try to live – off sunken treasure.

Scattered by the Winds of God

In May 1588, 130 ships and 30,000 men left Spain to subdue England. They failed. In the attempt about 40 vessels and 10,000 men were lost. The running battle up the Channel and the subsequent storms resulted in the most dramatic series of shipwrecks in British waters. The instructions given to the Spanish admiral, Medina Sidonia, were quite simple. He was to avoid battle until he had linked up with the invasion army gathered in the Low Countries by the Duke of Parma. Then he was to secure the Channel so that Parma could cross. But these plans were complicated by the English navy, which harried him all the way along the coast, by the Dutch navy, which prevented his union with the Duke, and by the weather, which shattered the unity of his force and obliged him to run northwards before the wind. The great fleet, now divided into small groups and single ships, attempted to reach home the long way. Even given favourable conditions, they could not do it without stopping somewhere to take on supplies and make essential repairs. But the conditions were not favourable; they were atrocious. As the Armada medal, ordered by Queen Elizabeth, stated, 'God blew with his winds and they were scattered.' The Armada captains hoped to find succour among Catholic groups on the west coasts of Scotland and Ireland. In the event, many ships were destroyed by rock and tempest, and survivors who landed did not find the natives as hospitable as they had hoped.

Much successful work has been done in recent years on locating many of the Armada wrecks. From a historical point of view the discoveries made by marine archaeologists are fascinating. None of the vessels was a 'treasure ship' in the same category as those on the bullion run from Havana, but they were carrying items of value – personal jewellery, plate, objects of religious devotion and chests of coin for the payment of troops. The stories of the doomed men who tried to get themselves and their possessions safely back to Spain make sad reading.

July 1588 and the Spanish Armada is intercepted off the Isle of Wight by Lord Howard's fleet. But Medina-Sidonia, the Spanish admiral, not to be deflected from his task of linking with the land forces of the Duke of Parma, will not grant the English a major engagement. A running battle begins. Many Armada ships are weakened by cannon shot. This will prove disastrous when they encounter storms and high seas on the homeward journey.

The fate of the Armada, 1588-9

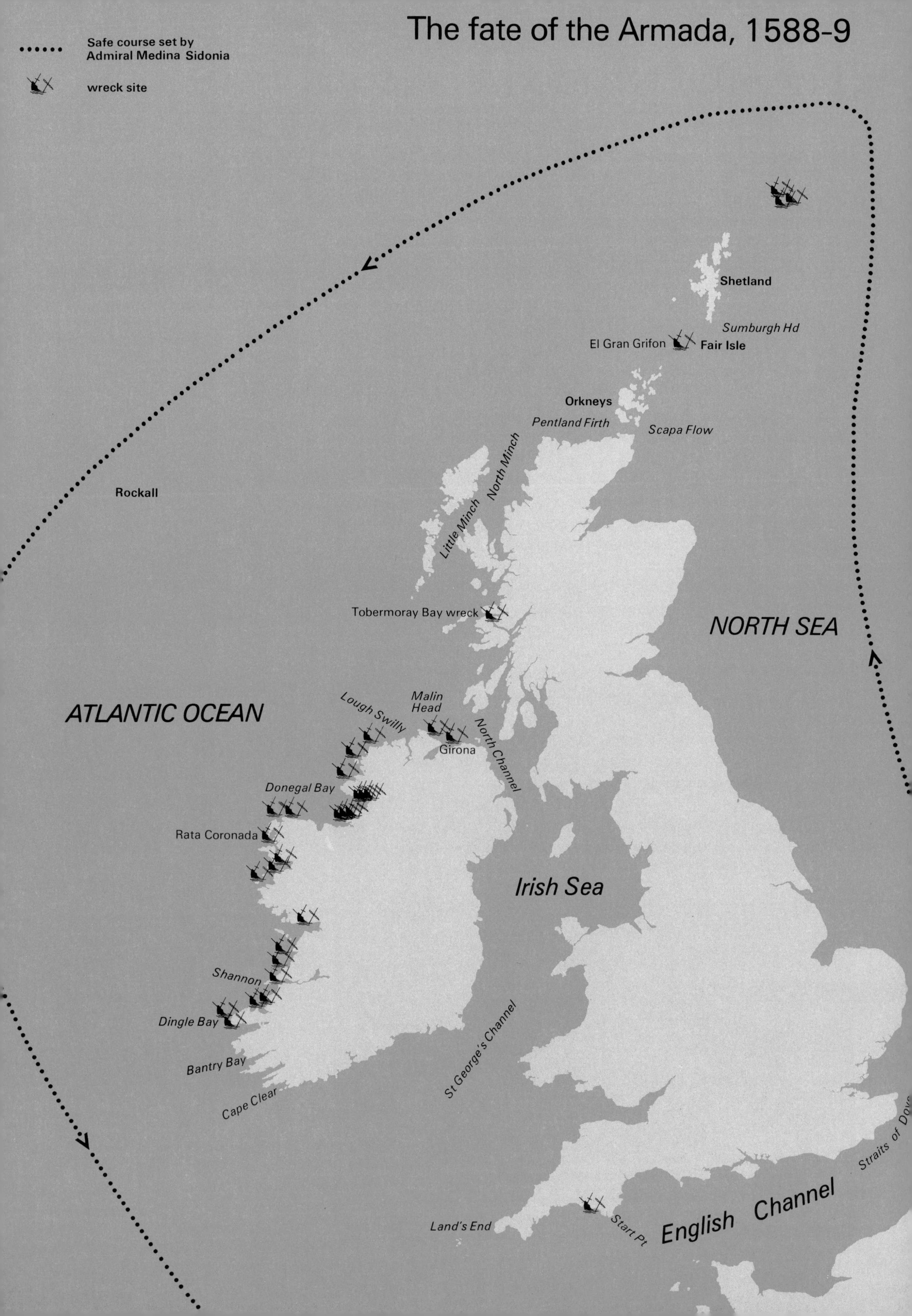

•••••• Safe course set by
Admiral Medina Sidonia

wreck site

Shetland

Sumburgh Hd

El Gran Grifon   Fair Isle

Orkneys
Pentland Firth   Scapa Flow

North Minch

Little Minch

ATLANTIC OCEAN

Rockall

NORTH SEA

Tobermoray Bay wreck

Lough Swilly   Malin
Head

Donegal Bay

Girona

North Channel

Rata Coronada

Irish Sea

Shannon

Dingle Bay

Bantry Bay

St George's Channel

Cape Clear

Land's End   Start Pt   English Channel

Straits of Dover

The Overloaded Galleons

Don Alonzo Martinez de Leiva's ship, the *Rata Coronada*, was a converted carrack, cumbersome but heavily armed and formidable. She safely negotiated the Scottish coastal waters and put in at Blacksod Bay on the western coast of Ireland to seek fresh water and provisions. There she was caught by a westerly gale and driven hard on to the beach. Fortunately for Don Alonzo and his men another ship, the *Duquena Santa Ana*, had anchored in a nearby bay. She was a transport hulk already carrying more than three hundred soldiers and crew, but room was found for the complement of the *Rata Coronada* and everything worth removing from her.

The *Duquena* was even more unwieldy than the *Rata Coronada*. As soon as she left harbour she was beset by heavy seas and changeable winds. She could make no progress southwards and was eventually obliged to run north-eastwards until she, too, was driven ashore on the coast of Donegal. Once again fortune smiled on de Leiva and his men. They heard that another Spanish ship had sought refuge not far away. She was the galleon *Girona*, an admirable vessel, propelled by both oar and sail. At the end of October the *Girona* set forth. She was now dangerously overloaded with about 1,300 men (her normal complement was 550), provisions, supplies and personal belongings. There was no question of reaching Spain, so de Leiva gave orders to return to Scotland and seek succour among the western lords, traditional enemies of the English.

They never made it. After only two or three days Don Alonzo was shipwrecked a third time. The *Girona* struck the rocks of Port na Spaniagh, County Antrim. Only a handful of the 1,300 officers and men (who included many of Spain's leading nobility) managed to scramble ashore through the breakers. For weeks afterwards bodies were washed up on the nearby rocks and beaches, to be searched and stripped by the local people. The wreck itself, or that part of it which was accessible, was looted by the lord of this region, James McDonnell. It was said that he was able to rebuild his castle on the proceeds. The *Girona* was soon forgotten. No record existed of her exact location. The Irishmen who did

From the sand and the rocky crevices of Port na Spaniagh (below left), Sténuit and his team retrieved numerous small objects of value which provide fascinating detail about the Girona's complement. The gold cross of St John probably belonged to Captain Spinola, a member of the order. The gold locket was made to contain a protective charm blessed by the Pope. The cameo mounted in gold and pearls was one of many. Most famous of all the Girona treasures was the beautiful gold salamander set with rubies.

One problem faced by diving teams in the 1960s and 1970s was the difficulty of establishing salvage rights over a discovered wreck and keeping rival groups away. When in 1969 a British team located the Armada ship Santa Maria de la Rosa *off Blasket Island, Co. Kerry, 'pirate' groups were immediately drawn to the spot by the lure of Spanish gold. While expedition organizers battled in the Dublin courts, frogmen engaged in a potentially more dangerous conflict on the site.*

know certainly had no intention of informing their English overlords and allowing them to claim the *Girona*'s treasure. Thus it was that a small fortune in jewellery, plate, and gold and silver coin remained where it had fallen for nearly four hundred years.

The man who found it was the Belgian diver Robert Sténuit. After years of archive work on old documents and maps Sténuit felt sure he knew the approximate location of the wreck, and in June 1967 he dived off Lacada. He immediately found cannon, cannon balls and 'pigs' of lead. The following spring he was back with colleagues and equipment to begin the salvage work. It was unpleasant work; the water was cold, the currents were strong, visibility was poor. Yet they went about it carefully and scientifically. The site was plotted. The location of every find was marked on the plan before it was removed. The remnants of the *Girona* had, Sténuit now discovered, been scattered over a wide area, although many of the most exciting finds had been washed into an underwater cave at the foot of the cliffs. When the word went around Northern Ireland that the foreigners had found treasure, groups of local divers began to converge on the area. Burly Irishmen tried to frighten off Sténuit and his colleagues. There were even fights underwater. Not until Sténuit obtained legal recognition as sole salvor through the courts was this nuisance removed.

The team spent three seasons in Port na Spaniagh and in that time they brought up over 12,000 artefacts, from massive cannon and anchors to tiny fragments of pottery and gold. Many of the items subsequently took on renewed value after research brought out their significance. They told not only about shipboard life but about the identity of members of the *Girona*'s complement. For instance an engraved ring was found that had been worn or carried by Jean Perrenot when he drowned. It was given him by his grandmother. Of treasure proper the salvors found 405 gold coins, 756 silver coins, a beautiful gold salamander (left) set with rubies, golden chains, cameos in settings of gold and pearl, rings, pendants and other items of Renaissance jewellery. At Sténuit's insistence these precious objects were not put up for auction but acquired for £132,000 for permanent display in the Northern Ireland National Museum.

The Tragedy of the Golden *Griffin*

She was out of the Baltic port of Rostock and she was built for service in heavy northern seas. She took her name from the golden griffin which was Rostock's heraldic emblem. She was a 650 ton *urca*, a great, solid, potbellied store ship, contracted to Spain by the German Hanseatic merchants. And she was the flagship of the Spanish Armada supply squadron. If any vessel could survive the storms of the North Sea and the Atlantic it should have been *El Gran Grifón*. But her planking was badly strained by blows received from English guns in the Channel, and in addition to the heavy weight of food and supplies she was carrying she was obliged to take on survivors from other craft during the journey round Scotland. Through the late summer of 1588 she wallowed through heavy seas around the northern islands, then ran into fierce south-westerly gales and was forced to run before the wind. The conditions were appalling: 'We were fit only to die, for the wind was so strong and the sea so wild that the waves mounted to the skies, knocking the ship about so that the men were all exhausted, and yet unable to keep down the water that leaked through our gaping seams.' Settling steadily lower in the water, the *Grifón* eventually reached Fair Isle, between the Orkneys and Shetlands. Her captain tried to beach her but strong currents wedged her on to the rocks of Stromshellier, where she began to break up. The crew scrambled up masts and rigging to reach the overhanging cliffs, salvaging what food and precious possessions they could. They must have succeeded in getting off any treasure the *Grifón* was carrying because the eventual excavators of the wreck found only one four-*real* coin.

It was different with the 'Tobermory galleon'. This as yet unidentified vessel went down off the Isle of Mull, and rumours immediately circulated that she had great treasure aboard. Swedish salvors using diving bells explored the wreck in the mid seventeenth century, and a hundred years later a visitor described watching divers coming up with 'the spoils of the ocean, whether it was plate or money'. At the beginning of the twentieth century an English consortium called the Pieces of Eight Company was at work on the site. Bronze cannon, quantities of gold

The Gran Grifón *was a northern urca of the type shown in this contemporary engraving. Squat and broad-bellied, she was not designed for speed and manoeuvrability but for coping with heavy seas and rough weather. She should have been able to cope with the 1588 storms but she had been damaged by gunfire and was badly overloaded. Her wallowing journey 'north about' became a nightmare as pumps failed to remove the water in the hold and she settled steadily deeper in the waves*

coin and a variety of artefacts are known to have been found, but no scientific record of discoveries exist. The latest excavators have had to contend with a seven-metre layer of mud covering the ship.

The quest for these and other Armada wrecks poses the question as to what we really mean by 'treasure' in this context. If it is material having current commercial value then many of the expeditions which have been launched to survey and salvage 1558 sites must be considered as complete wastes of time and effort. But if, as marine archaeologists would claim, anything that increases human knowledge has great value, then the Armada seekers have found treasure indeed. As a result of excavations during the last decade we now know a great deal more about 'the Enterprise of England' and its failure. The ships' ironwork – guns, shot, anchors, etc. – was of inferior quality. Many vessels were incapable of surviving several months at sea. Several were ill-provided with cannon. As all the new evidence is pieced together it begins to appear that we must reinterpret the entire Armada episode. The hastily assembled fleet was, it seems, intended more for show than anything else. Invasion was never more than an outside possibility; the Enterprise was a diplomatic bluff intended to coerce the English into agreeing to peace at any price. When the history of the Armada campaign comes to be rewritten it will owe much to the marine archaeologists who risked life and limb in the cold, murky northern waters.

As the North Sea storms worsened the battered ships of Philip II's great Armada struggled to round the British Isles and make for home. About forty vessels came to grief on the coast and islands of Scotland and Ireland.

Perils of the Deep

The East Indiamen

In their day (1600 to *c.* 1850) these were the finest merchant ships afloat. On their activities the commercial and colonial supremacy of Britain and Holland largely rested. The (English) East India Company (incorporated 1600) and the Dutch East India Company (incorporated 1602) were founded to wrest control of the Orient trade from Spain and Portugal. They sailed from Europe with cargoes of bullion and manufactured goods and returned with spices from the East Indies, silk, porcelain and lacquered furniture from China, tea, gems and cheap cottons from India. But even good ships can founder, and the East Indiamen were no exception. Between 1600 and 1800, for example, the British company lost over 200 vessels, many of which went to the bottom carrying rich treasures.

In 1792 the *Winterton* ran before an Indian Ocean storm and was thrown on to shoals off the east coast of Madagascar. She lies there still in five fathoms, and with her a consignment of gold and jewels which were valued at £400,000 at the time of loss. Five years earlier the *Hartwell* was making her maiden voyage. A month out from London found her approaching the Cape Verde Islands off the west coast of Africa. She was beset by foul weather, shipped too much water and began to sink. A subsequent inquiry put this disaster down to the ill-discipline of the crew. The cost to the company in lost cargo was £80,000. The *Cabalava* was a British vessel *en route* for China in 1818 carrying perfume, watches, muslin, lead and iron 'pigs', paper and £200,000 worth of Spanish silver

From the East India Company's spacious dockyard at Deptford sailed the magnificent ships which brought back the wealth of the Orient. Many of them, loaded with gems, ivory, gold, porcelain, silks and spices, never returned.

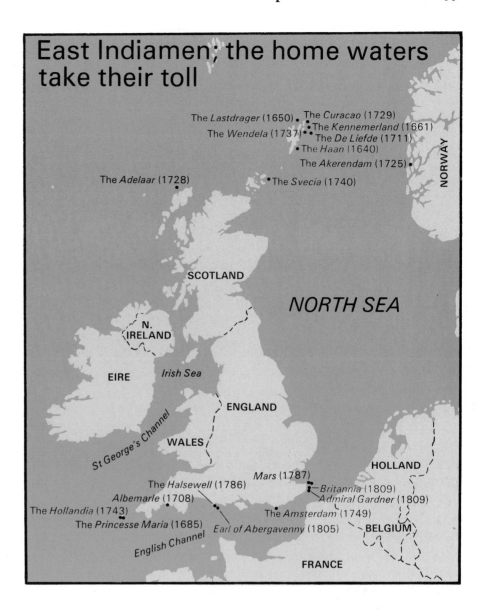

East Indiamen; the home waters take their toll

The *Lastdrager* (1650) • The *Curacao* (1729)
The *Kennemerland* (1661)
The *Wendela* (1737) • • The *De Liefde* (1711)
• The *Haan* (1640)
The *Akerendam* (1725) •

The *Adelaar* (1728) •
• The *Svecia* (1740)

NORWAY

SCOTLAND

NORTH SEA

N.
IRELAND

EIRE   *Irish Sea*

ENGLAND

St George's Channel

WALES

HOLLAND

Mars (1787)
The *Halsewell* (1786)   *Britannia* (1809)
Albemarle (1708)   *Admiral Gardner* (1809)
The *Hollandia* (1743)   The *Amsterdam* (1749)
The *Princesse Maria* (1685)   *Earl of Abergavenny* (1805)   BELGIUM

English Channel

FRANCE

All the pride of commercial empire is portrayed in this ceiling painting which adorns the headquarters of the East India Company in London. Generations of merchants dreamed of people in the East proffering their riches to a Britannia who ruled the waves. The East Indiamen and their crews tried hard to make that dream a reality.

pesos. She broke herself on a reef in a lonely stretch of ocean between Mauritius and the Seychelles. No record of a salvage attempt exists.

For every ship wrecked in the open ocean whose location is approximately known there are dozens which have vanished without trace. In the days before telegraph any vessel that went down with all hands was very unlikely ever to be found. A large number of richly laden East Indiamen fall into this category. For example, what became of the *Skelton Castle*? She left Portsmouth in 1806 with the *Matilda* and the *Union*. When the other commanders elected to put in at Cape Town for fresh water and victuals, Captain Vaughan of the *Skelton Castle* decided to sail straight on for Madras, taking advantage of the favourable wind. He was motivated, it seems, by a highly developed business acumen (or should we call it greed?). Company captains invariably indulged in trading on their own account, and Vaughan wanted the *Skelton Castle* to be the first ship of the season to reach India with European cargo, so that he could obtain the best price for his merchandise. After leaving Cape Town neither he nor his ship were ever seen again.

Only two years before, the *Prince of Wales* had vanished in the midst of a fleet of East Indiamen. She was the flagship of a homeward-bound convoy loaded with the profits of trade. Rounding the Cape, the vessels ran into a severe gale. Commodore Price ordered the fleet to lie-to and ride out the storm. It was the last signal he ever made. After a night of violent winds the *Prince of Wales* was seen no more. As well as company profits the flagship carried many personal treasures, principally those of Major-General Eccles Nixon who, after long service with the Madras army, had accumulated a 'noble fortune' and was returning home to enjoy it. Little attempt has been made, even by supreme optimists among the modern treasure-hunting fraternity, to retrieve the valuable contents of these distant wrecks, many of which are inadequately charted and lie in deep, distant waters.

This is not so with the East Indiamen which foundered within sight of home. For many Dutch and English vessels came to grief in the Channel or around the coast and islands of Northern Europe. The *Earl of Aber-gavenny*, a splendid ship of 1,200 tons, had scarcely left Portsmouth in February 1805 with £300,000 worth of cargo and specie when she ran into a gale which carried her on to the Shambles. She was badly holed on the rocks but managed to fend off into deep water and tried to reach Weymouth, firing her guns all the time as a distress signal. No one could possibly come to her aid in those conditions. Darkness fell. At about eleven o'clock she sank quickly with three hundred people aboard. Among the dead was her captain, John Wordsworth, younger brother of the poet. Not until the 1970s was the wreck of the *Abergavenny* located by local divers and a full-scale expedition planned.

In 1743 the *Hollandia*, outward bound for the Orient, foundered off the Scillies. Among other cargo she was carrying 130,000 guilders' worth of silver coin to lubricate the wheels of commerce. On the night of 13 July this proud, armed merchantman was thrust on to the rocks near St Agnes' Island and went down with all hands. Within weeks her owner had a salvage crew at work, but they had no precise information about the shipwreck. The islanders had heard the *Hollandia*'s guns being fired as a distress signal. They had found wreckage and bodies. But no one could locate the place where the vessel had sunk, within less than a few square miles. To help in the search the Dutch East India Company called in John Lethbridge and his impressive modern equipment. Lethbridge's diver was taken out and repeatedly lowered into the dark waters wearing his leather barrel. 'But the tide running strong at bottom and the sea appearing thick, the diver could not see distinctly through the glass of his engine, so returned without success. The wreck remains as a booty for those who can find it.' It had to wait over two hundred years for those successful seekers.

They came in 1970 and they were led by Rex Cowan, a solicitor who found life behind a desk too tame and went searching ancient wrecks and treasure. Months of patient research and a salvage

Receiver of Wreck

No matter how long a wreck had been on the sea bed, it belongs to someone and a treasure-salvor must reach an amicable arrangement with the appropriate authorities. In Britain the Merchant Shipping Acts of 1894 and 1906 require anyone retrieving objects from sunken vessels to hand them over to the Receiver of Wreck at the nearest port. If salvors can establish that they own the wreck or have acquired salvage rights, the property will be released to them. It is also theirs if no one claims it within a year. Rex Cowan and his team (below with the Receiver of Wreck for the Scillies), for example, had an agreement with the Dutch government (owners of all property previously belonging to the Dutch East India Co.) whereby they could dive on the *Hollandia*, one of the Dutch East Indiamen, as long as a quarter of all discoveries were made over to the Dutch.

The rapid growth of interest in treasure-diving in recent years has brought forth a considerable body of new legislation in many countries. In Britain, the most important is the Protection of Wrecks Act of 1973, which empowers the Board of Trade to declare any important site a protected area, to grant exclusive licence to a specialist salvor to work on it, and to punish by fine any unauthorized persons (in other words 'cowboys' or 'pirates') who interfere with it. Passing such legislation is one thing; enforcing it is another. It will, however, go some way to restricting the free-for-all that has been a feature of submarine archaeology for the past few decades. Another Scillies wreck, the *Association*, is known to have had within it a lot of silver and gold plate. Almost all of it has 'disappeared'. That indicates how important control is.

Many of the thousands of coins brought up from the Hollandia *were in as good condition as on the day they were minted. This was because they were concreted together in large clumps. While those on the outside of the clumps were badly corroded those in the centre were unharmed. These two eight-real silver pieces were made at the Mexico City mint in 1741.*

This model of a Dutch East Indiaman gives an excellent impression of the size and grace of the ships which were the queens of the sea in their day.

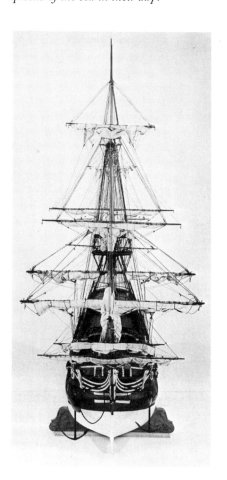

agreement negotiated with the Dutch government were followed by systematic search with a magnetometer. The 1970 season passed – unsuccessfully. The summer of 1971 was spent in fruitless labour. Then, on 18 September, the divers found the telltale signs of an ancient wreck – cannon, anchors and ballast. A couple of days later they met with an incredible sight – a mound three metres high and four metres in circumference; a mound of solid silver. When examined it proved to be composed of thousands upon thousands of concreted coins.

The work of raising the *Hollandia* treasure took several years. They were years well spent, for she was the most valuable Scillies wreck yet discovered and contributed considerably to the £1,000,000 plus of treasure taken from these waters in the 1970s.

But if the financial rewards were great, so were the expenses; Cowan certainly did not make his fortune. Nor was he looking to do so; it was the life of an underwater, historical detective that fascinated him. As he once said, 'The great treasury in ships lies not in silver and gold treasure but in the marvellous satisfaction in all the other things you discover.'

Many Dutch East Indiaman captains preferred to avoid the hazards of the Channel by sailing 'north-about' round the British Isles. The number of vessels that came to grief around the Scottish islands suggests that this route was scarcely less dangerous. The doleful catalogue includes the *Haan* (1640, Shetlands), the *Lastdrager* (1653, Isle of Yell), the *Kennemerland* (1664, Out Skerries), the *De Liefde* (1711, Out Skerries), the *Adelaar* (1728, Outer Hebrides), the *Curacao* (1729, Isle of Unst), the *Wendela* (1737, Isle of Fetlar) and the *Svecia* (1740, Orkneys). Of these the *De Liefde* has been the object of the most successful recent salvage operation. Early attempts to recover the ship's 200,000 silver coins achieved only modest success and the wreck was largely forgotten, although storms occasionally speckled the nearby beaches with ducatoons. It was the location of a cannon by naval divers that attracted two salvage outfits, Scientific Survey and Location Ltd and Static Devices Ltd, to the spot in 1965. In a series of dives spanning several years, thousands of coins and other artefacts were brought up. The most exciting find was 4,000 newly minted coins intact in a sea chest, preserved by a strange hard black substance which covered much of the site. As the years pass the sea occasionally yields up more secrets of missing East Indiamen. Only recently the wreck of the *Akerendam*, which vanished in 1725, turned up off the coast of Norway.

The Gold of the Eagle and the Bear

The double-headed eagle of the Hapsburgs fluttered proudly from the masthead of many a ship crossing the Pacific from the Philippines to Panama in the great days of Spain's overseas empire. The Manila galleons sailed annually from the Spanish oriental capital to the New World, where the treasures were carried across the Panama Isthmus and loaded on to the Atlantic bullion fleets. And what treasures! These proud vessels were laden with the varied exotic produce of the Orient – gold from Luzon, silk and porcelain from China, lacquerware and art treasures from Japan, ivory, gold, jade and amber from Burma and Thailand, ceramics and pearls from Borneo, gemstones and perfume from India – and always aboard were chests of coin, the lifeblood of international commerce.

Hundreds of these vessels lie at the bottom of the ocean with the more durable parts of their cargoes still intact. Many foundered in the open sea and their positions remain unknown. Some, however, are capable of salvage. To indicate the potential wealth of these wreck sites we might consider the case of a small *patache*, which struck the Calantas Reefs off the Philippines in 1735. Immediate efforts were made to recover her cargo. 1,518,000 pesos were salvaged before the work was abandoned, leaving a large quantity beneath the waves. Fifteen years later the *Pilar*, carrying two million pesos in coin, apart from other cargo, foundered in the mouth of Manilla harbour at the beginning of her journey because the captain was too proud to turn his leaking ship around. In 1802 the *Ferrolena* was smashed up on China's Cauchi Reefs, scattering gold and silver over the rocks and sand below. In 1734 the *Santa Maria Madalena*, absurdly overloaded, went down within minutes of leaving her anchorage at Cavite. And so it went on, year after year, yet in comparison with other areas, these eastern waters remain virgin territory for the marine archaeologist and the treasure-hunter.

A great treasure of the Russian Bear lay intact beneath a hundred metres of turbulent water until very recently. In 1904 the tiny island state of Japan had the temerity to challenge the might of Tsarist Russia. And it was to Japan's modern and efficient navy that the first victory went: they annihilated the Russian Pacific fleet. Tsar Nicholas's Baltic fleet was now dispatched to chastise the enemy. In her midst was the light battlecruiser *Admiral Nakhimoff*, carrying, not only armaments, but a large quantity of bullion and coin borrowed from European banks to help sustain the war effort. The Russian vessels met up with their adversaries in the Straits of Tsushima – and suffered another heavy defeat. The *Admiral Nakhimoff* tried to avoid the battle in order to land her cargo safely, but early on 28 May 1905 she received two torpedo hits. Rather than save his ship and allow her to fall into enemy hands, the captain deliberately sank his crippled vessels in a deep channel, notorious for its currents and bad weather.

The *Admiral Nakhimoff* defied all salvage attempts until 1980. Then a Japanese millionaire funded an expedition supplied with the latest kind of diving bell and other sophisticated equipment. His team was successful and soon began raising the estimated £20,000,000 worth of treasure. Only one major problem remains – the Soviet government is claiming the gold.

The battle of Tsushima was one of the most spectacular and devastating naval engagement of all time. Among the Russian vessels sunk by the Japanese navy was the Admiral Nakhimoff *carrying a fortune in bullion to the Tsar.*

Treasures Beneath Orient Seas

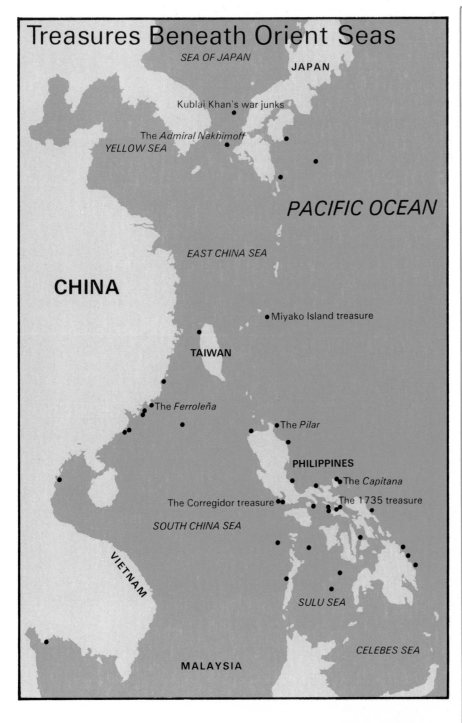

SEA OF JAPAN

JAPAN

Kublai Khan's war junks

The *Admiral Nakhimoff*

YELLOW SEA

PACIFIC OCEAN

EAST CHINA SEA

CHINA

Miyako Island treasure

TAIWAN

The *Ferroleña*

The *Pilar*

PHILIPPINES

The *Capitana*

The 1735 treasure

The Corregidor treasure

SOUTH CHINA SEA

VIETNAM

SULU SEA

CELEBES SEA

MALAYSIA

Kamikazi

Kamikazi – the holy wind! To many western ears the word recalls the far-eastern campaigns of the Second World War and the suicide fighter-pilots who crashed their aircraft into American warships. Its origin, however, is centuries earlier. In 1279 the great Kublai Khan had made himself master of mainland China and had begun to turn his attention to the conquest of the nearby islands. His fleet of a hundred war-junks set off across the China Sea on a career of loot and plunder. On they sailed towards Japan, a formidable and terrifying invasion force. Then, when they were off the coast of Honshu, a typhoon sprang up suddenly, scattering the fleet and swamping many of the vessels. This was the holy wind which saved the Japanese from conquest. It also sent to the bottom of the sea coin and many works of medieval oriental craftsmanship which would be priceless in today's art market. It is a treasure that no one is ever likely to raise. After seven hundred years its position and condition cannot be known. Any salvage attempt would be far too speculative.

Antipodean Treasures

It was in the opening years of the seventeenth century that European ships and men made their first contact with the coasts of Australia. For some that contact proved fatal. In 1611 the Dutch East Indiamen abandoned their coast-hugging route to the Orient and took the faster 'roaring forties' course from the Cape of Good Hope across the Pacific. In the wide expanse of ocean it was quite possible to be carried or to set a course too far to the east and end up on the savage reefs bordering the Western Australian coast.

One of the earliest vessels to be so lost was the *Vergulde Draeck* (the *Gilt Dragon*). She left the Low Countries in October 1655 carrying, among other cargo, eight chests of coin. At Cape Town she took on a consignment of ivory, then set off on the long haul across the Pacific. Before dawn on 28 April 1656 she crashed into the outer reef near the mouth of Moore River. Seventy-five passengers and crew reached the mainland and a boatload made a courageous journey across the Indian Ocean to Batavia, the Company's headquarters on Java. When a relief expedition returned they found no trace of the remaining survivors and could not locate the wreck. Not until 1931 were any clues to the disaster found. In that year a boy came across a skeleton and some coins on a beach north of

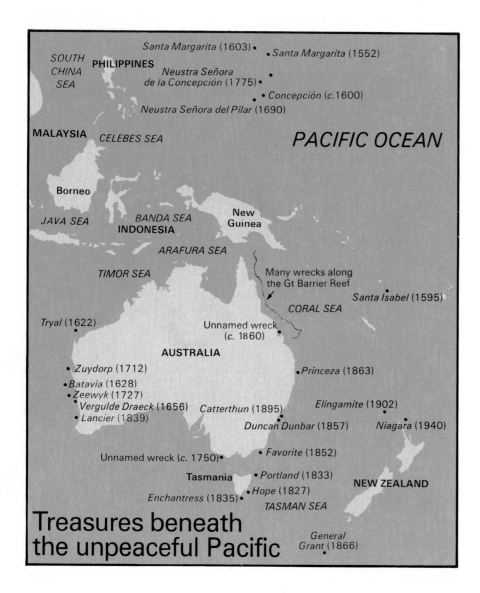

Treasures beneath the unpeaceful Pacific

The Silver of the *Batavia*
'. . . make efforts to bring up from the bottom the chest with eight thousand Rix dollars sunk from the lost ship *Batavia* . . . which would be a good service done to the . . . Company . . .' That was the order given to the explorer Abel Tasman in 1642 by the Dutch East India Co.'s governor at Batavia. But Tasman did not recover the chest of coin and nor, to date, has anyone else. The *Batavia* had struck the Abrolhos Islands thirteen years before, carrying twelve chests of money. One hundred and seventy people survived the cruel waves, only to find themselves pitched into a nightmare of savagery and blood-letting. A party of mutineers took over the little island settlement, butchering all who were not of their persuasion. A boatload of courageous sailors meanwhile sailed to Batavia and eventually company agents returned to revenge the dead and to salvage ten of the twelve treasure chests. The discovery of the *Batavia* in 1963 was a gruesome affair. An Australian team led by Hugh Edwards, Hec Donohue and Max Cramer not only dived to the shattered remains of the vessel, they explored the islands and uncovered the graves of brutally murdered, hastily buried men and women. They brought up cannon, navigational instruments, pottery and a number of coins from a chest that had been broken open and looted by the mutineers. But of that other chest, which had defied the company's Indian divers because it was pinned beneath a cannon, they found no trace.

Moore River. In 1957 some divers claimed to have discovered the *Vergulde Draeck* – and then lost her again, much to the amusement of sceptics. Then, in 1963, one of the original finders came upon the wreck once more and brought up ballast and elephant tusks. Proper salvage work began and a variety of items were retrieved – cannon, pottery, pewter, bronze items. Then the 'real' treasure was located – pieces of eight and gold eight-reales, thousands of them. Many of the *Gilt Dragon*'s relics are now on display in the Western Australia Museum. In the century following the loss of the *Vergulde Draeck* many other Dutch ships shared her fate.

On the other side of the continent lay the Great Barrier Reef and beyond that the Coral Sea and the wide scattering of coral ridges and islands that make up Melanesia and Micronesia. These have claimed an incalculable toll of ships, cargoes, and lives. In 1690 the thousand-ton Manilla galleon *Nuestra Señora del Pilar* sank off the southern tip of Guam on the last leg of her journey from Acapulco. She was carrying one and a half million pieces of eight. Stories of lost and found treasures abound along the Queensland coast. One tells of the survivors of a shipwreck reaching Mer Island with a large iron chest which they immediately buried. They were then eaten by the local inhabitants. Pearl divers off the Barrier Reef claimed to have found a chestful of Spanish coins in the middle of the last century. The owners of the company melted most of them down to make a silver dinner-service. The tales are many and varied. Sadly no authenticated discoveries of any significance have yet been reported.

We must travel more than four thousand miles to the south to reach the area associated with one of the greatest treasure mysteries of these far eastern waters. The *General Grant*, a fine American clipper of 1,103 tons, set sail from Melbourne in May 1866 carrying, among other Australian cargo, 2,576 ounces of gold from the new workings at Ballarat. Nine days out she was carried by contrary seas on to the craggy coast of one of the uninhabited Auckland Islands, south of New Zealand. She was driven hard into a large cave and there settled in six fathoms. The handful of survivors spent a dreary, uncomfortable eighteen months on the weather-lashed islet before being rescued. One of them was soon back to conduct the first of many salvage attempts, but heavy breakers prevented the team getting into the cave. Adverse conditions obstructed most salvage attempts, but those treasure-seekers who have entered the cave – one group made a thorough underwater search in 1969 – have uncovered a real mystery: they insist that there is no trace whatever of any ship having been wrecked there.

The Cruel Scillies

There is an old saying in the Scilly Isles that for every man there who dies peacefully in his bed nine are lost at sea. This cluster of a hundred and forty-five islands and rocks at the entrance to the English Channel has claimed thousands of ships and sailors over the centuries. Most of the lumps of jagged granite are covered at high tide, and the low-lying islands themselves all too frequently merge with the grey of sea and sky. Nowadays, when there are six lighthouses and a lightship around the Scillies and when vessels are equipped with radar and radio, wrecks are comparatively few. It was not always so. Countless ships have scattered their cargoes and crews over the Atlantic bottom and the island shores. The old prayer has frequently been answered which runs: 'We pray thee, O Lord, not that wrecks should happen but that if they should happen, that thou wilt guide them into the Scillies for the benefit of the poor inhabitants.'

Most of the vessels lost on this ten-mile barrier of rock were carrying prosaic cargoes – brandy, coal, wool, timber, grain and livestock – valuable, indeed, to the islanders but not qualifying as 'treasure'. How-

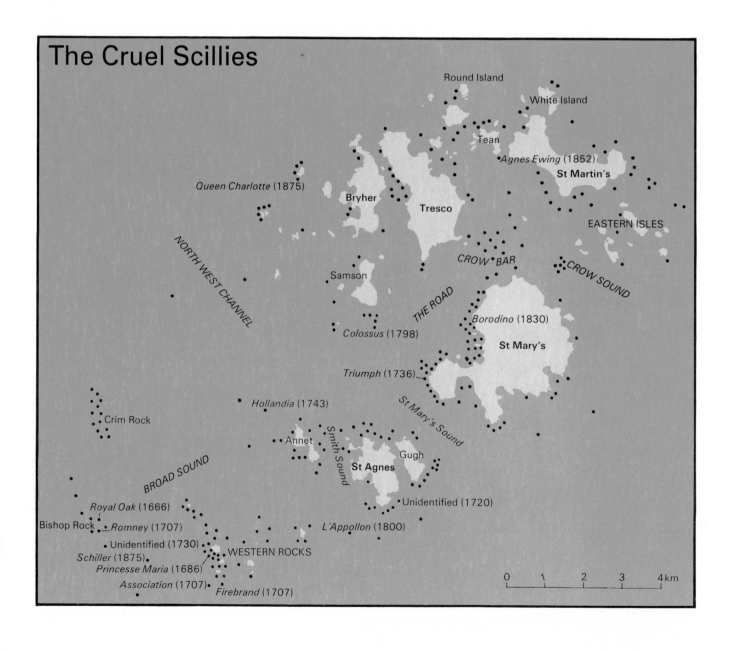

The Cruel Scillies

Round Island
White Island
Tean
Agnes Ewing (1852)
St Martin's
Queen Charlotte (1875)
Bryher
Tresco
EASTERN ISLES
NORTH WEST CHANNEL
CROW · BAR
CROW SOUND
Samson
THE ROAD
Borodino (1830)
St Mary's
Colossus (1798)
Triumph (1736)
Hollandia (1743)
St Mary's Sound
Crim Rock
Annet
Smith Sound
Gugh
BROAD SOUND
St Agnes
Unidentified (1720)
Royal Oak (1666)
Bishop Rock · *Romney* (1707)
L'Appollon (1800)
Unidentified (1730)
Schiller (1875)·
WESTERN ROCKS
Princesse Maria (1686)
Association (1707)·
Firebrand (1707)

0   1   2   3   4km

ever, there were exceptions. The most celebrated Scillies wrecks, the *Association* and the *Colossus*, are noted elsewhere, but they are not alone in carrying precious items to the ocean floor. The East Indiaman *Royal Oak* returning with her rich cargo from the Orient went down in fifteeen minutes when she struck the Bishop and Clerks in 1666. In 1730, a vessel bringing back wine from the Canaries became wedged on rocks close to Rosevean. Only with difficulty was her captain induced to leave the doomed ship; he was reluctant to abandon the large sum of money he had on board. Only ten years before, a well-laden Dutch vessel sank off St Agnes with all her cargo. In 1800 the loss of the French ship, *L'Appollon*, proved very fortunate for the islands. She was carrying a Napoleonic invasion force. As well as the six hundred soldiers, their considerable payroll was also lost. Another French ship, the *Pacquebot de Cayenne*, which foundered in Crow Sound in 1780, was also believed to be carrying a large amount of coin. Somewhere near Tean the outward-bound East Indiaman *Agnes Ewing* went down in 1852. The *Triumph* was carrying £10,000 in gold coin when she struck Steval Rock in 1736, and a century later the Dutch East Indiaman *Mercurias* foundered in the same area. One of the largest salvage operations of the nineteenth century followed the loss of the 3,421-ton steamer *Schiuer* on Retarrier Ledges in 1875. She was known to be carrying £60,000 in twenty-dollar gold pieces, as well as the property of wealthy passengers. Diving continued for almost a year, during which time most, but not all, of the specie was raised.

The greatest excitement of recent years among salvage operators in the Scillies was roused by the discovery of two Dutch East Indiamen. Not much was expected of the *Princesse Maria*, which struck the Western Rocks in 1686. She had remained above the waves for several days and was thoroughly looted. Even the King, James II, took part in the plunder, sending his royal yacht to the site and appropriating 13,000 pieces of eight for the royal purse. Yet when the wreck was located in 1973 it soon became obvious that the original scavangers had not taken everything. Coins, pewter objects and navigational instruments were retrieved, and, most remarkable of all, a pottery bellarmine jug with its contents – forty-three pounds of mercury – still intact.

The *Hollandia* was a different story. All members of the Scillies diving fraternity knew that this vessel had vanished without trace off St Agnes in 1743, carrying a very large consignment of specie. We have already seen how Rex Cowan and his team eventually solved the mystery in 1972, and the wealth of the treasure they salvaged. For every such successful expedition there are hundreds which fail. Every year groups of divers seek hopefully for the uncharted or unlocated wrecks which litter the sea bed around the Scillies. Those who search for gold beneath the seas know that theirs is no romantically adventurous occupation. They are aware of the presence of death. Every diver has lost a colleague or friend at some time and is conscious that any mistake or piece of bad luck could claim his own life.

The subaqua teams are entering the domain of long-dead seamen whose pathetic mementoes may be among the 'treasures' they recover. When the *Association* and her companion vessels went down in 1707 they took with them 2,000 officers and men of the British navy. Perhaps it is just that such riches as lie around the Scillies should only be won at great risk.

There are few accurate records of early treasure ships. The Hollandia *is an exception. This original drawing of the Dutch East Indiaman helped divers in knowing exactly what they were looking for. Most of the bullion aboard the* Hollandia *was carried at the back of the ship.*

Handfuls of Guineas

In October 1707 twenty-one English warships were returning home from a spell of duty in the Mediterranean. They were under the command of the fifty-seven-year-old Sir Cloudesley Shovell, Rear-Admiral of England. His flagship was the first-rate man-o'-war *Association*. This large, well-armed vessel was one of the finest in the Royal Navy. She was a working ship and her business was the destruction of enemy vessels and shore fortifications. Most of the 'tween-deck space was required for her 640 crewmen, her officers, cannon, ammunition, stores and victuals. But there was room for cargo, and the *Association* had plied commercially in the Mediterranean on behalf of the crown and private merchants. Thus it was that she carried several chests of coin, the proceeds of trade. There was also the admiral's own property – money, jewels and silver plate, from which he and his officers always dined. In addition there were boxes stuffed with plunder from captured enemy craft.

The fleet had a stormy voyage. So often had they been driven off-course that, as they approached the entrance to the Channel, none of the captains could pinpoint their positions with any accuracy. In the afternoon of 21 October, Sir Cloudesley summoned all commanders aboard the *Association* to discuss the situation. The consensus of opinion was that the fleet was close to the island of Ushant off the coast of Brittany. In fact,

Members of the Association *salvage team survey the treacherous Gilstone rocks. This granite reef is completely covered at high tide and many vessels have fallen foul of its hidden menace including Sir Cloudesley Shovell's ill-fated fleet.*

as the light failed on that grey day, the English fleet lay to the south-west of the Scillies and was heading straight for them. That night a strong south-westerly gale blew up. It did not worry the Admiral. Quite the reverse; with the open Channel before him, he could confidently run before the wind and be brought even sooner into Portsmouth harbour. Most of his captains realized their mistake in time. The sharp eyes and ears of the duty watch detected the sound of breakers and the flickering light from the beacon on St Agnes' Isle. Hurried orders were given. Ships veered away into deeper water. The *Phoenix* was badly holed, but her crew managed to beach her on Tresco. The *Eagle* and the *Romney* were not so fortunate. They went down with all hands. And the *Association* ran into Gilstone Rock. Next morning the islanders of St Mary's were down at the shoreline, busy with a familiar occupation: picking over the remains of dead men and dead ships for items of value. One woman found an elderly man lying on the sand. He was unconscious but still breathing. There was little clothing on him, but jewelled rings adorned his fingers. It was the work of but a moment to strangle the fellow and remove his jewels. Thus died Rear-Admiral Sir Cloudesley Shovell.

The *Association* was located in 1964 by members of the Naval Air Command Subaqua Club. Although they could not be certain of the wreck's identity the recovery of a bronze gun and a few seventeenth-century coins suggested that they were on the right track and they worked the site for several seasons. But Roland Morris was also

Early navigators had little help in detecting and avoiding rocks around the Scillies. One of the first attempts to map the hazards was Edmund Gostelo's 'Map of the islands of Scilly; showing all the rocks and ledges, with the soundings and bearings of the exact places where the Association, Eagle, Romney *and* Firebrand *was lost . . .' which was published c. 1720.*

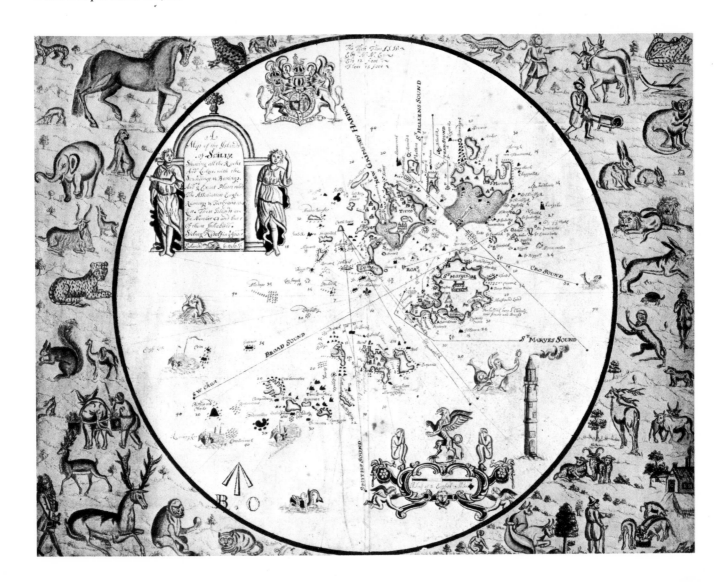

The Association *yielded a rich variety of treasures. There were cannon balls; nautical instruments and a variety of ship's and personal implements. Every diver came up from the sea bed with something of interest, such as an encrusted musket, a spoon, a fragment of pottery. But it was the coins that caught the popular imagination. There was millions of pounds' worth of gold and silver – English guineas and crowns, French écus, and the irregularly shaped pieces of eight. Exciting as all this was, it was not the specie that principally interested Roland Morris, the team's leader, and his colleagues. They were looking for something that would prove the identity of the wreck. The discovery of a silver plate bearing the arms of Sir Cloudesley Shovell, Admiral of the Fleet, was the triumphant reward for their persistent underwater excavation. Cloudesley Shovell had his flag in the* Association *and was aboard when she foundered on the Gilstone reef.*

interested. He was a Penzance *restaurateur* and part-time salvor. He obtained salvage rights to the 1707 wrecks from the Ministry of Defence. In 1967 and 1968 his divers brought up three bronze cannon and a variety of coins and artefacts. One day one of the men surfaced spluttering that he had gone through a crevice in the rocks and found the ocean floor carpeted with gold and silver coins. Still there was nothing to prove conclusively that the wreck was the *Association*, and that meant, as the law then stood, that anyone could dive on it. Morris and his men, as they carefully catalogued their finds and handed everything over to the Receiver of Wreck, had the frustration of seeing 'pirates' illegally hawking pieces of eight and other finds to tourists. At last a member of the team came up with irrefutable proof – a beautiful silver dish bearing Sir Cloudesley Shovell's coat of arms. The news was not greeted warmly by Morris's rivals. One of them phoned him anonymously offering to smash up his restaurant. Against this unpleasant background of hostility and bitterness the work continued until all that could reasonably be recovered had surfaced. Much of it came under the hammer in July 1969, when Sotheby's held the first ever sale of sunken treasure from a ship in British waters. Over 2,000 coins, items of plate, jewellery and ordnance changed hands for more than £20,000. At another sale six months later Morris himself was the most determined bidder. He paid £2,100 for that single, all-important plate.

Cuckold's Treasure

Sir William Hamilton has been unkindly lampooned as 'the man who shared his wife with an admiral and his treasure with the sea'. Emma Hamilton's relationship with Lord Nelson is well known. The story of her husband's treasure is less so. Sir William was British envoy to the court of Naples from 1764 to 1800, a time when, as we have seen, the leaders of fashionable society were vying with each other for the possession of classical antiquities. Hamilton's tastes were catholic and he was ideally placed to indulge them. He collected a large and impressive quantity of bronzes, terracottas, ivories, gems, gold ornaments, glass objects and coins. He sold it all, in 1772, to the British Museum. When he later resumed collecting he specialized principally in painted Greek vases, most of which came from tombs in the region of Naples. Hamilton's hoard was both large and selective, representing considerable research and expense, but once again he wearied of accumulating treasure and offered all his pieces for sale. Having failed to find a buyer on the Continent he sent them home in 1798, carefully packed into twenty-four crates aboard the seventy-four-gun warship *Colossus*. As the vessel approached the Scillies she was buffeted by severe north-easterlies, and her captain, George Murray, ordered the anchor to be dropped in the lea of St Mary's. Within hours the wind swung round to the south-east and built up to gale force. The overstrained anchor cable snapped and the *Colossus* was swept on to the Southern Wells reef off Samson Island.

The Treasure of the Colossus presented experts and volunteer workers at the British Museum with the biggest jigsaw puzzle in the world. Tens of thousands of fragments of painted Greek vases, part of Sir William Hamilton's collection, were salvaged from the sea bed and sent to the museum for cleaning, preserving and sorting. How many items it will be possible to recreate in whole or in part, cannot yet be estimated.

Sir William Hamilton was, as his portrait suggests, a sensitive man of refined tastes. He spent most of his adult life as special envoy and plenipotentiary to the Court of Naples, and while in Italy he accumulated his collections of antiquities. Most of the Greek vases he obtained came from tombs in the region of Naples. In 1791 he married the celebrated beauty, Emma Hart. Her relations with Lord Nelson later created a public scandal and a favourite theme of cartoonists such as Gilroy, who depicted the antiquarian examining objects which bear obvious reference to the lovers.

Only one life was lost, but all Sir William's precious crates sank with the ship. Salvage work was set in hand immediately, and sixteen cases were saved. The rest of the Hamilton collection remained on the sea bed until it became the subject of one of the most dramatic salvage operations of recent years.

Once again, Roland Morris was organizer of the rescue. He had worked on a number of Scillies wrecks since the *Association*, and in 1973 he determined to see what was left of Sir William's vases. Taking advantage of a new law (the Protection of Wrecks Act 1973), Morris obtained sole right to salvage of the *Colossus*. His men discovered the pottery beneath a thin covering of sand. The boxes had long since decayed and their contents were scattered, smashed into a myriad of fragments, some as big as a man's hand, others no larger than a thumbnail. In two seasons' diving the team gathered over 35,000 pieces. Each was carefully cleaned, wrapped and packed, ready for the experts, and it was to the British Museum that this gigantic jigsaw puzzle was dispatched. Probably the task of reconstruction would have been beyond even the top British specialists if Sir William Hamilton himself had not posthumously helped them. For that dedicated collector had had his fine pieces drawn with accurate and loving care by an expert draughtsman, and the British Museum possessed the folios containing these drawings. Even with the help of this master plan it will be many years before all the fragments of the *Colossus* treasures are fitted together.

De Profundis

There are probably no lost treasures which will remain technically inaccessible to man for all time. But there are treasures which will take vast reserves of courage and ingenuity to recover. It was so with the gold of the *Egypt*. This P&O liner of just under 8,000 tons was outward bound from London in May 1922 when she collided with the freighter *Seine* in fog off Ushant. Her wireless operator had time to signal the ship's position before she went down, so there was no secret about her location. Yet the *Egypt*, and her cargo of £1,054,000 in gold and silver *en route* for Indian banks, had to be written off. She lay at a depth of 120 metres, twice as far as any diver had ever penetrated and lived.

The problem, of course, was pressure. The human body and its life support systems would be squeezed and crushed if they penetrated the 60 to 70 metre barrier. For years men experimented with armoured suits, lead-encased air pipes and other devices. Divers lost their lives trying out these contraptions. Even suits that would convey a man to the ocean bed and enable him to live there proved to be failures because they gave him no manoeuvrability. Therefore, the underwriters had to consider the *Egypt*'s precious cargo as lost.

Not so Giovanni Quaglia. Quaglia was an irrepressible Italian salvage expert who specialized in the impossible. In 1929 he began his quest for the *Egypt*'s bullion. A year passed during which his salvage crew worked unproductively in one of the world's worst areas of storm and fog-beset sea. The project swallowed capital, for SORIMA, the salvage company, used highly trained divers and the most up-to-date equipment. Quaglia's technique was based on the use of the 'iron man', an armoured diving suit weighing half a ton perfected by the Hamburg firm of Neufeldt and Kuhnke. The diver, encased in this mass of metal, was there to direct operations carried out from the surface. By means of a telephone link to the salvage ship he guided the cranes and winches which lowered explosives and steel grabs into place. But even with this sophisticated equipment it took months to locate the *Egypt* in the Atlantic's murky depths, and when she was found she presented another problem to the salvors: she had settled in an upright position, which meant that the excavators would have to tear their way through three deck levels to reach the strongroom. Quaglia's personal fortune followed SORIMA's working capital into the undertaking. Work had to stop while the Italian sought more capital – not easy in the years of the Great Depression.

When the work resumed there were frequent interruptions caused by current, which carried the salvage ship away from the wreck and banged the 'iron man' about dangerously at the end of his cable. Eventually the cumbersome suit was replaced by an observation chamber which gave the occupant greater visibility. Painfully slowly the *Egypt* was ripped apart and probed. Not until 22 June 1931 did the grab bring up treasure – a single gold sovereign. By the end of the month Quaglia had amassed a pile of ingots and coins. He reported to Lloyd's in London and was given a hero's welcome. Every diving season he returned to the wreck site and did not abandon his task until 1935, by which time he had recovered ninety-five per cent of the *Egypt*'s treasure. To gain experience and learn about the problems of working in this stretch of water they did a 'dummy run' on another wreck in the vicinity. Quaglia dared not begin on the *Egypt* until he had the necessary equipment and technical skills.

As Giovanni Quaglia and his salvage company applied themselves to the considerable technical problems of opening up a steel ship over 120 metres beneath the surface of the Bay of Biscay, the world waited for news of his audacious recovery effort. The Illustrated London News *provided its readers with a series of drawings showing how the work was being done.*

THE "EGYPT" SALVAGE : DIRECTING OPERATIONS FROM A DIVING-SHELL.

DRAWN BY OUR SPECIAL ARTIST, G. H. DAVIS, FROM INFORMATION RECEIVED.

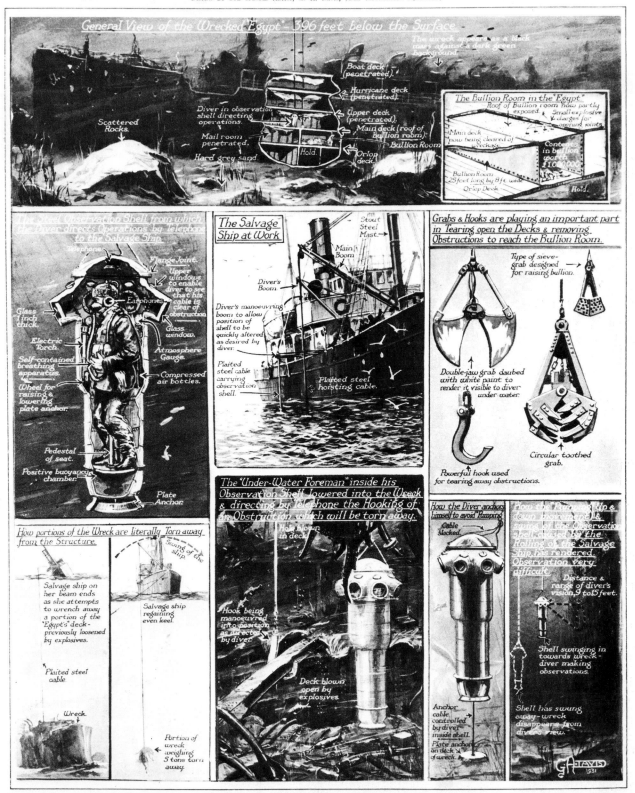

GUIDED BY AN UNDER-WATER FOREMAN AT 396 FT. DEPTH : EFFORTS TO SALVE THE "EGYPT'S" £1,000,000 OF BULLION.

The world awaits with interest the result of efforts by Italian divers of the "Artiglio," the new salvage ship of the Sorima Company, of Genoa, to salve the gold and silver, worth about £1,000,000, from the bullion-room of the P. and O. liner "Egypt," sunk on May 20, 1922, twenty-five miles S.W. of Ushant, in 66 fathoms, or 396 feet, of water. The great depth renders ordinary rubber diving-suits useless and many new types of salvage gear became necessary. Steel diving-suits with flexible arms and legs, of German make, were first used, but proved inadequate, so the Sorima's own engineers devised a chamber just large enough for one man, fitted with many windows, and connected by telephone to the surface. In this shell the diver is lowered to the wreck, and, assisted by co-ordinated team-work on the surface, acts as under-water foreman. Though unable to work himself, he directs the lowering and placing of explosive charges and operation of hooks and "grabs." The "Egypt" lies on hard sand, practically upright, and, as the observation chamber can only be lowered vertically, four decks had to be blown and torn open to get to the bullion-room. With the ship rolling, the diving-shell far below, suspended on plaited steel cable, "pumps" up and down and swings in all directions, giving the diver only momentary glimpses of his objective. The salvors recently reached a point practically right above the bullion-room and began desperate efforts to penetrate the roof and secure the treasure before winter gales should end this year's operations. Mr. David Scott, in his book, "Seventy Fathoms Deep," gave a graphic description of the work, which is unique in that the Sorima is the first company to specialise in treasure-hunting at well over 200 feet. The first "Artiglio" blew up off Quiberon on December 7, 1930.

The Bell of Doom

She was a thirty-two gun French frigate called *Sprite* or, in the language of the men who built her, *La Lutine*. She was a fast, manoeuvrable vessel laid down in an age which saw the finest sailing warships ever built, the second half of the eighteenth century. However, she was destined to be famous, not because of her part in the epic naval struggle between Nelson and the admirals of Napoleon Bonaparte, but because of the treasure she took with her to the bottom of the North Sea – and because of her bell. Early in the conflict between Britain and revolutionary France, the *Lutine* was captured. In October 1779 she was sent from London on an important solo mission. She carried money to pay the troops occupying Texel Sound against France's Dutch allies, and bullion for the merchants of Hamburg, who were giving Britain valuable assistance in the war. Her precious cargo was insured for £1,200,000, most of it with Lloyd's of London.

Withing hours of her departure she fell foul of shoals between the Dutch islands Yerschelling and Vlieland and went down will all hands save one (the lone survivor died before he could give any information about the shipwreck). For the underwriters the loss was a severe disaster; for although the wreck was in fairly shallow water, it could be, and was, claimed by the enemy.

The Dutch began salvage work immediately but were hampered, as all other attempts were to be hampered, by bad weather and shifting sands. The wreck was broken up and scattered over a wide area of the sea bed at depths varying from ten to twenty metres. It was then covered by a deposit of silt. Using rafts anchored over the site, the salvors 'fished' for treasure with hooks and tongs. In this way they recovered 58 bars of gold and 35 bars of silver as well as a quantity of coin. This was only the first of many attempts to raise the *Lutine*'s bullion, attempts bedevilled by diplomatic wrangling as well as the natural hazards of the site. Lloyd's never officially relinquished possession of the wreck, but long after the end of hostilities the Dutch government continued to claim it. Every attempt at salvage was strenuously opposed by the English insurers. It was 1826 before the Dutch relinquished their rights and only then after they had reached the conclusion that nothing more was likely to be found. This meant that Lloyd's could now claim fifty per cent of the value of any salvage.

Over the next hundred years or so nine major expeditions were mounted. The only one to achieve a measure of success was that of 1857–60 which raised 41 gold bars, 64 silver bars and a quantity of coin, as well as various fragments of the ship. During this salvage attempt the ship's rudder was recovered (now made into a table and kept at Lloyd's) and also the Lutine Bell. This famous ship's bell was hung in the insurers' premises in Leadenhall Street, where it has remained ever since. It is rung whenever the tragic news reaches London that a vessel is missing. It also signals the happier information that a ship, feared lost, has safely reached a harbour.

Since the mid nineteenth century more money has gone into *Lutine* salvage efforts than has ever come out. Suction pumps, dredges and other sophisticated equipment have been used, but all to no avail. The thick, ever-shifting sea bed still covers millions of pounds' worth of precious metal.

Gold Fever

Priam's Treasure

From the pile of gold and silver on the rough wooden table, Heinrich Schliemann took a 3,000-year-old pendant and a pair of earrings and placed them on his beautiful young wife, Sophia. 'Helen,' he whispered.

As well as being the most romantic moment in the history of archaeology, this was for Schliemann the culmination of a quest that had obsessed him for most of his fifty-one years. He had been fascinated by Troy ever since, as a child in Germany, his father, a Lutheran pastor, had read him Homer's stories of Agamemnon's siege, the Trojan Horse and

'No sooner has one set foot on Trojan soil than one is astonished to see that this noble mound of Hissarlik seems to have been intended by Nature herself to be the site of a great citadel.' With his remarkable instinct Schliemann recognized at first glance the site of the famous city the experts said had never existed.

Heinrich Schliemann was a determined man who usually got what he set his mind upon. He mastered fourteen ancient and modern languages, allowing himself six weeks to become fluent in each. In twenty years he rose from office-boy to tycoon. But the steel-willed businessman was also a warm romantic. He decided to marry a Greek woman and accordingly instructed his agent, 'Try to find me a wife with a Greek name and a soul impassioned for learning.' The girl found for him was a seventeen-year-old beauty, Sophia Engastromenos, who became for Schliemann a second Helen, the embodiment of Greek grace, gaiety and dedication to art and learning. The moment when Schliemann decked his wife in ancient Trojan treasures and, as it were, reincarnated Homer's tragic heroine, was a moment of poetry for him.

the fall of Priam's capital. For most boys brought up on the tales of the Greek heroes, Homer's *Iliad* was myth with little or no historical foundation – but not for young Heinrich. He vowed he would find the ancient city that scholars agreed did not exist.

First, however, he needed the money to do it. His belief in himself was total and he undertook everything with complete dedication. By 1860 he was a millionaire and in 1863, at the age of forty-one, he retired from his work in banking to devote himself to travel, study and archaeology in the land of his beloved Hellenes.

Schliemann walked and rode among the groves and hills that Homer had loved. He looked out over the sea that Agamemnon had crossed with his battle fleet to invade Troy and bring back the beautiful Helen. He even married a Greek woman.

By the time of his marriage Schliemann had already, to his own satisfaction, located Troy. Those experts who were prepared to concede that the ancient city had existed sited it near the little village of Bunarbashi. Schliemann went there, *Iliad* in his hand, and decided that Bunarbashi simply did not fit the details of Homer's story.

Immediately, he travelled on to the only other possible site. This was the mound of Hissarlik, an hour's distance from the Dardanelles. It took him very little time to make up his mind: 'After walking round the ground for half an hour ... all doubts concerning the identity of Hissarlik with [Troy] vanish.'

In the spring of 1870 Schliemann returned with his wife to begin excavations. He hired a hundred labourers, bought valuable equipment, worked himself from dawn till dusk – probing, measuring, prising finds carefully from the earth, cleaning, examining. The scholarly world laughed. They labelled Schliemann a dilettante, a wealthy businessman with no academic credentials, playing at archaeology. He ignored them. He was supremely happy and he was producing some incredible results. Starting at the top of the mound he almost immediately discovered walls, pottery, weapons and ornaments. In four seasons, between 1870 and 1873, he produced evidence for nine periods of occupation at Hissarlik. In the second and third levels from the bottom he found the remains of massive walls and an impressive gateway that had been badly scorched by fire. This, he confidently asserted, was the city that had fallen to Agamemnon.

By June 1873, Schliemann's reports and the artefacts he had dispatched to various museums had created considerable interest in the archaeological world. What happened next took the world by storm. The archaeologist and his wife were at the excavations early on a clear June morning, supervising the work. The men were digging earth away from the walls of 'Priam's palace' when Schliemann suddenly noticed the gleam of metal. Bending down for a closer look, he saw the circular rim of a copper object. That was interesting enough, but in the cavity behind he felt sure he recognized the glow of gold. He did not dare let the labourers know of his discovery so he ordered them to take their meal-break. Then he approached the spot with Sophia. While Heinrich prised items loose with his knife, his wife wrapped them carefully in a shawl and removed them to a safe place. One by one the objects were brought up from their burial place – a copper cauldron and plate, a jug and two cups of pure gold, copper lances, and ceremonial knives of silver; then, most exciting of all, a group of silver vases whose weight indicated that they were not empty. Glancing inside, Schliemann saw that they were packed with

'Priam's Treasure' was lost during the Second World War, and now only old photographs and engravings of it exist. They do scant justice to the 3,000-year-old golden head-dresses, rings, pendants, earrings, and other items of adornment of simple yet beautiful design.

pieces of jewellery. It was a stupendous discovery. The treasure-hunter in Schliemann triumphed over the archaeologist. He scrabbled away eagerly at earth and stone, not pausing to make observations about the exact location of his find, not bothering to preserve fragile items intact as long as he collected all the pieces. He was even careless of his own safety, for his frenzied digging beneath the ancient wall threatened to bring tons of stone down on top of him.

When all was removed to the site hut, the finds were spread out on a table – jars, dishes, weapons, two beautiful diadems, sixty golden earrings, necklaces, gold buttons and other ornaments, bracelets, goblets and no less than 8,750 gold rings.

Schliemann was convinced that what he had found was a chest containing personal treasures buried by a member of Priam's family in the very hours when the city fell: in fact he was wrong. The hoard that he confidently labelled 'Priam's Treasure' predated Homer by at least a thousand years and came from the Early Bronze Age. During the last century similar hoards have been found in Asia Minor and Greece. Almost certainly they are the personal wealth of ancient aristocrats, buried for safety at times of crisis and never reclaimed.

Schliemann was determined to preserve Priam's Treasure intact and smuggle it out of Turkey. He and Sophia bundled the precious items up, put them in baskets and sent them to the US consul in Constantinople, who conveyed them to Greece under diplomatic protection.

The outraged Ottoman government was determined to regain this

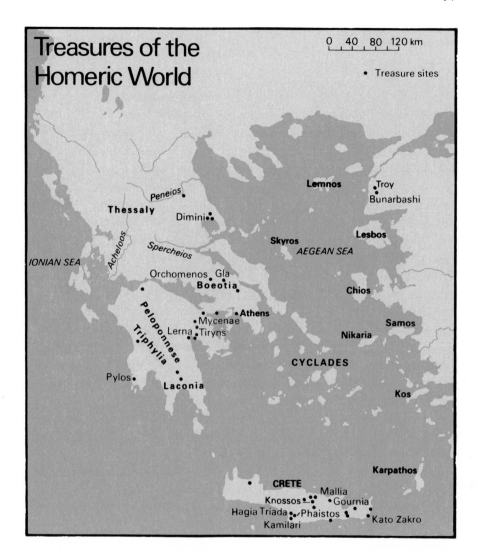

Treasures of the Homeric World

famous treasure. Official protests were made to the Greek government. Agents were sent to break into Schliemann's hotel suite. Then the Turks took the archaeologist to court in Athens. He was interrogated and spent several weeks under virtual house arrest. Meanwhile Priam's Treasure had been dispersed and hidden by Sophia's relatives. Schliemann lost the case and was ordered to pay 50,000 francs to Turkey in damages and restitution. Almost as a gesture of contempt he paid over five times the required amount.

After some years Schliemann donated his major Trojan discoveries to the Berlin Ethnological Museum. There they remained for over sixty years until the tide of Hitler's war turned against Germany. They were moved for safety, first to the Prussian State Bank, then to the air-raid shelter at Berlin Zoo. As enemy troops closed on the capital, the Nazis thought it wise to disperse Schliemann's gold and silver, along with other national treasures. Some went to Lebus Palace on the Polish border; some to Schönebeck on the Elbe, and some to Petrusche Palace near Breslau. From these locations they disappeared. In the confusion and devastation of the last days of the war, Priam's Treasure, which had escaped being plundered in another conflict 4,000 years before, now fell a victim to twentieth-century human locusts. Whether it was carried off to Russia, or looted by local people, or buried without trace beneath tons of rubble, will probably never be known. The story of Priam's Treasure is, surely, another epic worthy of Homer.

Consorting with Spirits

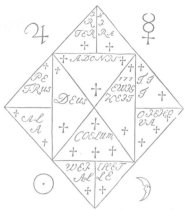

For some men the quest for buried treasure becomes an obsession. Schliemann and Layard devoted years of their lives to seeking out antique splendours. It was knowledge as much as valuable relics that they were seeking. Others were motivated by sheer greed and were prepared to use the most bizarre methods to enrich themselves.

Sorcery has always been closely linked with treasure-hunting. Buried hoards were thought to be guarded by demons, dragons and spirits, and so could only be safely recovered with the aid of powerful magic. In 1527, John Curson of Kettering consulted a local priest, who told him that a cache of gold and silver worth £3,000 lay concealed. But it was within a nearby barrow guarded by a male and a female spirit. Curson enlisted the aid of two accomplices and, at the astrologically propitious time, approached the mound in the black of night. He then began a complicated ritual of incantations and spells. The darkness and the weird proceedings must have been extremely unnerving. But that was as nothing to the shock that came next. From below their feet came a deep, rumbling growl, caused by nothing more than stones falling into and echoing round the burial chamber; but to the trembling hearers it sounded like the angry roar of a roused demon. They threw down their implements and fled. It was some time before Curson could find more stout-hearted companions. When he did so the ceremony was repeated. Again they were disturbed, not by spirits this time, but by the local magistrates who had heard of Curson's unlawful activities. Some of the excavators were caught and the whole story came out at the subsequent

Cabalistic signs, a secret language for communicating with spirits, were only a part of the stock in trade of magicians. The Key of Solomon was a book which told how to conjure up Parasiel, the demon in charge of treasures. Another useful tool was the magician's sword, whose blade and hilt were inscribed with mystic names. It had to be polished at the first or fifteenth hour on the day of Mercury, then solemnly sprinkled with water while a long incantation was pronounced over it. The seeker then had to describe a circle on the ground with the sword on a night when the moon was in the sign of Leo. Then he had to light a lamp which was fuelled by oil mingled with the fat of a newly dead man, having a wick made with threads from his shroud. If all these rites were correctly performed the treasure would be found.

The Spell

John Dee

Dr John Dee, the most remarkable English scholar of the reign of Queen Elizabeth I, was a man who excelled in most branches of knowledge. He was a mathematician, astronomer, astrologer, philosopher and alchemist. He also ventured deep into the mysteries of the black arts. He claimed to be able to conjure spirits by means of a crystal globe. He had his own divining rods which, he claimed, revealed the whereabouts of precious metal. By means of this device he offered to discover for the Queen a gold or silver mine. In return he asked for a patent, making over to him all treasure trove found in the kingdom. Doubtless he planned to use his various arts to locate buried hoards. Elizabeth, it seems, was not satisfied that she was on the best end of the proposed deal and nothing came of it. Dee, like all alchemists, turned most of his mental energies to the task of discovering the philosopher's stone which would change base metals into gold. He failed, of course, but he enjoyed the patronage of the Queen and several leading courtiers and so made a reasonable living. It was when he took up with Edward Kelly that things began to go wrong.

Kelly was a resourceful young man who turned his agile wits to necromancy, alchemy, astrology and anything that would persuade people to part with money. He had already had his ears cropped for fraud or coining and had also been in trouble for conjuring spirits of the dead in the churchyard at Walton-le-Dale, perhaps with the intention of locating buried treasure. He introduced himself to Dee in 1582 as an expert in the art of conjuring demons. He also presented the magus with an old parchment which he claimed to have discovered in Wales with the aid of one of his spirits. It was in cypher, but Dee, who was an expert in codes, soon translated it into Latin. It purported to be a catalogue of treasure buried by 'Gordano' and other chiefs of the Arthurian epoch on both sides of the Bristol Channel. Dee's manuscript notes can still be seen in the British Library (*Sloane MS* 3188, fols 86, 87) with the 'treasure' sites listed in his own hand: 'Gilds

D. Dee avoucheth his Stone is brought by Angelicall Ministry.

cros, Branxes Suters croces, Marsars got cros, Huteos cros, Fluds grenul, Mons mene, Mountegles arnid, Lan sapant, Corts nulds, Mnrr Merse'. All these sites are, or were, close by clear landmarks – crosses, hills and trees. Any modern treasure-hunter going after them would obviously have more difficulty than his sixteenth-century counterpart. He

would also show himself to be more credulous than John Dee. It seems unlikely that Dee believed this to be a forgery, for he fell completely under Kelly's spell and the charlatan spent many years as Dee's house guest. However, Dee never went in search of the ten treasures, preferring instead to rely on Kelly's necromantic skills as a source of income. The two men toured many foreign courts, seeking rich and gullible patrons. The truth about his companion only dawned on Dee after Kelly declared that he had received an instruction from the spirits that they were to have their wives in common.

Sibly Del

Ames Sculp

EDWᴰ KELLY, A MAGICIAN.

in the Act of invoking the Spirit of a Desceased Person.

Dʳ Dees Works

inquiry. At those proceedings one of the excavators made this rueful comment about the tumulus, which rounds off the incident for us: 'it hath been dygged ... but he can not tell whoe dydd dygg it'.

The treasure-hunter very often inhabited a complex and sinister underworld. Amylyon, Judy and Smith were three unprincipled sixteenth-century rogues who traded upon human gullibility and greed. They obtained royal licence to excavate for treasure in East Anglia. Not content with carrying out their own searches, they sought out necromancers and blackmailed them into helping them. They extorted money from landowners who had carried out their own clandestine searches. They confiscated banned books of magic, only to use them themselves. Court records of the sixteenth and seventeenth centuries are full of cases against men who 'claimed to obtain treasure by invocation of spirits', or 'digged for treasure in sundry places'.

Some practitioners put their faith in the divining rod, which according to a French treatise of 1693 could discover 'springs of water, metallic lodes, hidden treasure, thieves and escaped murderers'. One night in 1628 a solemn group of men met in the cloisters of Westminster Abbey. They were led by Davey Ramsey, courtier, merchant and inveterate treasure-hunter, William Lilly, astrologer, and John Scott, diviner. Slowly they paced the echoing flagstones until, in a corner of the cloister, Scott's rods dipped. Immediately labourers were set to work. All they found was a coffin and none of them dared to open it. When they moved into the abbey itself an even more disturbing phenomenon met them: a sudden violent, shrieking wind blew up, extinguishing their torches and sending the treasure-seekers running.

Reliance on the occult sciences to help unearth treasure persists to the present day. In the early 1950s, for example, a medium was employed at Arginy in the Rhône valley to help locate one of the treasures of the Templars. He apparently made contact with eleven of the knights' spirits but, aggravatingly, they only gave him the most cryptic information.

The connection between treasure-hunting and the occult continues to the present day. Mediums are still consulted by individuals anxious to locate hidden hoards. One celebrated twentieth-century magician was Aleister Crowley, seen here in the robes of the mystic Order of the Golden Dawn.

The spirits of the recently dead were believed to be especially informative on a variety of subjects, including the whereabouts of buried treasure. Just what the notorious Edward Kelly was after in this escapade at Walton-le-Dale churchyard is not clear.

The hopes of would-be treasure-hunters have always been kept alive by the fact that some people do find buried hoards. This fifteenth-century peasant, with or without the aid of necromantic mumbo jumbo, unearthed some old pots of coins.

The Golden Man

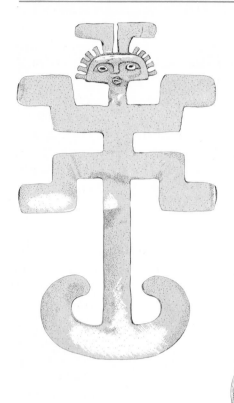

Sir Walter Raleigh, glittering courtier and poet, was mesmerized by the gold of El Dorado. In 1592, Spanish documents fell into his hands which seemed to establish the whereabouts of the fabulous kingdom. Raleigh, whose earlier colonial ventures had failed, determined to secure it for England. He travelled 250 miles up the Orinoco and found nothing. Yet he remained convinced that the Golden Man's kingdom of Guiana was there, studded with 'more rich and beautiful cities, more temples adorned with gold than either Cortés found in Mexico or Pizarro in Peru'. Moreover, he had a map to prove it. For twenty years, most of which were spent in the Tower of London, he dreamed of returning to find the empire of gold. At last King James I allowed the prisoner to stake everything on one last gamble. He found no shimmering city. All that faced him on his return was the block.

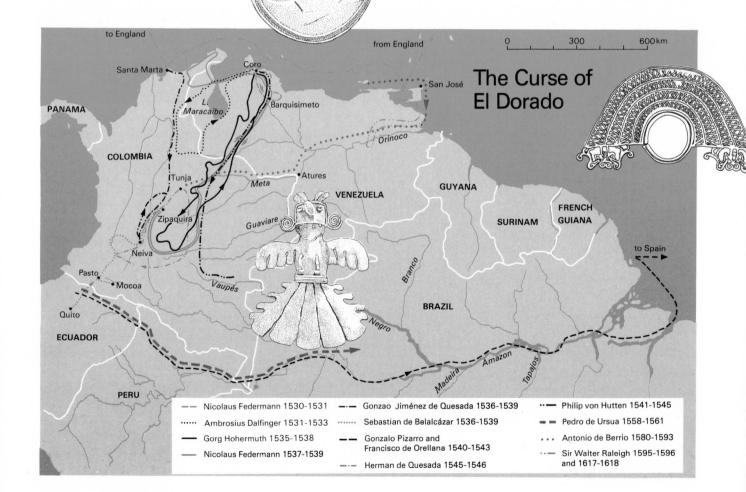

The Curse of El Dorado

—— Nicolaus Federmann 1530-1531	—·—· Gonzao Jiménez de Quesada 1536-1539
········ Ambrosius Dalfinger 1531-1533	·········· Sebastian de Belalcázar 1536-1539
—— Gorg Hohermuth 1535-1538	——— Gonzalo Pizarro and Francisco de Orellana 1540-1543
—— Nicolaus Federmann 1537-1539	—·—· Herman de Quesada 1545-1546
—··— Philip von Hutten 1541-1545	
——— Pedro de Ursua 1558-1561	
····· Antonio de Berrio 1580-1593	
—·—· Sir Walter Raleigh 1595-1596 and 1617-1618	

Three hundred million dollars: that was the value put on the Guatavita gold in 1807 by Alexander von Humboldt. Humboldt was not, like Raleigh, a romantic adventurer who believed a thing because he wished it to be true; he was a methodical, efficient German scientist who travelled through the Americas collecting specimens, making notes and drawing sketches, then spent many years writing up and publishing his findings. And it was his calculated opinion that vast quantities of votive offerings lined the bottom of the lake. If he was right, most of them are still there.

The last expedition to go in search of a golden civilization in the jungles of South America was that led by Colonel Percy Fawcett in 1924. Travelling with only two companions, his son and a friend, this experienced explorer began his quest in the Matto Grosso. On the 30 May following, he cabled his position to an American newspaper. Nothing was ever heard of his party again. Subsequent search parties unearthed various stories about Fawcett's fate at the hands of hostile Indians – but no remains were discovered.

The quest for El Dorado, the Golden Man, was the longest treasure-hunt in history and the most costly in human life. In 1519, Hernando Cortés conquered the kingdom and wealth of the Aztecs. In 1532, Francisco Pizarro seized the golden kingdom of the Incas. From these two Indian empires an unbelievable stream of riches flowed to Spain. It seemed only reasonable to assume that the vast unexplored regions of South and Central America would yield greater treasures yet. It was known from the existence of artefacts that somewhere in the forbidding interior there were mines of silver, gold and emerald. Also there were strange tales.

As the *conquistadores* moved inland, looting shrines and graves for the precious objects stored there over the centuries, they heard tales of El Dorado, who ruled a mountain kingdom where gold was commonplace. What especially caught their imaginations were accounts of the ceremony which took place at the inauguration of a new monarch:

> The first journey he had to make was to go to the great lagoon of Guatavita, to make offerings and sacrifices to the demon which they worshipped as their god and lord. During the ceremony which took place at the lagoon, they made a raft of rushes, embellishing and decorating it with the most attractive things they had ... they stripped the heir to his skin, and anointed him with a sticky earth on which they placed gold dust so that he was completely covered with this metal. They placed him on the raft, on which he remained motionless, and at his feet they placed a great heap of gold and emeralds for him to offer to his god. On the raft with him went four principal subject chiefs, decked in plumes, crowns, bracelets, pendants and earrings all of gold ... when the raft reached the centre of the lagoon ... the gilded Indian then made his offering, throwing out all the pile of gold into the middle of the lake, and the chiefs who had accompanied him did the same on their own accounts.

The legend was basically true. A wealthy and powerful Chibcha kingdom had existed in the eastern cordillera of the Andes, and its people had worshipped the god of Lake Guatavita. But before the Spaniards arrived the empire had gone into decline. In Europe the simple legend grew and grew in the retelling. Someone calculated that 50,000,000 precious trinkets lay on the bed of Guatavita. Fantastic details of El Dorado's realm abounded: he had a personal bodyguard of fierce women warriors, the Amazons; he lived in a city made of gold; he ruled a headless race of people whose faces were in their chests. Soon adventurers were flocking to South America, braving jungle, arid mountain, cannibals and wild animals in a desperate bid to reach and conquer the kingdom of gold.

Three Spanish *conquistadores* converged on Lake Guatavita in 1539. They took loot in plenty from the Indian villages of the area but found no gilded capital. So they assumed that it must be somewhere else. So convinced were the Spaniards of its existence that they claimed all the territory between the Andes and the Orinoco and called it the Province of El Dorado. In 1568, Gonzalo Jiménez de Quesada arrived as governor of this province and set out from Bogotá with a thousand soldiers and an army of Indian porters to find the golden land. He returned four years later with 66 Spaniards, 4 Indians, 18 horses and a mind turned by the unspeakable horrors he had encountered. He was succeeded by Antonio de Berrio, who made three expeditions between 1584 and 1591. He did not find El Dorado but believed that he had located the king's realm in the highlands of Guiana, a thousand miles from Guatavita. At Trinidad,

Lake Guatavita is one of five sacred lakes lying at 3,000 metres in the eastern cordillera of the Andes. Its sides are steep, its depth formidable. The notch cut in its rim by Antonio Sepúlveda (just visible on the left of the picture) is still a feature of the landscape. And its green waters conceal one of the world's greatest treasures.

Indians throughout a wide area of South and Central America have panned gold for centuries. They were doing it when the first Europeans arrived in the continent and they are still doing it today. The techniques have, however, changed a little. Before the construction of the airport at Cripori it took seven weeks by outboard canoe such as this to reach the gold mining area.

de Berrio was captured by Sir Walter Raleigh, destined to become the most celebrated of all pursuers of the El Dorado myth. Raleigh launched two expeditions to find the fabulous kingdom, sinking all his wealth into the project and promising discoveries which would make his sovereign rich above all earthly princes. It was his failure to do so which led to his execution in 1618.

This put an end to the quest for the legendary king, but adventurers had by no means given up hope of dredging Lake Guatavita for its presumed treasures. The first to turn his mind to the task was Hernán Quesada. In 1544 he dragooned an army of Indians into lowering the level; day after day throughout one long dry season a chain of workmen emptied Guatavita's water over the brink of the crater. Under the watchful eye of armed guards, the Chibcha passed full gourds from hand to hand up the hill. Imperceptibly the lake's rim receded. Hernán prodded about among the exposed mud and weed. And there they were: votive offerings of crude workmanship (*tunjos*) in gold or gold and copper, flat, two-dimensional figures representing the long-dead worshippers who had come to commend themselves and their work to the spirits of the lake. The three-metre strip around Guatavita's brim which now lay exposed did not yield much treasure but it did suggest that the legend of El Dorado's golden ablutions was true, in which case a vast hoard of precious offerings lay in the depths towards the centre of the lake. Then, having got thus far, Quesada gave up his excavations in favour of the potentially more rewarding quest for El Dorado.

Further success had to await the arrival of a man with sufficient capital to drain the lake properly. In 1578, Don Antonio Sepúlveda, a wealthy wine merchant, set 8,000 Indians to the task of cutting a gigantic notch in the rim of the crater. When this was done, much of the water flowed out, leaving a twenty-metre-wide strip of mud and weed around the edge. From this Sepúlveda and his men gathered scores of *tunjos*, pectoral discs, carved serpents and eagles, a staff covered with gold plates and hung with golden ornaments, and an emerald the size of a hen's egg. When he ordered the cut to be deepened the sides of the channel collapsed, killing hundreds of diggers and bringing work to a standstill. All Sepúlveda's profit went to pay back the government's share of the project. The wine merchant, a ruined man, was eventually buried within a stone's throw of the lake.

In 1811, Colombia gained its independence, and several European businessmen offered to drain Guatavita. Despite the use of modern engineering techniques, these expeditions only brought ruin to their backers. Between 1905 and 1909 the British firm Contractors Limited did actually succeed in pumping out the crater, but before the thick layer of mud could be excavated it had baked hard. Contractors Limited went bankrupt in 1913. A sale at Sotheby's of all the beautiful finds failed to save the company. Other twentieth-century attempts to lift the treasure of Lake Guatavita all met with the same result. Then, in 1965, the long treasure-hunt came to an end: the Colombian government declared Guatavita a protected area of natural and cultural interest. The god of the lake remains in possession of the offerings made by generations of long-dead El Dorados.

The Curse of El Dorado

1530–1531
Nicolaus Federmann
The first to discover the hostility of the country and people.

1531–1533
Ambrosius Dalfinger
Amassed a large amount of loot but was forced to bury much of it. Killed by Indians.

1535–1538
Georg Hohermuth
Lost 300 men. Suffered appalling hardship. A broken man physically and mentally.

1536–1539
Gonzalo Jiménez de Quesada
Devoted most of his life to the quest for El Dorado and died in poverty at Bogotá.

1536–1539
Sebastián de Belalcázar
Reached Guatavita. Later arrested for cruelty and murder. Died on his way back to Spain to face trial.

1537–1539
Nicolaus Federmann
On his second expedition reached Guatavita. Returned to Europe to face trial for embezzling his employers' funds.

1540–1543
Gonzalo Pizarro and Francisco de Orellana
Travelled right down the Amazon. Pizarro and many men perished in the jungle.

1541–1545
Philip von Hutten
Forced by hostile natives to return to the coast where he was killed by a rival.

1543–1546
Hernán de Quesada
First man to explore Lake Guatavita. Made a fruitless expedition into the Ilanos. Killed by a thunderbolt.

1558–1561
Pedro de Ursua
Travelled down the Amazon. Murdered by mutineers.

1578–1579
Antonio Sepúlveda
Drained part of Lake Guatavita. Bankrupted. Died in poverty.

This votive offering brings us close to the very heart of the El Dorado legend. For here, in gold, is the king and his attendants on their raft about to sacrifice to the god of Guatavita.

1580–1593
Antonio de Berrio
Made three fruitless trips to the middle Orinoco.

1595–1596 and 1617–1618
Sir Walter Raleigh
Made two fruitless expeditions along the Orinoco. Executed on his return to England.

1801
Alexander von Humboldt
The first man to describe accurately Lake Guatavita and its environs.

1823–1825
José Paris
Attempted to drain Lake Guatavita. Went bankrupt.

1898–1901
Company for the Exploitation of the Lagoon of Guatavita
Forced to abandon attempts to drain Lake Guatavita.

1905–1913
Contractors Limited
Drained Lake Guatavita but unable to raise the treasure. Went bankrupt.

Mr Pepys' Treasure

The most unlikely people, given the opportunity, can become possessed by 'treasure fever'. Take, for example, Samuel Pepys, the famous diarist. In 1662 he held a responsible post as clerk of the king's ships. He was a justice of the peace and a respected member of City society with powerful friends and patrons at court. Yet on more than one occasion in the autumn of that year he was to be found – coat and wig laid aside – up to his knees in London clay, frantically searching for buried gold.

The story of the great Tower treasure-hunt begins some years before. During the period of Cromwellian rule in the mid-seventeenth century one of the lieutenants of the Tower was Sir John Barkstead, a swaggering bully of a man who enriched himself while in office by extorting money from wealthy royalist prisoners. With the restoration of the monarchy in 1660, Barkstead fled abroad. He was, however, captured, tried and condemned to be hanged, drawn and quartered. His head was set up over the walls of the fortress he had once ruled. A woman who had been Barkstead's mistress believed that the ex-lieutenant had buried his ill-gotten gains within the Tower before his hasty departure. She took two men into her confidence, a Mr Wade and a Captain Evett. They appealed to the Earl of Sandwich for permission to excavate within the castle, offering him and the king a share of the proceeds. The nobleman readily agreed and, as great lords do not descend to such mundane tasks as supervising digging operations, he appointed his protégé, Samuel Pepys, to assume responsibility for the excavations. In his diary Pepys noted the progress of the work day by day as well as his hopes and fears about the success of the enterprise.

He was very excited at the prospect of finding the gold, estimated at £7,000 (a figure later raised by the female informant to £20,000, doubtless to keep Pepys interested), and immediately presented his warrant to the lieutenant of the Tower. Permission was given for work to start immediately; that very afternoon (30 October) Pepys, Wade, Evett and their assistants went to the fortress. By the light of a candle they started digging in the basement of the Bell Tower. It was soon clear that Wade and Evett did not know the exact location of the hidden hoard. Six hours of back-breaking work revealed nothing and it was agreed to postpone the search until the female informant had been questioned more closely. It was the first of many setbacks, but Pepys was undeterred. He had been bitten by the treasure-hunting bug and one of the symptoms of the resulting infection was dauntless optimism. That night he wrote in his diary: 'our guides did not seem at all discouraged... being confident that the money is there [that] they look for, but having never been in the cellars, they could not be positive to the place, and therefore will inform themselves more fully...'

He could scarcely rid his mind of thoughts of Barkstead's treasure and waited with impatience for the reappearance of his colleagues. Two days later they were back with more precise information and everyone returned to the Bell Tower, expecting their picks and shovels to strike at any moment upon the butter firkins in which the gold had reputedly been buried. But after two or three hours, Pepys records, 'we went away the second time like fools'. He took his associates to the nearby Dolphin tavern and there questioned them closely about their female accomplice: 'though we have missed twice, yet they bring such an account of the

The Bell Tower at the Tower of London was so called because of the bell mounted on top which signalled the times when prisoners might exercise and must be locked in for the night. It was in the earth beneath this tower that Colonel Barkstead was supposed to have buried his treasure.

Samuel Pepys

Colonel Barkstead

probability of the truth of the thing, though we are not certain of the place, that we shall set upon it once more, and I am willing and hopeful in it'. It was agreed that at the next attempt 'the woman herself will be there in a disguise'.

She dutifully turned up and confirmed that they were digging in the right place, whereupon Pepys and company set to again with a will. All day they laboured, pausing only for a light meal – 'upon the head of a barrel dined very merrily' – by which time it was clear that there was nothing buried in the Bell Tower. Pepys now had serious doubts, though he was far too gallant to suspect the lady of any deceit: 'we were forced to give over our expectations, though I do believe there must be money somewhere hid by him, or else he did delude this woman in hopes to oblige her to further serving him, which I am apt to believe'. And a week later, after a further meeting with Wade and Evett, he could still write: 'I have great confidence that there is no cheat in these people, but that they go upon good grounds.'

It was now decided that the treasure was buried in the lieutenant's garden; further excavation had to wait for better weather. Even then Pepys had no enthusiasm for wielding a spade himself. While his colleagues laboured he 'did sit all day till three o'clock by the fire in the Governor's house ... reading a play of Fletcher's, being *A Wife for a Month*, wherein no great wit or language'. Then he went out to visit the excavation site where four grimy, sweating labourers stood in a deep, empty hole: 'having wrought below the bottom of the foundation of the wall, I bade them give over, and so all our hopes ended'.

Thus the great Tower of London treasure-hunt came to nothing. The last glimpse we get of poor Pepys is on his return that evening to his comfortable home in Seething Lane – or, perhaps, not so comfortable. He was cold and not a little annoyed, and Mistress Pepys, apparently, was in no better mood: 'and so home and to bed, a little displeased with my wife, who, poor wretch, is troubled with her lonely life'. Poor wretch, indeed – obviously an early example of a 'treasure widow'.

A Fortune in Ivory

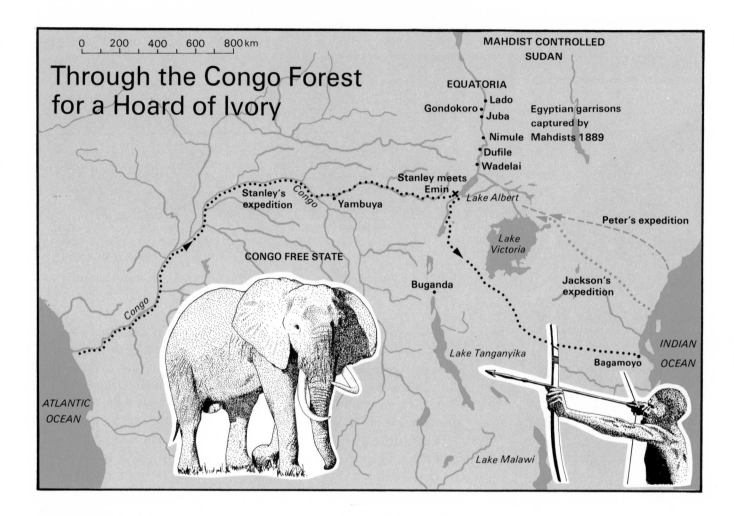

KHARTOUM FALLEN! GORDON DEAD! That was the alarming news which reached Europe in February 1885. The Mahdi's revolt in the Sudan against the British-backed Egyptian government had cost the life of one of England's greatest soldiers and several of his men. Moreover it had cut off other garrisons in Equatoria (the southern Sudan province) and left them at the mercy of the advancing Mahdists. The governor of Equatoria was the German-born Emin Pasha and he held out with troops still loyal to Cairo. Public opinion in Europe demanded that a relief expedition be sent to rescue him. There was no lack of volunteers to lead such a mission, for Emin Pasha had with him two hundred tons of ivory. The Upper Nile region was teeming with elephant. The herds had only recently been hunted by man, and some of the creatures who roamed the savanna carried tusks of 75–100 kg each. Ivory was the main source of income derived from Equatoria and, until the revolt, Emin had sent regular shipments downriver. This was no longer possible but the governor still sent out his hunting parties, and the government warehouses were full to bursting with ivory. As Emin retreated southwards he had to bury large caches of tusks but some he took with him to his new headquarters at Wadelai.

The first relief expedition to get under way was led by the famous explorer Henry Morton Stanley and was supported by the avaricious Leopold II, King of the Belgians and of the Congo Free State. Stanley travelled up the Congo river in the early months of 1887 and established a

At the end of Stanley's gruelling march through the Congo forest, Emin came to meet him on the shore of Lake Albert. The contrast between the two men was striking; the burly, tough Stanley was exhausted and in tatters, while the tiny, dapper German appeared in 'a clean suit of snowy cotton drilling, well-ironed and a perfect fit'. Any observer might well have wondered who was the rescuer and who the rescued. The nineteenth-century artist who did this picture has unfortunately missed this point and idealized Stanley.

Some of Emin Pasha's vast hoard of ivory at Wadelai.

base at Yambuya under the command of Edmund Barttelot, who was ordered to wait for the arrival of Tipu Tip, an Afro-Arab slave and ivory trader who had promised Stanley 600 porters. He was then to follow on with the bulk of the supplies. Meanwhile Stanley and 389 men went ahead into the unexplored rain forest of Ituri. The next ten months were months of sheer hell. Food ran out. Porters deserted. Heat and humidity sapped men's energy. The column was attacked by hostile natives. But worst of all were the depredations of the mosquito and tsetse fly which felled the members of the expedition one after another. Stanley lost two hundred men before reaching Emin Pasha. Worse was to come. There was no sign of the rear column. Eventually, Stanley was forced to retrace his journey through the forest. He discovered a depleted and demoralized base. Tipu Tip had failed to arrive. Discipline had broken down. Barttelot had been murdered. Many Africans had deserted, others had been flogged to death. Stanley gathered together the tattered remnants of his expedition and returned to Equatoria. But now he discovered that Emin did not want to leave. He believed that he could hold out and that he should not desert his post. Stanley sourly remarked that Emin was 'charmed with his African life, where he is king'.

By now, other adventurers, hearing of Stanley's difficulties, were *en route* for Equatoria. Frederick Jackson, an agent of the Imperial British East Africa Company, left the east coast in 1889 and reached Buganda, to the north of Lake Victoria. He was beaten in the westward race by Carl Peters, representative of a rival German company, who started later but travelled by a more direct route. In the event both men were too late to rescue Emin Pasha. Stanley, using cajolery, bribery and threats, at last forced the reluctant governor to leave his post. Together rescuer and rescued made their way to Zanzibar, which they reached at the end of 1890.

And the ivory? Stanley and Emin only had enough porters to bring a fraction of it down to the coast. The rest was buried. Emin hoped that the area around Lake Albert would be ceded to Germany in pursuance of certain treaties made by Carl Peters, and that he and his ivory would be placed at the disposal of the new colonial power. But by the Treaty of Berlin this region was declared to be within the British sphere of influence. Emin was murdered by Arab slavers in 1892 before he could return to the Upper Nile or reveal the whereabouts of his ivory hoards. As for Stanley, the veteran explorer had had enough of Africa. He never returned.

The Rape of Africa

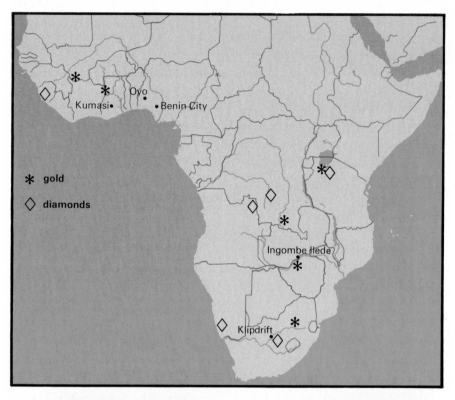

The Benin kingdom of the lower Niger was famous for its magnificent bronzes. These sculptures were used as votive offerings in shrines and graves and were savagely looted by colonial conquerors.

(left) A gold burial from Ingombe Ilede

One of the more ancient civilizations of West Africa was that of Nok. Iron-working was practised by the Nok people in the second century BC and they developed a lively style of terracotta sculpture.

Asante Gold

In 1873 a British punitive expedition led by Sir Garnet Wolseley was dispatched to the Gold Coast (modern Ghana) to bring the Asante people to heel. The member states of the Asante confederation had for centuries controlled the production of gold and the manufacture of golden objects in the region of the middle Volta. These objects adorned shrines and provided symbols of kingship for the Asantahenes, the rulers of the region. During their raid upon Kumasi, the capital, the British looted thousands of these examples of native art. They had no qualms about possessing themselves of the traditional wealth of a 'warlike and savage' people. The most exquisite artefacts were tiny weights made in the shape of birds, animals and men. They were used for weighing gold dust. The most important single treasure, however, was the Golden Stool, the symbol of the Asantahenes' power in which, it was believed, the soul of the nation reposed.

Sub-Saharan Africa has yielded unique treasures to both invaders and archaeologists. Centuries before the Europeans found their way to the fringes of the continent and named them the Gold Coast and the Ivory Coast, African traders were exchanging gold for salt, ivory for iron, copper for cowrie shells. An eleventh-century king from the upper Senegal region crossed the desert by camel and distributed so much largess in the streets of Cairo that the market price of gold fell alarmingly. A thousand years ago Arab dhows went across the Indian Ocean to load gold and ivory at Kilwa, Mozambique and Sofala. A series of graves in Zambia's middle Zambezi, excavated in the early 1960s, gave evidence of the wealth of these early traders. Among the grave goods which adorned and surrounded the skeletons were bracelets of beads, gold and copper, coils of copper wire and uniform X-shaped ingots (trade currency). The Nigerian cultures of Oyo and Benin were ancient and their craftsmen were highly skilled workers in bronze and ivory. At the end of the nineteenth century these areas came under British control. Tombs and shrines were plundered, first by agents of the Royal Niger Company and later by troops and officials sent by the colonial government.

Most African metal production was surface mining and river panning. The rich mineral deposits of South Africa and Namibia had to wait until white settlers and modern technology arrived. Diamonds were discovered along the lower Vaal in 1867 and there was a rush of prospectors into the area. The typical lawlessness of the boom towns that sprang up was intensified by the rival claims of the Cape Colony and the Boer states to the diamondiferous zone. Incidents like the murder of John Johnson of Klipdrift were rife. Johnson was killed for his diamonds, but his murderers never found where he had hidden them.

Treasure Inc.

Treasure-hunting has always been big business. Though some fortunate individuals have, by accident or design, dug up buried hoards in back gardens, barrows or open fields, there have always been some troves whose excavation has required considerable capital. And so powerful is the lure of gold that there has never been a lack of businesslike merchants, worldly wise courtiers, even kings and emperors ready to back wild schemes.

The name of the Emperor Nero would not figure in anyone's top ten of the world's shrewdest and most level-headed monarchs, but in 65 AD he became involved in a treasure-hunting expedition that was extravagant even by his bizarre standards. The scheme originated with one Cesselinus Bassus, a native of Carthage who was much given to dreams. In one of his visions Bassus believed the whereabouts of a great treasure was revealed to him. It had been hidden in a deep cave near the city by Dido, the legendary Queen and foundress of Carthage, and comprised an immense fortune in gold bars. The Carthaginian travelled to Rome and told his story with fervour. The Emperor, whose government was almost bankrupt, was more than ready to be convinced and he immediately set in motion plans for an expedition to retrieve the hoard, making lavish promises of how the wealth would be expended for the good of the people. The bottom of the imperial coffers was scraped to finance a fleet of triremes, and Bassus was soon back in Carthage supervising the excavations. Paid with Nero's money, an army of local labour spent months in digging over a very wide area. They found nothing. The officials sent to protect Nero's interests grew steadily more sceptical. Bassus produced further visions and wrote letters to Rome brimming over with confidence. But inevitably the time came when he ran out of dreams and the Emperor ran out of patience. The Carthaginian was summoned to the capital to pay the price for disappointing Nero. Bassus knew only too well what that meant; he preferred to take his own life. The ships and men returned to Italy. All Nero could do was confiscate Bassus' property to defray part of the cost of the failed quest for Dido's gold.

William Phipps was not psychic but he, too, believed that he had discovered the whereabouts of a great treasure and he likewise resorted to his sovereign for financial backing. Phipps was born into the large family of a poor Massachusetts blacksmith in 1651. He began his working life as a ship's carpenter, but being a forceful and hard-working man he had his own ship by the age of twenty-three. On one of his journeys he heard about the wreck of the *Nuestra Señora de la Concepción*, a Spanish bullion ship which had sunk off Hispaniola in 1641, and he determined to salvage her cargo. Such a project, he realized, would need more funds than he possessed. His ships would have to be manned with reliable sailors, provisioned for weeks at sea, armed against attack by Caribbean pirates, and he would have to hire skilled divers. He sailed to England, presented himself at court, and obtained backing from the king and several leading personalities. The agreed share-out of net profits was to be 10 per cent to the king, 12 per cent to each of the shareholders, and the remainder (6 per cent) to Phipps. The arrangement may well have offended the Bostonian's business principles but he was in no position to haggle.

The Emperor Nero ruled Rome from 54 to 68 AD. His extravagance was one contributing factor to the bankruptcy of his government. When news reached him of the possibility of unearthing a fabulous hidden treasure in the province of Africa he seized eagerly on the chance of discovering a fortune.

Phipps invested in the latest equipment, including a Catalan bell. Unfortunately this piece of diving apparatus was not very efficient (Edmund Halley's improved diving bell patented five years later was much more successful – see above, page 123), and Phipps' native divers preferred to work without it. The second expedition in 1687 to the Silver Bank, off Hispaniola, was crowned with success. The divers quickly located the main strongroom, and each man came up time after time with bar silver, plate and pieces of eight. After six weeks they had accumulated 1,138 lb of gold coins alone. But greater riches lay in the *Nuestra Señora*'s hold, just beyond their reach. Phipps was furious to think that this treasure might elude him, and his men were on the verge of mutiny. He urged his divers to one more supreme effort. Time and again they surfaced with blood streaming from their noses, too weak to scramble aboard, but they managed to get ropes around one of the chests. It was broken open on the deck of Phipps' ship, the *James and Mary*. The crew gathered round, jostling each other for a good view. As the lid flew back there were gasps and cries of astonishment. Rubies, emeralds and diamonds flashed back the sunlight; gold and pearls gleamed; oriental statues grinned inscrutably. It was a king's ransom, more wealth than any man present can ever have dreamed of. As well as the coins and jewels, Phipps took back to Deptford over 63,000 lb of silver and 347 lb of plate. All the investors received a sixtyfold return on their capital and Phipps had a clear profit of £11,000 plus a number of 'trifles' he had not considered worth inventorying.

The rest of the galleon's treasure remained on the sea bottom until another enthusiast appeared employing sophisticated technology and having the finance to fund it. This was Burt Webber, an electronics expert and subaqua diver. He founded Seaquest Incorporated in 1976 and set about selling it to wealthy Americans. He had no difficulty; capital poured in from businessmen who knew that they could enjoy expenses-paid vacations in the West Indies on the company, that they might, indeed, see a good return on their investment, and that in the event of failure their losses could be set against income tax. Webber hired a converted minesweeper, the *Samala*, and fitted her out in Miami. He personally developed a new type of magnetometer which functioned close to the sea bed instead of on the surface. At the end of 1978, Webber's divers struck lucky. The Spanish treasure was no longer held tidily together in chests and sacks. It lay spilled among the sand and the grotesquely beautiful coral. It was under boulders and within rocky crevices. But metal detectors tracked down piece after piece; sand was removed by suction pumps; rocks were floated away by using air bags. Month after month the work went on, the *Samala* usually staying on site for two weeks at a time. The excavation is not finished yet (October 1979) but already the investors in Seaquest Incorporated have every reason to be satisfied. Silver plate, fragments of Ming porcelain, a bronze astrolabe, and over two tons of coins have been raised. Their value on the international antique market can be calculated only in millions.

Seaquest Incorporated is only one of thousands of companies that have come into existence on both sides of the Atlantic in the twentieth century for the purpose of locating and exploiting buried and sunken valuables. The modern treasure-hunter may have the heart of a romantic and adventurer but he must have the head of a businessman.

Commander F. A. Worsley was certainly an adventurer. He was captain of the ill-fated HMS *Endurance*, the ship in which Ernest Shackleton

William Phipps' story is one of rags to riches. Born into the large family of a poor Massachusetts blacksmith in 1651, he began his working life as a ship's carpenter but he was ambitious and dedicated. By the age of twenty-three he was trading in his own ship and had become a respected Boston merchant. He heard by chance of the wreck of a Spanish treasure ship. Despite setbacks he carried out the greatest salvage operation of the age and became a very wealthy man.

travelled to Antarctica in 1914 and which was caught in the pack ice off Caird coast. Worsley was among the company which endured months of appalling hardship in the frozen wasteland. And in 1922 he was again with Shackleton as sailing master of the *Quest* when the great explorer died. But when he planned an expedition to find the pirate hoards of Cocos Island he formed a company, Treasure Recovery Limited, and set about convincing potential investors that he could provide them with a handsome return for their stake. First of all he made a detailed study of such documentary evidence as there was concerning the activities of the pirates associated with Cocos Island. He interviewed previous treasure-seekers. He carried out a reconnoitring visit and located those areas where loot was more likely to be concealed. But, above all, Worsley brought the advantages of science to the quest for buried gold, in the shape of a 'portable radiometer', an instrument 'that has been in use for a decade by big mining companies run by practical men, whose only aims and determination are to pay big dividends'. The radiometer was, in effect, the first metal detector. It was an electrical device which passed a current between electrodes stuck into the ground.

This late seventeenth-century chart of the silver bank shows the wreck site of the Nuestra Señora. *After William Phipps' successful salvage operation treasure-hunters swarmed over the reef. But most of the remaining gold and silver were inaccessible until the development of twentieth-century diving techniques.*

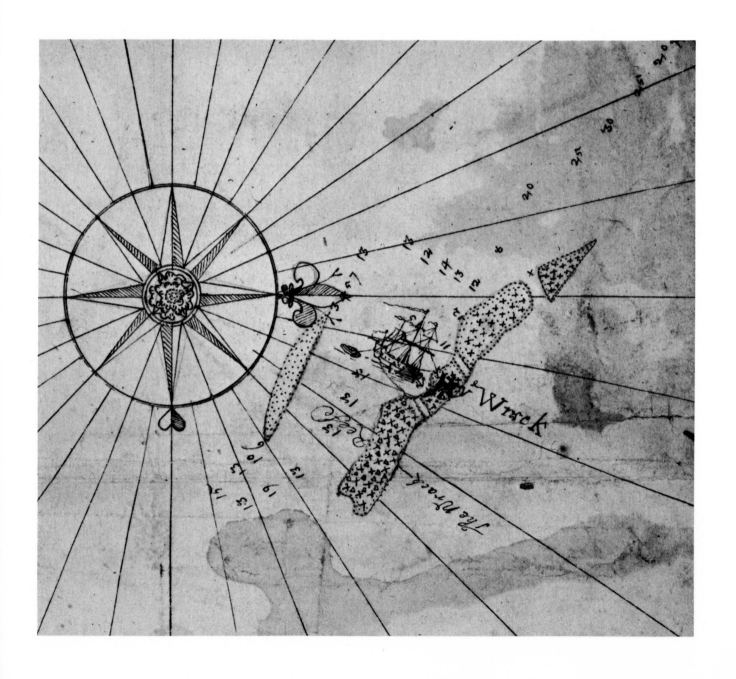

The readings produced were plotted on a grid. Any extra-efficient conductors, such as gold and silver, showed up as irregularities on the grid. The man who confessed to always having been fascinated by treasure islands claimed to have banished 'romance' from his quest. But, as in so many cases, the quest was its own reward. Treasure Recovery Limited never paid a dividend.

Nor is it only the inherent difficulties of the quest which may swallow up invested capital. Sometimes there are political and legal battles to be fought. Governments are now much more sensitive than they used to be to finds located within their boundaries or territorial waters. Or even in international waters beyond their boundaries: before Seaquest Incorporated began searching for the *Nuestra Señora*, Burt Webber thought it wise to come to an arrangement with the Dominican Republic – they agreed to provide a base and naval protection in return for half the treasure. Another venture, Platoro Incorporated, was less fortunate. After the company had salvaged treasure from a 1554 galleon off Padre Island, the Texas state legislature confiscated the finds. Treasure-hunting is big business – and risky business.

For the latest expedition to the Silver Bank the salvors, Seaquest Inc., have chartered a converted British minesweeper, the Samala. *She now carries the latest sensitive magnetometers and sonars, not for locating the sinister instruments of sudden death but for finding a 340-year-old treasure.*

'Where Gold Goes, Blood Flows'

They call the mountain Victorio Peak after the Apache chief who roamed the desert trails of New Mexico with his braves, attacking stagecoaches. And somewhere on that mountain is a cave stacked from floor to ceiling with Victorio's loot. There are gold bars, jewels, coins and a diamond-studded crown. This is no dream treasure. Several people have actually seen it – or so they claim. There is just one major obstacle to the recovery of the hoard: Victorio Peak is now in the middle of the US army's White Sands missile range.

Victorio flourished in the middle decades of the last century. Among the travellers who reputedly fell victim to him were the servants escorting the personal treasure of Emperor Maximilian of Mexico, deposed in 1867. Soon after that the chief was killed and the knowledge of his hiding place died with him. It came to life again in 1937. One day in that year, Milton 'Doc' Noss was deer-hunting over the peak when he stumbled across the partially concealed entrance to a cave. He pulled away some of the rocks, squeezed inside and was confronted by the sight of a lifetime. As well as the carefully stacked treasure there were twenty-seven skeletons chained to stakes. Presumably they were captives who had been used to carry the gold to its hiding place, then left to die so that they could not reveal it.

Moving the gold out, Noss knew, would be a difficult task, especially if secrecy was to be maintained. In order to make the job easier he dynamited the mouth of the cave to enlarge the entrance. All he did was seal it up with tons of rock. Now he had no choice; others must be let in on the secret in order to help excavate the treasure. He took his son, Marvin, and a local businessman, Charles Ryan, into partnership. All was set for the trio to tunnel into the cave, convey the hoard to an aeroplane and fly it across the border into Mexico. Then the whole enterprise fell to pieces. Noss and Ryan had a fierce argument which ended in Doc being shot dead. The same day Marvin was badly injured in a plane crash. Noss's widow was anxious to complete her husband's work but she would not take anyone into her confidence after what had happened to Doc. 'Where gold goes, blood flows,' she would say when talking about Victorio's treasure.

In 1953 the army took over the area as a missile range and only service personnel had access to Victorio Peak. Then, like Doc Noss, two ser-

It is hot (over 80°F) and dusty on Victorio Peak, a desolate spot in the San Andres Mountains of New Mexico, but this did not deter Norman Scott and his colleagues of Expeditions Unlimited from toiling away with machines, explosives and bare hands in a frantic race to find a fabulous treasure in March 1977. Scott had with difficulty obtained permission to search for a limited period on the peak, which is part of the US army's White Sands missile range. 'Operation Gold Finder' was slick, well equipped and heavily capitalized. It had to be; the site of Indian Chief Victorio's reputed hoard was a cave whose entrance was blocked with tons of fallen rock, high in the mountains seventy kilometres from the nearest road.

Gold in the washing up on the day Doc struck it rich

SAN ANDRES MOUNTAINS, New Mexico

'FUNNY thing about gold,' drawled the 81-year-old woman in the white cowboy hat as she looked up the big dusty hill, where Geronimo the Indian chief once sent his braves on the warpath against the U.S. Cavalry.

'Where gold goes, blood flows. Been a lotta blood flowed because of that hill, good buddy, and it's my guess it ain't done flowing yet. You'll see.'

Even when she drank her diet-free Cola and munched the candy bars kept in her handbag, old Mrs Ova Noss didn't for one second take her eyes off the armed soldiers scrambling across the dried-up bushes and blood-red sand of Victorio Peak high above.

She kept an even closer watch on the army of prospectors with picks and shovels, hillbillies and helicopters, radar-sounding equipment, and crumpled maps they constantly consulted.

They were looking for Apache gold. And she knew it. More than that, she'd seen it, or read the lot.

She could never get out of her head that almost all of the hoard that is estimated to be worth £150,000 million.

Missiles

Legend says that the hoard was hidden by Victorio, the Apache chief, who buried in U.S. dollars part of New Mexico what he and his braves stole from passing stage coaches and looted from the treasure-crowded wagon train of the fleeing deposed Emperor Maximilian.

Now 30 prospectors are spending eight hours a day clawing and scrabbling their way across the peak that bears Victorio's name.

They haven't much longer to strike gold. The U.S. Army which now uses the area as its White Sands missile-testing range, has given the prospectors until sundown today.

After that, the site, where the first atomic bomb was tested in the 1940s, goes back to Army use.

Sometimes the Army major who is supervising the great treasure hunt — nicknamed Operation Gold Finder — stepped across to Mrs Noss and suggested that maybe she ought to go in the shade because ... 'Heck, lady, it's 80 degrees out here, and you run bum bad in all this desert sun and 'wind.'

Crown

But Ova Noss just adjusted the parasol above her head so she couldn't see the grey thin-eared circling high overhead any more and said with Wild West grit: 'Ain't no one bodging me, mister. Leastways not till we get that gold.'

One way and another Mrs Noss has been looking up at, climbing across, tumbling through, or just plain thinking about the 600ft-high Victorio Peak in the aptly named Dead Man's Valley for the past 30 years.

Now she is closer to seeing the legendary treasure of hidden gold, jewels and crowns than at any time since a Nov-ember day back in 1937 when her late Doc and her husband Doc clawed through a tiny funnel right at the top of the mountain and discovered more gold than there is in the whole of Fort Knox.

'We had a little stone home-stead called Rock House just around that hill there,' she said. 'I remember one time we had a chicken piled up high around the stove and I even cooked a gold crown up in my kitchen oven. Yup !

'Do you know how many diamonds were in that crown when I got all the sand off ? Two hundred and forty-three ! I counted them.

'Then I took it to the meat scale and it weighed 7lb. Think about that boy, and you won't wonder what I'm doing here in all this heat no more.'

Sure, she said, she'd have liked to hang on to that crown and the 80 gold bars her husband took out of the mountain.

But he darn it was fearful of bandits and for safety's sake buried the lot in four places on the peak and then died before he told her where.

'I'll never forget the day we found it,' said Mrs Noss, who was wearing jeans just like the men. 'Doc had been hunting deer with a whole gang of fellows and I was cooking down in the pass.

'He said he was chasing a real big buck across the peak when he just kinda fell over the rocks that were in front of a cave. He saw an opening and pulled the rocks back.

'And there it was ! Gold ingots, hundreds of them,

piled up like cordwood and two chests and a conquista-dor's helmet.

'There was something else 27 skeletons chained to posts. They'd all had their Achilles tendons cut. We figured they were slaves, or something, and had been left bars in our hands and one of there so they couldn't tell where the treasure was.

handbag, and from under-neath the candybars produced a pile of faded snapshots that show just what's she's saying. There, you thought I was a crazy woman didn't you ?'

The most striking picture is of her husband with a bar in his hand, a six-gun at his hip and a black Stetson on his head. He is darkly handsome and looks like Errol Flynn dressed as Wyatt Earp.

Mrs Noss was quiet for a moment while she looked up at the bulldozers, shovelling tons of earth and rocks in their search for her cave.

'Trouble was Doc got too keen and tried to dynamite the cave to make it easier to get to but he brought the walls down and roof in, sealing it off, instead, she went on.

Doc didn't tell anyone about his troubles, though. Instead he struck a deal with Charlie Ryan, a businessman from the gun-slingers border town of El Paso.

Ryan built an airstrip in the desert and landed a DC3 plane ready to airlift the gold over the border to Mexico and a fortune.

But Milton Noss — nick-named Doc because he was a chiropodist before he turned prospector—changed his mind and went into Truth or Consequences a nearby town, and told Ryan he wasn't going to work with him. That was the undoing of Doc.

Ryan lost his temper and shot him. One bullet passed right through Doc's head.

In her handbag, Mrs Noss still carries the coroner's photograph of her husband slumped dead over his car bonnet. Ryan was acquitted in court. Self-defence, they said.

'A couple of hours before Doc's death, his son, Marvin, who had been mapping the area from the air, was severely injured when his plane crashed into the side of Geronimo Peak.

'It was one heck of a day,' said Mrs. Noss. 'You know how I heard about Doc being dead ? I read it in the paper. Well, I just hollered and then I went straight to the mortuary.

Promise

That came right after an army captain claimed he had been inside the cave with another serviceman and had seen the gold too.

'It was piled high like rocks,' said Captain Leonard Fiege. His testimony was examined by the State Department, and he passed a lie detector test too.

He is one of the group of six claimants to have hired professional treasure hunter Norman Scott and funded the £600,000 ten-day search which is due to end today.

Of course, if the gold is there and they do ever find it, it might spend just as much time being argued over in court as it has spent in Victorio's Peak.

Suspicion

Meanwhile no one trusts anyone. The prospectors are being watched by the claimants who in turn are being watched by the soldiers, while the FBI is watching all three.

And Ova Noss is keeping her eye on everyone.

Ova Noss remembering : She held a fortune

Fortune hunters at work on the desolate, dusty mountain site 45 miles from the nearest road

Operation Gold Finder certainly caught the popular imagination. Newspaper reporters monitored the progress of the excavators and covered the story from almost every conceivable angle. They interviewed elderly Ova Noss, widow of the man who reputedly discovered the treasure in 1937. She recalled the day when, on a hunting expedition, her husband had stumbled upon the cache. She described how he took her, excitedly, to the cave and showed her 'more gold than there is in the whole of Fort Knox'. She told reporters how she had washed a golden gem-studded crown, then weighed it on her kitchen scales. It came to fourteen kilos. Unfortunately, Mr Noss buried his finds for safety and soon after was killed in a brawl with his partners.

vicemen discovered the cave by accident. They reported their discovery and, predictably, were not believed, even though they came unscathed through a lie-detector test. However, they persevered, and in 1963 were given permission to conduct a brief private search for the gold cave. They found backers and raised $150,000 to equip the search party but they failed to relocate the treasure. A few years later another unsuccessful attempt was made.

Not surprisingly, the authorities were very reluctant to allow any further searchers within the prohibited area. But there were still enthusiasts who insisted that they knew that millions of dollars' worth of gold and gems lay concealed on Victorio Peak. In the 1970s, Lee Bailey entered the story. He fought a long battle with state and federal officials over the right to excavate on the missile range. At last he obtained permission of a New Mexico court to test his theory. Grudgingly, the army allowed him to work on the site for ten days. It was clear that a gigantic effort would be necessary and Bailey enlisted the aid of Norman Scott and Expeditions Unlimited Incorporated, a treasure-finding company. In March 1977 a battalion of prospectors moved in, equipped with bulldozers, helicopters and metal detectors. Day after day they toiled in the blazing sunshine. Scott obtained permission to extend the search period to fourteen days. But after thirteen he called a halt. His men could find no trace of Victorio's gold. There, for the foreseeable future, the matter rests. If the Apache treasure was ever there it is there still.

The Cost of the *Atocha*

Melvin Fisher is the archetypal treasure-hunter, a mixture of restless adventurer, confident opportunist and unsinkable optimist. He emerged from the Second World War as a young American engineer who could find no comfortable niche in civilian life. He tried a variety of jobs and then got hooked on scuba diving. Soon he turned his hobby into a way of living: he fished for lobsters, he sold diving gear, he gave diving lessons. But already he had become obsessed by thoughts of treasure. He made many unsuccessful expeditions, financing them by a variety of money-making schemes. Then at the age of forty he sold everything he had, took a group of other enthusiasts into partnership and formed Treasure Salvors Incorporated. In the summer of 1964 they struck it rich: from one of the Florida coast's many Spanish galleon wrecks they retrieved one and a half million dollars' worth of gold and silver coins and trinkets.

A wise man would have invested his share of the profit in securities or started a sound business. But Mel Fisher was not a wise man; he was a treasure-hunter. He had already decided to go after the richest wreck site off the Keys – that of the *Nuestra Señora de Atocha* and the *Santa Margarita*

Mel Fisher is the archetypal treasure-hunter. Gold fever is in his blood, and he has devoted the greater part of his life to the quest for sunken riches. His longest, most difficult and, ultimately, most rewarding salvage operation was the lifting of the Atocha *bullion.*

(see above page 115). He believed he knew approximately where the remains of these much-sought ships were, and once again he gambled everything on finding them. Four years later his resources and much borrowed capital had gone and Fisher had seen not the merest trace of the galleons. But there was no question of giving up. Somehow, he raised more money. And he hired another team member, Eugene Lyon, an academic currently researching for a doctorate in the Archives of the Indies in Seville. Fisher asked him to ransack the archive building, with its fifty million largely uncatalogued documents, and find information about the 1622 treasure fleet. 'Put me within a quarter of a mile of the *Atocha*,' he said, 'and I'll pay you ten thousand dollars.' It was a mammoth task, but Lyon went patiently to work, straining his eyes to decipher the 350-year-old scrawl of official reports and cargo lists. And, one by one, the details began to emerge. Soon he had a piece of vital information for Mel Fisher: 'the area you have been searching is 100 miles from where the 1622 fleet foundered'.

All the gear was moved to the new location, and in 1973 the ballast stones of a wrecked wooden ship were discovered. But was it the right ship? Days of work brought various finds, including some golden articles. Then three silver bars were found. Careful note was made of the markings, and details were sent to Lyon. He checked through the 901 ingots listed in the *Atocha*'s cargo catalogue. And he found them. Fisher's search was at an end. Now it only remained to bring up the treasure. But that was to prove a long, difficult and costly task. Currents and storms had spread the ship's remains over a wide area and the rate at which valuable objects were discovered was too slow. They did not compensate for Fisher's mounting expenses. But the *Atocha* was to demand a higher price. One of the expedition's boats capsized in a storm. Trapped aboard were Mel's twenty-one-year-old son, Dirk, and the boy's young wife.

Still Fisher continued diving on the wreck. Then came another shock: the State of Florida claimed everything the salvors had found as their property and confiscated it. Now Fisher had to fight for his treasure in the courts as well as under the sea. It took five years to establish his right to the *Atocha*'s contents, by which time Fisher's men had located most of the ship's fabulous cargo. Since then they have discovered the wreck of the *Santa Margarita*. Success and vindication have come to Mel Fisher at last – but at what a cost.

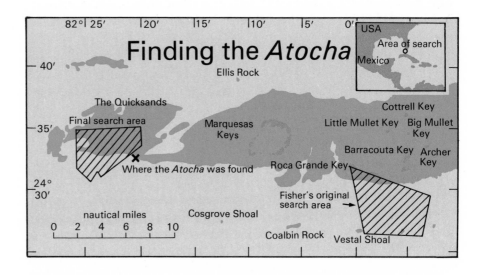

Pirate Gold

Hyenas of the Seven Seas

Say 'treasure' to most people and the chances are that they will think of pirates – pirates and desert islands and faded maps on which *X* marks the spot. They will do so because the romantic myth of the 'sea dog' built up by Defoe, Byron, Scott and Robert Louis Stevenson has become a part of our culture. Yet myth it is, and the ironical fact must be recorded that of all the legends and accounts of buried treasure that have ever been told or committed to paper those concerning pirate gold are among the least well authenticated. Piracy is as old as maritime commerce and is still with us today, but its heyday was in the sixteenth to nineteenth centuries when sailing vessels regularly travelled the established routes to the Americas and the Orient laden with bullion, jewels and other precious cargo. Thousands of vessels fell prey to seaborne brigands, many of whom operated from remote island bases. The leaders of these pirate bands usually died, as they had lived, violently, and without revealing the whereabouts of their loot. Thus the stories abounded of treasures buried on tropical beaches or concealed in submerged caves, their locations marked by signs on trees or rocks or by the bones of slaughtered pirate comrades. In fact few of these criminals had the desire or opportunity to conceal their plunder. They were, for the most part, rough, undisciplined men who had no thought for the future but squandered their money in port on liquor and women and started each new venture penniless. Yet the legends have persisted and, by the law of averages, there is probably

The Barbary pirates or corsairs were for centuries a scourge of the Mediterranean. They originated in the Christian–Muslim conflicts at the time of the Crusades. Pirate chiefs were petty princelings operating out of bases on the North African coast and preying on the rich trade of Venice, Genoa, Constantinople, the Levant and western Europe.

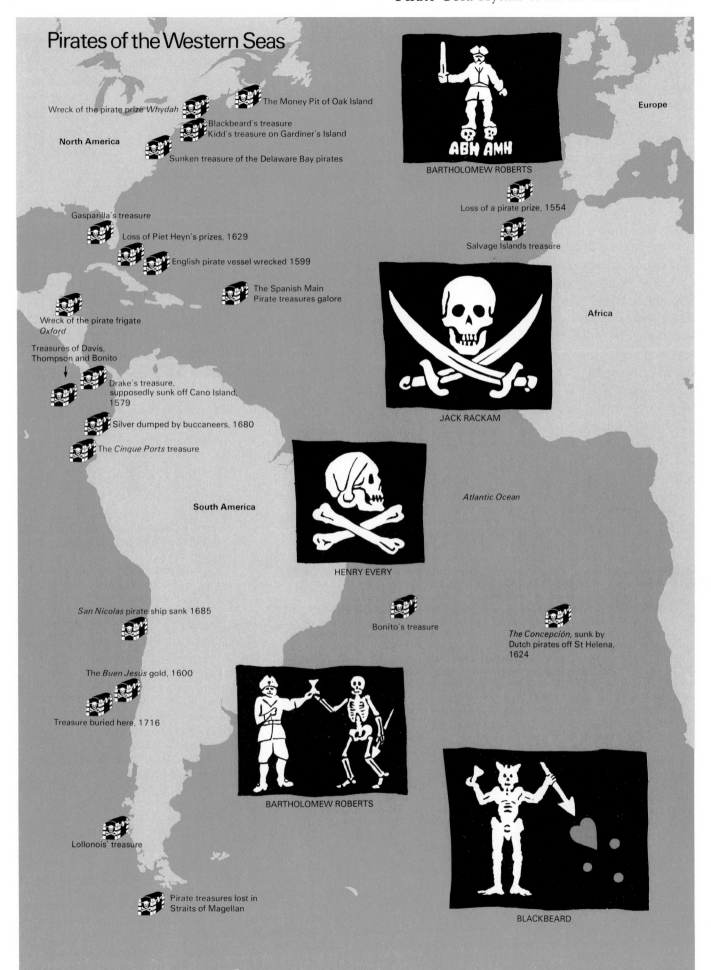

Pirates of the Western Seas

Wreck of the pirate prize *Whydah*

The Money Pit of Oak Island

North America

Blackbeard's treasure

Kidd's treasure on Gardiner's Island

Sunken treasure of the Delaware Bay pirates

Gasparilla's treasure

Loss of Piet Heyn's prizes, 1629

English pirate vessel wrecked 1599

The Spanish Main
Pirate treasures galore

Wreck of the pirate frigate
Oxford

Treasures of Davis,
Thompson and Bonito

Drake's treasure,
supposedly sunk off Cano Island,
1579

Silver dumped by buccaneers, 1680

The *Cinque Ports* treasure

South America

San Nicolas pirate ship sank 1685

Bonito's treasure

The Concepción, sunk by
Dutch pirates off St Helena,
1624

The *Buen Jesús* gold, 1600

Treasure buried here, 1716

Lollonois' treasure

Pirate treasures lost in
Straits of Magellan

Europe

Loss of a pirate prize, 1554

Salvage Islands treasure

Africa

Atlantic Ocean

BARTHOLOMEW ROBERTS

JACK RACKAM

HENRY EVERY

BARTHOLOMEW ROBERTS

BLACKBEARD

truth in some of them. To sort truth from fiction, however, is a well nigh impossible task.

The most notorious pirate of the eastern American seaboard was Blackbeard, alias Edward Teach, alias Edward Thatch, alias Edward Drummond. For about two years (1716–18) he was the scourge not only of merchant shipping but also of rich plantation owners whom he plundered virtually at will, until he was at last gunned down by a Royal Navy captain. Despite his reputation as a free-spending carouser, he was believed to have buried part of his loot on a beach on Plum Island off the New England coast. On Christmas Day 1928 two fishermen, crossing this beach, came across a freshly dug hole in the bottom of which they could still discern the imprint of a heavy iron-bound chest. Such, at least, was their story. Was it merely a tavern tale, or had some unknown seeker really located and made off with Blackbeard's treasure?

Juan Fernandez, a small island five hundred miles off the coast of Chile, was the home for four years of the marooned Alexander Selkirk, the unfortunate mariner who provided Defoe with the inspiration for *Robinson Crusoe*. A few years after Selkirk's rescue Juan Fernandez was according to legend chosen by a Spanish adventurer as the hiding place for his ill-gotten gains. He buried his chests inside a cave, the entrance to

The romantic image of likable rogues of the stamp of Long John Silver who wandered the seven seas and buried their treasure on distant tropical isles is captured in this nineteenth-century painting. In fact there was nothing remotely romantic about these bloodthirsty criminals. Lolonois (above) plundered Caribbean settlements with unprecedented savagery. Once he tore the heart out of a Spaniard and ate it in front of other prisoners to encourage them to reveal the whereabouts of their valuables. He died violently at the hands of Darien Indians. One of his followers is supposed to have concealed his treasure on an island off the coast of Chile. Blackbeard (right) deliberately made himself appear more ferocious before a battle by twining smouldering slow fuses into his hair and beard. He was killed in a long and bloody naval engagement in 1718, reputedly after concealing his ill-gotten gains on Plum Island. There was certainly nothing romantic about the few members of the fair sex who took up piracy. Despite Defoe's touching account of Mary Read's accidental involvement with buccaneers and her subsequent faithfulness to the captain, she (above right) was almost certainly taken aboard as a common whore. She dressed as a man and went willingly into battle. She died of fever in a Jamaican prison in 1720.

which was marked by a cutlass, an axe, a crowbar and the body of a slave.

The Salvage Islands are a barren group of rocks in the North Atlantic between Madeira and the Canaries. In 1804 a mutinous Spanish crew killed their captain and concealed the treasure their ship was carrying on the largest isle in the group. Their object, it seems, was to return to the West Indies from where they had come, wreck the ship there and masquerade as *bona fide* survivors of a maritime tragedy. When opportunity arose they would return to claim their loot. But their ship really was wrecked. All the crew perished save one who just had time to tell the story of the treasure before he, too, died. The tale was passed on to a British captain, Hercules Robinson, who took HMS *Prometheus* to the Salvage Islands and set the crew to digging up the beach. They found nothing, and it was forty years before Robinson, now an admiral, was able to return for a second search. By this time the 'Salvage Islands Treasure' was common knowledge; in Tenerife, Robinson heard news of another British party which had spent three months on Great Salvage Island some years before and had subsequently turned up in Marseilles £40,000 the richer.

Another deserted Atlantic island has been searched frequently for the treasure of Benito de Soto, a nineteenth-century renegade who preyed on Brazilian and Argentinian commerce. Long after the pirate had been captured and hanged, a one-time member of his crew died, leaving a chart of Trinidad Island, midway between South America and Africa, showing the location of Benito's treasure. The first seekers, in 1880, discovered that the area of beach containing the treasure site was covered by thousands of tons of rock, the result of a landslide. This obstacle has thwarted all subsequent attempts to reclaim the treasure. The tropical heat and the amount of rubble make work with hand-tools virtually impossible. The treacherous reefs which ring the island make the landing of heavy machinery equally impracticable. Any modern treasure-hunter looking for Benito's plunder would have to be prepared to hazard a very large sum on what might turn out to be a wild goose chase.

More certainty can be attached to many sunken pirate treasures than to the legends of buried hoards. Vessels 'on the account' were just as subject to the hazards of storm and rock as were merchantmen and warships. In April 1717 the *Whydah* was wrecked off Cape Cod. She was a merchantman carrying African gold and ivory to the Americas which had been captured by a pirate called Bellamy. He was sailing her to New Zealand to sell the cargo when she foundered in fog off North Eastham. Occasionally storms throw up coins on the Cape Cod beaches, but the bulk of the *Whydah*'s treasure lies on the sea bed under a covering of sand seven metres thick. Silver ingots and other items have been washed up on the shore of the Delaware Channel, further to the south. These are probably from the wreck of one of the pirate ships which used the bay as a base in the second half of the seventeenth century. The pirate vessel *San Nicolas* is known to have foundered off Atacoma, Chile, in 1685 but her exact whereabouts are unrecorded. Some miles to the south, off Valparaiso, five hundred gold bars and a quantity of coin lie sprinkled across the ocean floor. They have lain there since 1600 when the Spanish caravel *Buen Jesús* was attacked by Dutch pirates. Rather than see his precious cargo fall into enemy hands, the ship's captain jettisoned it before the encounter.

Kidd's Treasure

Some personalities and exploits become so firmly embedded in popular folklore that no amount of fact or prosaic research can remove them. There seems to be no good reason why myths should gather round particular men but they do, and fact and fiction become inextricably mixed. It is true of heroes like King Arthur and Robin Hood and it is true of villains like Captain Kidd.

William Kidd has two claims to fame in the popular imagination: he was the most notorious of all the pirates, and he buried a fabulous treasure. In reality he wasn't and he didn't. The details of this unfortunate man's voyage in the *Adventure* galley, his trial and execution have been recorded so often that we need only give the barest outline of them here. In 1696 he was commissioned by King William III and backed by a consortium of leading politicians to suppress piracy and confiscate pirate loot. Kidd was a weak and ambitious man. When after several months he had failed to take a legitimate prize his crew forced him to go 'on the account'. Kidd plundered several ships in the Indian Ocean but the richest was the *Quedagh Merchant*, carrying £60–70,000 worth of varied cargo. £10,000 worth was sold off and distributed to the crew. Kidd transferred to the merchantman and sailed westwards. At Anguilla he learned that he had been outlawed and that naval patrols were searching for the *Quedagh Merchant*. At Mona Island he sold more cargo and bought a sloop, the *San Antonio*, with the proceeds. He transferred some of his plunder to this vessel and left the *Quedagh Merchant* at Hispaniola with some of his men. Determined to clear his name, Kidd reported to Lord Bellamont, Governor of New England, one of his patrons. On the way he entrusted some of his treasure to John Gardiner of Long Island.

Captain William Kidd was of obscure origin; he served with credit against the French in the West Indies. In 1695 he came to London and received the king's commission to arrest pirates. Upon reaching the town of Madagascar he joined with the pirates instead of hunting them down. He was arrested in July 1699 and sent to London for trial. It was March 1701 before he was brought before the bar of the House of Commons, which was interested in the political implications of his case. There was a move afoot to bring down some of Kidd's powerful backers. But Kidd, hoping that Lord Bellamont and others would stand by him, refused to implicate his patrons. They, for their part, were delighted to let Kidd be their scapegoat. At his subsequent Old Bailey trial he was inadequately defended. His conviction for piracy and murder was a foregone conclusion. It was partly the deliberate distortions of Kidd's backers and partly the popular love of larger-than-life characters that turned the weak and ineffective privateer into the ferocious pirate of legend. The image is neatly conveyed in this print (right) sold in large numbers by a London toy theatre.

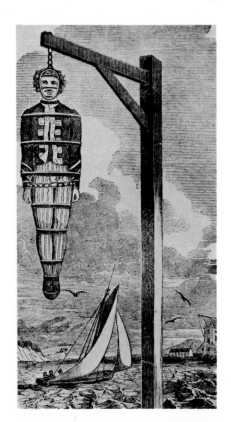

A FULL
ACCOUNT
OF THE
ACTIONS
Of the late Famous
PYRATE,
Capt. KIDD.

With the Proceedings againſt Him, and a Vindication of the Right Honourable *Richard* Earl of *Bellomont*, Lord *Coloony*, late Governor of *New-England*, and other Honourable Perſons, from the Unjuſt Reflecti-ons caſt upon tehm.

By a Perſon of Quality.

DUBLIN:
Re-printed for *Matthew Gunn*, Bookſeller in *Eſſex-Street*, 1701.

Immediately after the trial a broadside was published purporting to give a full account of all Kidd's crimes. It was evidence such as this that made him a celebrity, a bold pirate who ranged the seven seas seizing rich prizes at will. Since it was known that only a few thousand pounds of pirate loot were recovered from Kidd and his associates it was readily believed that other caches must lie concealed in distant places. For some considerable time after his death it was possible for the curious and the lovers of the macabre to gaze upon his remains. William Kidd was hanged at Wapping Old Stairs on 23 May 1701 (above right). He was hanged twice – the first time the rope broke. Then his tarred body was displayed on a gibbet at Tilbury Point, 'at such place on ye said Point where he may be seen quite plain by persons passing into and out of ye river . . . as a great terror to all persons from committing ye like crimes'.

Bellamont clapped Kidd in chains, appropriated some £14,000 worth of goods from the *San Antonio* and from Gardiner, and sent the pirate to England for trial. Kidd was condemned and on the eve of his execution he attempted to buy a reprieve with a letter to the Speaker of the House of Commons promising to lead the authorities to the rest of his treasure, which he valued at £100,000. This was an exaggerated estimate of the value of the merchandise he believed still to be aboard the *Quedagh Merchant*. In fact his crew had sold off most of the cargo, distributed the proceeds and set fire to the ship.

Kidd's treasure was thus all appropriated by his backers and his crew. This has not prevented generations of enthusiasts seeking it in scores of locations, some of them thousands of miles from any spot the pirate ever visited. In 1762 a New York farmer was plagued by nocturnal diggers who repeatedly pockmarked his land with holes. In 1846 there was a rush of excavators to the Hudson River after a local woman dreamed that the treasure was located somewhere on its banks. Early in the 1950s two separate expeditions set off in a blaze of publicity, one from England and one from Canada. Nothing was subsequently reported about them: newspapers are not interested in failures. In 1956 treasure was found on the Japanese island of Yokoate-Shima – silver bars and chests of gold coin. For no very good reason it was attributed to William Kidd. All the obvious sites – Anguilla, Mona Island, Hispaniola and Gardiner's Island – have been dug over many times. It is the ventures to unobvious places that cause one to marvel at the gullibility of man. Produce a faded map purporting to give the true location of Kidd's treasure and someone will be found prepared to risk life and fortune in the quest for this particular mythical gold.

Probably the single most important contribution to the legend of Kidd's treasure is the letter he wrote from Newgate Prison to Robert Harley, Speaker of the House of Commons, shortly before his execution. In it he claimed 'I have lodged goods and treasures to the value of £100,000' in the 'Indies'. He was probably referring to the goods left aboard the Quedagh Merchant *and he was certainly exaggerating their worth. He asked to be conveyed to the hiding place aboard a naval ship and to be pardoned if the treasure was successfully recovered. The appeal was regarded, probably rightly, as a desperate attempt to postpone the carrying out of the sentence. It has not been so regarded by generations of treasure-hunters.*

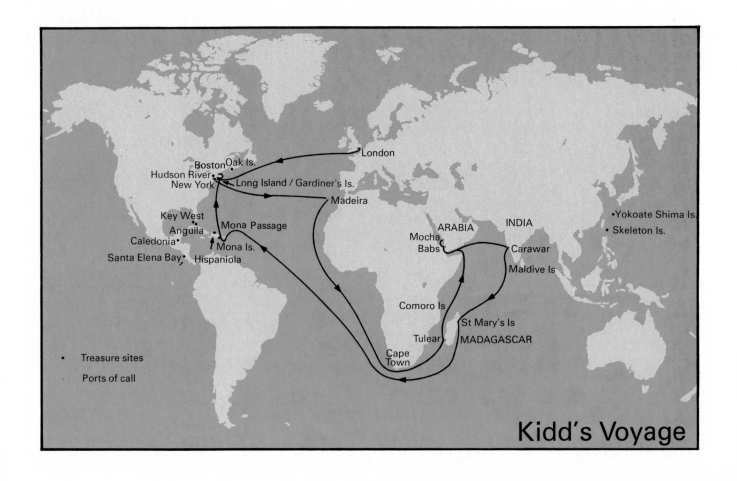

Kidd's Voyage

The Kidd Maps

An old chest with a false compartment containing a map – such is the stuff of pirate legend. One twentieth-century collector amassed five such chests, as well as a bureau which also contained a concealed treasure chart. This was Hubert Palmer, an Eastbourne solicitor who kept a small private museum of Kidd mementos. The bureau, bought in 1929, carried a brass plate inscribed, *Captain William Kidd, Adventure Galley, 1669*. Unfortunately, the style of the piece clearly dates its manufacture to some fifty years later. However, Palmer discovered or claimed to discover the map, not in one of the obvious secret compartments with which such desks were usually provided, but in a brass tube concealed inside one of the sliders supporting the fall front. The chests came into his possession complete with impeccable pedigrees (or so it is claimed). One had belonged to Thomas Hardy, captain of Nelson's *Victory*, who had it from Ned Ward, Kidd's boatswain. From these pieces of furniture the collector eventually found himself with four maps of the same island, which were pronounced by experts as genuine seventeenth-century productions. According to words on a couple of the maps, the treasure island was located in the 'China Sea'. Kidd's name or initials 'authenticated' the drawings, and the date 1669 appeared on some of them. This was long before the pirate's last voyage and seems to relate the maps to a period of his life about which nothing is known. No bearings are given which would pinpoint the island but locations of various hoards are shown. Hubert Palmer, shown in our pictures with two of his chests, died in 1951, and his collection was dispersed soon afterwards. Some charts fell into the hands of adventurers, who mounted unsuccessful expeditions to look for the island. Some observers have remarked its similarity to Oak Island, Nova Scotia, the scene of another famous treasure-hunt. If the 'Kidd maps' are genuine, they pose more problems than they solve. Or could it be that the Eastbourne lawyer concealed beneath his respectable exterior the spirit of a practical joker and the skill of a forger?

A FOURTH CHEST WITH BRASS-BOUND PLATE: "WILLIAM & SARAH KIDD. THEIR CHEST."

Collector is shown withdrawing hidden treasure chart.

A FIFTH CHEST CARVED WITH THE BLACK FLAG AND INSCRIBED: "1699. CAPN. KIDD."

Note.—The collector is holding false bottom with real treasure island chart of Kidd.

Treasure Island

If any spot on earth deserves the nickname of 'Treasure Island' it is the forest-covered expanse of volcanic rock lying by itself in the Pacific some five hundred miles from Panama. Cocos Island merits the title both because of the immensity of the pirate plunder reputedly concealed there (valued as highly as £50,000,000 by some researchers) and also by virtue of the large number of expeditions mounted to recover it, expeditions connected with such illustrious names as Sir Malcolm Campbell and Errol Flynn.

Cocos Island was a favourite haunt of pirates during the seventeenth, eighteenth and early nineteenth centuries. It was off the shipping lanes but close enough to the wealthy Spanish colonies along the South and Central American shores, which were frequent victims of the sea raiders. Deposits of loot on Cocos are associated with William Dampier and Edward Davis, who are known to have plundered the Peruvian settlements in the 1680s. Over a century later Bennet Grahame, alias Bonito, was employed in the same game and, according to one exaggerated claim, he buried 'three hundred and fifty tons of bullion' on the island. Such stories are largely speculation, but the treasure of the *Mary Dear* has documentary evidence to support it and forms part of a well-authenticated series of events.

In 1820 the sun was setting in blood upon Spain's American empire. Simon Bolivar, the great nationalist hero, had made himself master of Colombia, while in the south José de San Martin had liberated Chile. The anti-colonial forces now began to converge on Peru, the source of Spain's bullion trade. They were assisted by the eccentric Englishman Lord Cochrane, who mounted an attack on Lima and Callao from the sea. The wealthy citizens panicked and cast around for some means of escape for themselves and their valuables. They approached Captain Thompson, a Scot whose brig, the *Mary Dear*, lay at anchor in the harbour. There was very little haggling; the Spaniards were desperate to escape and able to offer a staggering fee. Almost immediately Thompson's incredulous sailors found themselves stowing below a cargo of silver plate, jewel chests, gem-studded holy relics, gilded chandeliers and candelabra hurriedly removed from the cathedral, paintings, statues, rare books and bags of coin. The *Mary Dear* left harbour on the next tide, bound for Spain.

Or so Thompson's passengers thought. His crew had other ideas. The realization that fabulous wealth was theirs for the taking proved too much for them. They told the captain what was in their minds and indicated that he could either lead them or become their first victim. So Thompson turned pirate. The Spaniards were murdered, and the *Mary Dear*, carrying the most easily acquired haul ever made by buccaneers, set course for Cocos Island. It was the natural place to go – to hide from Spanish vengeance, to take stock of the situation, to conceal the loot. The bulk of the treasure was buried and Thompson devised a ruse which, he hoped, would allay suspicion. He took the *Mary Dear* close to the coast of Central America, fired her, and took to the longboats with his men. They landed in Mexico only to discover that some of their victims' bodies had been washed ashore and that the authorities were on the lookout for them. Under torture, members of the crew confessed. Thompson, however, was able to bribe his guards and escape.

Cocos Island is one of the most inhospitable places to go looking for buried treasure. It lies off the coast of Central America, 87°2' west and 5°32' north; about twenty square miles in extent, Cocos is covered with thick tropical vegetation, its climate hot and humid. Out of the forest, mountain peaks rise to almost a thousand metres. It has two safe anchorages, Wafer Bay and Chatham Bay, both of which are on the north side. Fortunately for prospective treasure-hunters, the vast hoards deposited by Bennet Grahame, William Thompson, Edward Davis and other pirates are believed to lie within easy reach of these harbours.

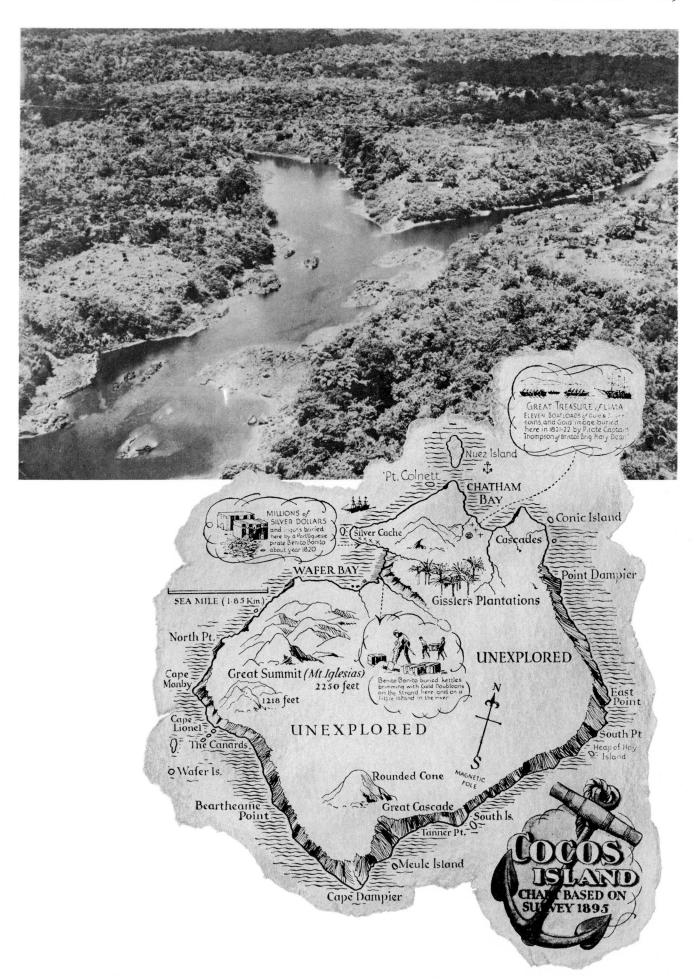

GREAT TREASURE of LIMA
ELEVEN BOATLOADS of Gold & Silver
coins, and Gold Image buried
here in 1821-22 by Pirate Captain
Thompson of Bristol Brig Mary Dear

Nuez Island

'Pt. Colnett

CHATHAM BAY

Conic Island

Cascades

MILLIONS of
SILVER DOLLARS
and Ingots buried
here by a Portuguese
pirate Benito Bonito
about year 1820

Silver Cache

Point Dampier

WAFER BAY

Gissler's Plantations

SEA MILE (1·85 Km.)

North Pt.

UNEXPLORED

Cape
Manby

Great Summit (Mt. Iglesias)
2250 feet

1218 feet

Benito Bonito buried kettles
brimming with Gold Doubloons
on the Strand here, and on a
little island in the river

East
Point

Cape
Lionel

UNEXPLORED

South Pt

The Canards

Heap of Hay
Island

Wafer Is.

N

Rounded Cone

MAGNETIC
POLE

S

Beartheame
Point

Great Cascade

South Is.

Tanner Pt.

Meule Island

COCOS
ISLAND
CHART BASED ON
SURVEY 1895

Cape Dampier

An engraving of Cocos Island made for Middleton's Complete System of Geography.

The captain managed to return to Cocos Island once or twice for some of his treasure but the bulk of it was still there at his death. Thompson told a friend called Keating about the cache shortly before he died; Keating in turn appropriated more pieces, before passing on the information to another. So word of the *Mary Dear* treasure travelled down the generations, as did various maps and documents describing it. These stories and written records would provide tempting bait for scores of treasure-hunters over the years. Who would not be attracted by an inventory such as this:

Commander Worsley, the explorer and one-time companion of Edward Shackleton, was convinced he had the machine which would lead him to the Cocos Island treasures. It was the portable radiometer. Current passed between electrodes stuck into the ground revealed the existence of buried conductors such as gold and silver.

We have buried at a depth of four feet in red earth
 1 chest: altar trimmings of cloth of gold, with baldachins, mon-
    strances, chalices, comprising 1,244 stones.
 1 chest: 2 gold reliquaries weighing 120 pounds, with 624 topazes,
    cornelians and emeralds, 12 diamonds.
 1 chest: 3 reliquaries of cast metal weighing 160 pounds, with 860
    rubies and various stones, 19 diamonds.
 1 chest: 4,000 doubloons of Spain marked *8*, 5,000 crowns of Mexico,
    124 swords, 64 dirks, 120 shoulder belts, 28 rondaches [small
    shields].
 1 chest: 8 caskets of cedar wood and silver, with 3,840 cut stones, rings,
    patens and 4,265 uncut stones.
28 feet to the north-east at a depth of eight feet in the yellow sand
 7 chests with 22 candelabra in gold and silver, weighing 250 pounds,
    and 164 rubies.
12 armspans west, at a depth of ten feet in the red earth
The seven-foot Virgin of gold with the child Jesus and her crown and
    pectoral of 780 pounds, rolled in her gold chasuble on which are 1,684
    jewels. Three of these are four-inch emeralds on the pectoral and six are
    six-inch topazes on the crown. The seven crosses are of diamonds.

Among the hundreds of hopefuls who have been drawn by the magnet of Cocos treasure is August Gissler, who obtained exclusive excavation rights in 1891 and devoted seventeen years of his life to the quest. He

amassed a total of thirty-three gold coins, enough to prove that some sort of treasure existed but not enough to recompense him for the wasted years. In 1926 Sir Malcolm Campbell the racing motorist and adventurer searched for several days without success. Three years later two separate expeditions arrived both of which claimed some success. Pierre Mangell believed he had found the right spot in a cave but the rising tide repeatedly filled his excavations. Peter Bergmans actually found chests brimming with gold, accompanied by a skeleton in another cave. Unaccountably, he left the treasure intact and when he returned for it he could not find the cave again. In 1935 Commander Worsley's team went to Cocos equipped with the latest electronic devices (see page 190). Worsley's backers, like so many others, put more money into Cocos than they took out.

After the Second World War the flow of treasure-seekers resumed. Every expedition leader who set foot on Cocos' equatorial beaches believed that he would succeed where all his predecessors had failed. Ian MacBean, a Canadian Scot, went to the island in 1964, having studied every book and document he could lay hands on. He and his companions spent days wading through mangrove swamps, hacking through dense forest and digging into loose sandy soil. For them, too, the search was its own reward. Shortly after this, the Costa Rican government decided to issue no more permits to treasure-hunters but such an obstacle was seen by eternally optimistic adventurers as simply a challenge. As recently as 1975 the Industrial and General Marketing Company was founded, an impressive-sounding enterprise with the aim of recovering the Cocos Island treasure.

Ian MacBean believed that he too would succeed where other treasure-seekers had failed. He arrived with a group of technicians, a pile of machinery, and information culled from the Curzon-Howe Papers. He and his companions cut through thick jungle, scrambled up rocky slopes and endured attacks by tropical insects, as they sought a treasure-filled cave. But even excavation with a motor-powered drill failed to locate the pirates' hoard.

In 1933 Worsley and some of his colleagues made a preliminary exploration of Cocos Island in preparation for their full-scale expedition the following year. They landed in Wafer Bay. Worsley confessed, 'I have always been fascinated by treasure islands', but claimed that no romantic spirit imbued his quest: 'The policy adopted in organizing the search includes the bringing together of the leading personnel of all recent treasure expeditions, pooling their knowledge, and utilizing it in a scientific manner.'

The Money Pit

The search for the treasure of Oak Island has lasted almost two hundred years, swallowed up well over a million pounds and cost six lives. Like most other treasure stories of the American seaboard it has persistently been connected with pirates. Oak Island is one of a cluster of islets in Mahone Bay, Nova Scotia, some eighty kilometres south of Halifax. In 1795 three lads from the nearby township of Chester were exploring the deserted eastern end of the island when they came across a tree with a lower limb which had been used to support a block and tackle. The equipment was still in place and beneath it there was a slight depression in the ground. Brought up on popular legends, the boys immediately thought of 'pirate gold'. They came back time after time to dig in their secret pit, only to discover that it was much deeper than they could have expected. It was a well-constructed shaft some four metres across with a succession of wooden platforms. At ten metres they had to give up and seek help. In 1804 the first professional excavation attempt was made. Its backers, like all those who were to involve themselves later with the Oak Island mystery, worked on the simple principle that since someone had gone to considerable trouble to create an elaborate pit they must have concealed something of great value in it. Just how elaborate the shaft system was they soon discovered to their cost. They penetrated to thirty metres, removing successive platforms. Then the hole began to fill rapidly with water. Some of the tightly fitting obstructions had acted as airlocks. Unknown to the excavators, two tunnels connected the money pit with a nearby beach. When the air pressure was released sea water flooded into the diggings.

Over the years various expeditions went to Oak Island, digging a succession of fresh shafts all around the original money pit and turning the whole site into a muddy morass. It was not until 1845 that the secret of the flooding was discovered. A succession of drains and filters had been constructed beneath the high water level of a cove – work demanding considerable skill and hard labour. Efforts to dam the tide failed and fresh excavations caused a collapse in the Money Pit which, the excavators believed, carried treasure chests to the bottom of the flooded workings.

More and more syndicates came and went, equipped with drills, cranes, mechanical excavators and explosives. In 1894 a drill went through a barrier of cement at about fifty metres and came up with fragments of wood, metal and parchment attached to it. But the seekers could not reach whatever lay at the bottom of the shaft. By then the whole area had become so pockmarked with deep holes that further excavation was rendered very hazardous. This did not deter hopeful seekers after the 'obviously' important Oak Island Treasure. The twentieth century brought wealthy treasure-hunters equipped with electric pumps and expensive mining gear, as well as cranks armed with 'gold detectors', divining rods and radar devices. In 1965 four excavators were buried when their shaft caved in. In 1971 a Canadian company working the site lowered a television camera to the bottom of the shaft. Dimly it revealed what appeared to be the outline of chests – wooden treasure chests? Intact after 200 years most of which they had spent under water?

The work goes on. The eastern end of Oak Island is by now totally

For 175 years Oak Island, off the coast of Nova Scotia, has been excavated by treasure-hunters who are convinced that they will find pirate loot, the French crown jewels or Inca gold. Whatever is at the bottom, it is certain that someone went to a lot of trouble to prevent it being found.

A cutaway view of the pit on Oak Island. Everything down to the ninety-foot level was actually found by searchers after 1795. The rest of the drawing is based on core drilling and speculation by searchers.

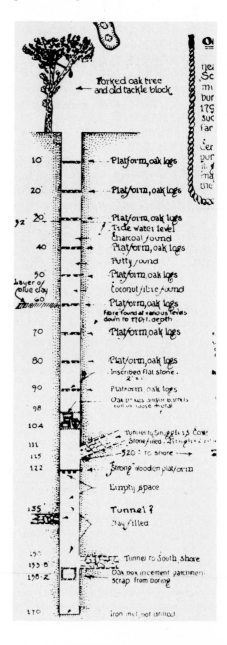

Prince Edward I.

CANADA

• Moncton

Saint John

• Halifax

Nova Scotia

Bay of Fundy

• Oak Is

UNITED
STATES

C. Sable

• Portland

NORTH ATLANTIC OCEAN

Boston

• C. Cod

Location of OAK Is

Modern machinery is brought to the aid of treasure-hunters probing the Money Pit mystery. A new shaft has been dug beside the original one so that excavators can tunnel into the original pit.

devastated. The only people to profit from the excavations are the businessmen who run the Buccaneer and Captain Kidd motels and the Oak Island Museum; the fishermen who take visitors on sightseeing trips; and the locals who in sundry ways supplement their incomes from tourism.

Yet the tantalizing facts remain that the shaft and tunnel complex was constructed by someone, and constructed for a purpose. The favourite candidate is, inevitably, William Kidd. Some support seems to be given to this identification by the marked similarity of Oak Island to the 'Skeleton Island' of the Kidd maps discovered earlier this century. But there is no evidence to show that Captain Kidd travelled as far north as Nova Scotia, nor that he possessed the skill and leisure necessary for so elaborate a construction as the Money Pit. Another theory requires us to believe that the American seaboard pirates joined forces to create a communal bank and that the Money Pit was their vault. It seems an unlikely solution; collaboration and making provision for the future were not common characteristics of pirates. If not buccaneers, then perhaps the crew of a Spanish bullion ship: this idea, canvassed as recently as 1978 in a well-argued book by D'Arcy O'Connor,* envisages

* *The Money Pit.*

The search for Oak Island's treasure goes on. Despite millions of pounds poured into earlier fruitless expeditions, despite the lives already lost, despite the muddy morass created by previous excavators, men are still determined to unravel the secret. Dan Blankenship is here seen carrying out a survey in 1970.

a damaged mid-seventeenth-century galleon limping homewards. Her captain realizes she will never reach Spain with the heavy cargo so he has it landed and concealed on Oak Island, elaborately safeguarded from pirates by the system of shafts and tunnels. The ship sets sail again and is overwhelmed by Atlantic storms. No one survives to reveal the secret or reclaim the treasure. This scenario fits most of the known facts but is quite incapable of proof. And would a random Spanish ship have had aboard the necessary equipment and men with the requisite engineering skills? Wilder theories which connect Oak Island with Incas, Vikings or the lost manuscripts of Francis Bacon can safely be jettisoned.

Ruper Furneaux* has presented what appears to be the most plausible solution offered so far. He dates the construction to about 1780, when the War of American Independence was in full swing. The British garrison at New York was under pressure and might have to withdraw hurriedly to Halifax. In order to safeguard his war chests, the British commander-in-chief had a secret repository prepared by the Royal Engineers. If this is the explanation, did the British ever have to use the pit? If they did, did they come back for their treasure? Whatever solution one accepts to the Money Pit mystery, it only seems to lead to new questions.

* *The Money Pit Mystery*, 1972.

Caribbean Criminals

The word *buccaneer* strictly speaking only applies to the Caribbean-based pirates of the sixteenth and seventeenth centuries. Colonies of ruffians grew on the deserted or sparsely populated Greater Antilles, made up of deserters, shipwreck victims and insubordinates deliberately marooned by their captains. From the natives they learned how to make *boucan*, fire-cured strips of meat, and this became their staple diet. They took to the water, trading in meat, hides and tallow, which they exchanged for guns and powder. Their way of life ensured that they were strong, fit and excellent shots, characteristics which stood them in good stead when they attacked passing ships and Spanish settlements. They were later joined by bands of official settlers from France, Holland and England who found seaborne brigandage more congenial and remunerative than the patient tilling of the soil. For years the Caribbean was a lake virtually dominated by bloodthirsty gangs with leaders who rejoiced in names like Montbars the Exterminator and Lolonois the Terrible. By the mid seventeenth century some of these gangs were so large that they could successfully raid and hold to ransom large towns such as Campeche, Panama and Maracaibo.

One of the later buccaneer princes was José Gaspar, alias Gasparilla. For over thirty years he and his crew were the scourge of the Caribbean

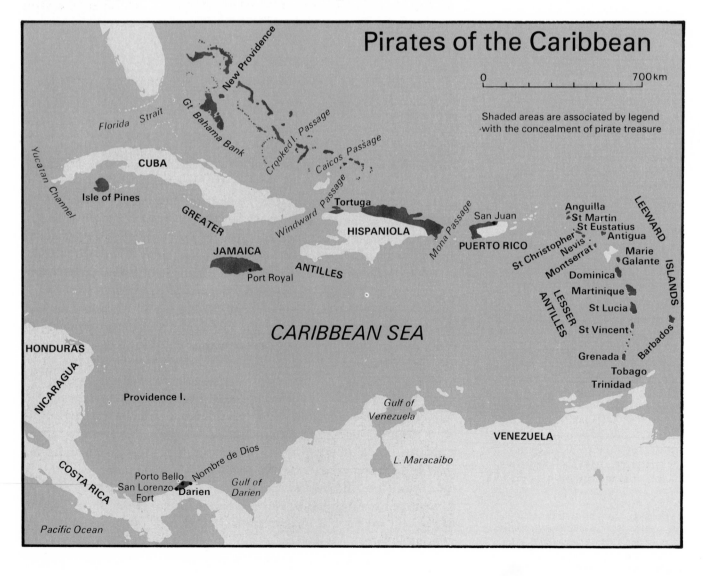

Panama Plunder

The most audacious enterprise in Henry Morgan's career was the raid on Panama in 1671. This leader of the Jamaica-based buccaneers eventually won respectability, a knighthood and the governorship of Jamaica but all that was in the future when he led a fleet of thirty-six ships across the Caribbean. Morgan and his men fought their way over the isthmus, overpowering the garrisons which guarded the bullion packhorse route. It was a long, hard march, and at last the pirates fell upon rich, ill-defended Panama. But its people fought well, and in the conflict the city of gracious wooden houses was set ablaze. Morgan's men were thus thwarted of some of their richest prizes. However, enough was found amid the ruins and extorted from trembling citizens to make the expedition highly profitable. Yet when, weeks later, the time came for the sharing out of loot Morgan distributed a mere 200 pieces of eight to each man. By this time the pirates were back on the Caribbean coast and the men were convinced that their leader had concealed the bulk of the hard-won plunder. An early reporter of these events agreed with them, declaring that Morgan buried his followers' rightful proceeds 'having designed in his mind to cheat them as much as he could'. The story of Henry Morgan's buried loot affords a slim pretext for a treasure-hunt but this has not prevented many hopefuls seeking it along the coast of Darien.

The pirates were bloodthirsty villains often given to gratuitous cruelty.

and accounted for well over a hundred well-laden merchant vessels. He made his headquarters on an island at the mouth of Charlotte Harbor on the Gulf of Florida. Modestly he bestowed upon it his own name. Here he built houses, quarters for prisoners awaiting ransom, a harem, farms and accommodation for the slaves who worked them and warehouses for his loot. Not all the pirate plunder was stored in these warehouses. From time to time Gasparilla paid his crew their share of the booty. It was then up to each man to guard his own portion. Since not one of the pirates trusted another all of them hid their personal treasure on Gasparilla Island and neighbouring islands, using it as occasion and need arose. But sometimes a man succumbed to tropical disease, was killed in a brawl or failed to return from a voyage. Then his wealth would remain hidden – perhaps to this day. That, at least, is what the scores of hopefuls believe who every year tread the beaches and scrub-covered interiors with faded maps or metal detectors. As for Gasparilla, his end came in 1821 when he was leaving the island for the last time. An American patrol vessel shot his ship from under him and sent him to the bottom of the Gulf of Mexico accompanied by most of his treasure.

Gasparilla's ship has yet to be discovered. It is not so with the *Oxford*, a buccaneer frigate which haunted the Main for years and ended its days as part of Henry Morgan's flotilla. In 1669 there was a drunken brawl on board during which someone accidentally fired the powder magazine. In recent years the scattered debris of the pirate vessel has been found, but little gold or silver has yet come to light among the wreckage. The same is true of the scores of stories of buried treasure relating to virtually every island the buccaneers are known to have inhabited.

The Island of Sin

As soon as a pirate ship was seen approaching, a cannon was fired at Fort Charles. Merchants left their shops. Craftsmen and apprentices threw down their tools. The law courts were suspended. Men, women and children rushed into the streets and made for the harbour. As the buccaneers' vessel slid to its mooring it was greeted with cheers, singing and dancing. For this was Port Royal, Jamaica, the pirates' capital.

Cromwell's navy captured Jamaica in 1655–6 and within a few years the buccaneers had adopted Port Royal as their city of pleasure. Here they came at the end of their voyages to spend their loot on drink and women. It was said that there was in this town 'more plenty of running cash (proportionately to the number of inhabitants) than in London'. Port Royal was notorious the world around for profligacy, wantonness and drunkenness. Duelling and brawls were common sights. Inebriated seamen abused the townspeople. In return the trademen of Port Royal devoted all their energies to relieving the sailors of their cash. It was nothing for a man to spend 3,000 dollars in a single night and to be thrown out on to the cobbles when his pockets were empty. In this centre of debauchery men lived wildly and violently. Eccentricity was the norm. Citizens were not surprised to see a captain sitting in the middle of the street astride a keg of wine and to be invited to drink with him – at

gunpoint. This state of affairs suited everyone, not just the keepers of taverns, brothels and gambling dens. The government in London could not afford constant naval patrols to defend Jamaica but as long as Port Royal was the buccaneers' favourite haunt the island's security was no problem. The pirates safeguarded the Jamaicans from attack, they spent freely, they traded captured merchandise, they bought farm produce to provision their ships. More pirate gold flowed through Port Royal than was ever buried on deserted coral strands.

On 7 June 1692, disaster struck this sinners' paradise with a suddenness and completeness which would have satisfied fully any preacher's vision of the visitation of divine wrath. Just before midday there was a terrifying rumbling. The earth opened and swallowed houses, shops, taverns, ships, forts, markets, and over 2,000 people. The sea gushed in over broken walls and rubble-strewn streets. When its surging and roaring had ceased, the gentle waves, littered with flotsam, covered nine-tenths of old Port Royal.

The pirates' port now exchanged one legend for another. From being the living city of sin it became the dead city of treasure. Pirate plunder worth millions, it was said, lay in its submerged buildings and ships. It was partly true, but only partly. The survivors of the disaster made sure they recovered all that was recoverable with the techniques available at the time. Port Royal was the headquarters of Caribbean skin divers who hired themselves out to the leaders of salvage expeditions. They were

Port Royal, Jamaica, was soon rebuilt after the earthquake of 1692, and for many years local divers explored the submerged part of the old town looking for valuable relics.

much employed in the summer and autumn months of 1692. So were the new diving bells. Yet there was much treasure that could not be reached. Although this most important marine archaeological site attracted explorers from time to time, and although the Jamaica House of Assembly passed an act for the recovery of treasure submerged in 1692, no major expedition was undertaken until 1959 and it was another five years before systematic excavation led by Robert Marx resulted in dramatic and exciting discoveries.

The work was not easy. Another earthquake in 1907 had caused further collapse among the submerged ruins and the site was covered in a thick sediment. Marx used a suction pump to clear the area he and his companions were working on and to dredge up small artefacts. Success came immediately. He discovered a collapsed wall, and reasoned that anything underneath it must have escaped the first salvors. Carefully the sand was sucked away and the cavity beneath was probed. Marx's fingers touched a pewter spoon, and another. Then came a large dish and a neatly stacked pile of plates. Other locations yielded more pewter – tankards, bowls, porringers, candlesticks, wine funnels and tasters – the most extensive collection of late seventeeth-century pewterware ever found. And there were other discoveries – over 5,000 fragments of clay pipes, a pocket watch, ceramics, silver plate, brass ship's fittings. And a chest; a chest which crumbled when touched leaving only a brass lock plate and its contents – hundreds of gleaming, freshly minted pieces of eight. Here was a pirate treasure indeed.

The divers who swam among the sunken ruins of Port Royal came across many different kinds of treasure. These small cannon were from the English warship Swan, *which sank during the 1692 earthquake. Most impressive of all the finds was the excellent collection of pewter (opposite).*

Orient Plunder

Before the discovery of Australia, the Indian and Pacific Oceans were conceived of as one vast, open tract of water, around whose northern fringes passed ships bearing the luxuries of the East to wealthy customers in the West. Silk, porcelain, spices, tea, pearls, gemstones, gold and ivory and the coin to pay for them were borne along well-worn trade routes by the East Indiamen. They were a prey to European pirates operating from such bases as Madagascar; to Arabian and Indian brigands sallying out of ports around the Persian Gulf; and to bands of criminals infesting the offshore waters of China, Malaysia and Indonesia. It is scarcely surprising, therefore, that legends of buried hoards are associated with many desert islands of the eastern seas.

Olivier le Vasseur's piratical career in the seas between India and Africa came to an end on 7 July 1730, when he was hanged on the French island of Réunion. On the gallows he scattered a sheaf of papers with the cry, 'My treasures are for him who can find them.' Truth or macabre jest? If the latter, the antics of fortune-hunters over the last two and a half centuries must have caused considerable mirth in the pirates' Valhalla. One of the papers contained a cryptogram, a coded message supposedly giving directions to the pirate's treasure. In 1923 the then owner of le Vasseur's documents searched on Mahé Island in the Seychelles, believing that the cryptogram was connected with inscriptions carved on rocks

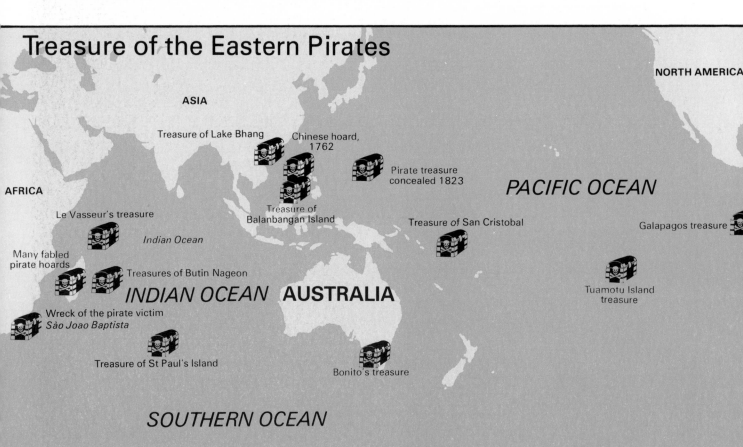

Treasure of the Eastern Pirates

NORTH AMERICA

ASIA

Treasure of Lake Bhang

Chinese hoard, 1762

Pirate treasure concealed 1823

PACIFIC OCEAN

AFRICA

Le Vasseur's treasure

Indian Ocean

Treasure of Balanbangan Island

Treasure of San Cristobal

Galapagos treasure

Many fabled pirate hoards

Treasures of Butin Nageon

INDIAN OCEAN AUSTRALIA

Tuamotu Island treasure

Wreck of the pirate victim
Sào Joao Baptista

Treasure of St Paul's Island

Bonito's treasure

SOUTHERN OCEAN

ANTARCTICA

along the shore (certainly the code, when broken, reveals a message which by itself is gibberish). He made a dramatic discovery – two skeletons, possibly of pirates. In 1949 the quest was taken up by Reginald Cruise-Wilkins, who went to the Seychelles on holiday and was bitten by the treasure-hunting bug. He devoted years to unravelling le Vasseur's puzzle and concluded that the various clues were somehow bound up with the twelve labours of Hercules. In his various digs Cruise-Wilkins came across a number of intriguing finds, including the statue of a woman and the skeleton of a horse. He now believes that he has located the hiding place of the pirate's treasure. Unfortunately, to get to it would require a great deal of rock-moving machinery which he cannot afford.

Can we really believe in criminals possessing the education and ingenuity and having the leisure and energy necessary to leave to posterity such elaborate mysteries? Even if we can, there is no proof that Mahé is the island le Vasseur chose to hide his loot. Mauritius, Réunion and St Mary's Isle are equally possible as hiding places. The former two islands are certainly connected with a colleague of le Vasseur, Butin Nagéon de L'Estang, who is supposed to have buried treasure there.

Captain John Avery plagued the eastern seas between 1691 and 1696. He plundered many East Indiamen and other ships belonging to wealthy Indian princes. This early print shows his vessel, the Fancy, *taking the* Gung-i-Suwaie, *returning from Mecca with £534,000 in silver and gold.*

If legend is to be believed, the remoter islands of the South Pacific are littered with pirate treasures. Despite the reasonably well-authenticated account of Captain Thompson's Cocos Island cache at least two expensively equipped expeditions have searched for some of the captain's loot 3,000 miles away in the Tuamotu archipelago. Several seventeeth- and eighteenth-century pirates were familiar with the Galapagos Islands, and this fact led to one of the most bizarre treasure-hunts of all time. In 1923 the beautiful Baroness Antoinette de Wagner travelled from France to that remote corner of the Pacific accompanied by three admirers. There they lived a 'back to nature' existence practising nudity and free love and at the same time making a desultory search for treasure. The rare callers in this earthly paradise were either accepted into the community, if the Baroness fancied them, or seen off at gunpoint. In 1944 the bodies of two of the men were discovered on the shore of Marchena. Of their companions there was no sign. Dead and buried? Or living luxuriously somewhere on the proceeds of a discovered pirate hoard?

In 1823 some wealthy Spaniards fleeing from Peru with their possessions were seized by British pirates who made off across the Pacific with their loot. They reached the Mariannas, where they buried their treasure. Then the villains fell out among themselves. During the conflict their ship was burned, and only three survivors escaped in a boat and reached Honolulu. Two of them hired a schooner and returned to collect, not telling the captain the object of the voyage. Before the ship reached its destination one of the pirates was mysteriously killed. The captain had by now guessed what was afoot and, believing that he had the sole survivor at his mercy, tried to force him to reveal the treasure. Whereupon the desperado filled his pockets with scraps of lead and iron and leaped overboard. No chart, no cryptogram was left to guide future seekers to the Mariannas' Treasure, but this has not deterred bands of optimists from looking for it.

The British navy was involved in the war against piracy in eastern waters until well into the present century. This gang of cut-throats provided a picture for a sailor's scrapbook in the 1930s.

Pirate Kings and Kingdoms
If any island away from the Caribbean ought to be rich in buried treasure it is Madagascar. On this large, well-watered isle many seventeenth-century pirates made their base, and from here they preyed on the shipping of the Indian Ocean. The tribes of Madagascar were frequently at war among themselves and this made it easy for the well-armed pirate leaders to establish control over their own petty kingdoms. One French brigand called Misson seems to have been imbued with political ideals. He established a city state around Diego Suarez Bay in the north of the island. The name of his capital was Libertatia and there pirates of many nationalities, local people, and freed slaves lived a kind of primitive communism based on the pooled plunder of pirate raids. For several years peace and prosperity and a new generation of cross-breed children began to grow up. Then Libertatia was unexpectedly attacked by a local tribe. The pirates loaded what treasure they could on to two ships and hid the rest. Soon after leaving harbour Misson's vessel sank in a storm. No account exists of any part of the Libertatia treasure being recovered.

The native pirates who infested the waters of South East Asia operated as large gangs from secure mainland bases and in the pay of petty princelings. They, therefore, had little cause to conceal their loot. Yet there are some legendary hoards in the area. The wealth of notorious plunderer Laka Bhang, a nineteenth-century ruffian, is reputedly walled up in a cave on some small island at the north end of the Gulf of Tonkin. Somewhere on the west coast of Manilla a hoard of gold and pearls lies buried which was concealed when the British took the island in 1762. A few years later the British East India Company established a depot on the tiny island of Balanbangan off the northern coast of Borneo. In March 1775 the stockade containing bullion, specie and trade goods was attacked by pirates. Realizing that their only salvation lay in flight, the British buried some of the gold and silver before they made a dash for their ships. There, as far as anyone knows, it remains to this day.

Bias Bay, some sixty miles from Hong Kong, was for many years the headquarters of the notorious pirate queen Lai Choi San. Her crews were tough, well armed and merciless.

Pirates and Perils of the Indian Ocean

The familiar waters of the Indian Ocean which were the haunt of European and local pirates are, to this day, littered with the wrecks of unfortunate merchantmen, which fell foul of sea brigands. Far worse than the British, Dutch and French pirates, most of whose careers were short, were the rogues who operated out of Indian and Persian Gulf bases. For them piracy was a way of life, a trade passed on from father to son. If they could not capture a rich prize, they had no hesitation in sending her to the bottom. Such was the fate of the well-laden *Thomas*, sunk off Kutch in 1688 by the infamous Beyt pirates. Such, too, was the end of the East Indiaman *Bombay*. She was attacked by the fleet of Kanhoji Angria in 1707. The Angria family were virtually undisputed masters of the Malabar coast, and foreign merchants had to pay for their protection. Unfortunately, in 1707 the East India Co. were out of favour with Kanhoji. After a long engagement, the *Bombay* was blown out of the water, her crew and cargo scattered over the waves.

Sometimes it was the pirates themselves, together with their treasure, who were sent to the bottom. Rahma bin Jabir was a particularly repulsive criminal. He had 200 wives and boasted that he never changed his shirt until it was blown off in battle. Finding himself involved in a conflict with a superior British force off Bahrain, he ignited his own powder magazine and blew his ship to pieces.

French pirates attacked the brig *Fly* in 1808 off Kais in the Persian Gulf. To protect his treasure the captain dumped it overboard, having first taken bearings on nearby landmarks. Sadly his prudence did not save the discarded chests of coin, for, though he was subsequently released by his French captors, he fell almost immediately into the hands of local Joasmee pirates and was obliged to buy his life by revealing the whereabouts of the treasure.

But for every rupee, doubloon and guinea successfully salvaged from the ocean, hundreds of thousands more remain on the sea bed, in locations of which most are in sight of the silver sands and nodding palms of tropical coasts and islands. Only in recent years have divers begun seriously to research these Indian Ocean wrecks and to raise some of their treasures.

One of the most fascinating and successful salvage operations is that of the *Sacramento,* which made its first – and last – voyage in 1647. It was a time when Portugal found herself beset by enemies at home and abroad, and her supply lines constantly harassed by pirates. Macao, her Far East base, was in danger of falling to Spain. And Macao housed a prize which the Portuguese could not afford to lose. A man named Manuel Tavares Bocarro worked in the city as one of the world's finest gunfounders. It was vital to convey his stock of bronze cannon to safety, so two first-rate ships were designated to load the weapons and transport them to Lisbon. All went well for the *Sacramento* and the *Nossa Señora de Atalaya* until they ran into bad weather off the lonely coast of South-east Africa. Both ships were driven on to the rocks and broke up quickly, the *Sacramento* foundering near the modern town of Port Elizabeth. She was found there in 1977 by two local salvage experts, David Allen and Gerry van Niekerk. In a hazardous operation, hampered by pounding surf, strong currents and vicious rocks (not to mention 'pirate' diving teams), the two South Africans raised the *Sacramento*'s load of forty beautifully decorated

David Allen, on the right in the top picture, has excavated many sunken wrecks around the South African coast. He is shown here with one of the forty magnificent bronze cannon recovered from the seventeenth-century Portuguese ship Sacramento. *The detailed ornamentation on the barrel is still quite clear (centre). It shows the arms of the city of Macao, where it was cast, the crest of the governor of Portuguese India, and the date of manufacture – 1640. (Below) The stretch of coast which claimed the* Sacramento *and other ships looks peaceful but can be treacherous in bad weather.*

bronze cannon. Some of these very valuable pieces were themselves containers of other once-precious cargo. From barrels and touch-holes flowed a trickle of yellow tumeric and black peppercorns, exports of the fabled Spice Islands. After 330 years at the bottom of the sea they still preserved their characteristic flavours. The site also produced fragments of Ming porcelain.

There are thousands of wrecks in this part of the world's oceans. Many of them contain eminently salvage-worthy cargo; most of them are unlocated because the nearby land was scantily populated, and few shipwreck survivors ever reached civilization. Among the many that are known about are the Portuguese vessels *São Jõa* (1552), *São Jeronimo* (1552), *São Bento* (1554) and *Santo Alberto* (1593), all homeward bound with bullion and precious oriental cargo.

Of a much later period is the well-known tragedy of the *Birkenhead*, a British transport paddle-steamer carrying troops and a £3,000,000 payroll to South Africa in 1852. The courage and discipline of the soldiers as the vessel sank rapidly at the Cape, off Danger Point, has become a legend; 454 men perished out of a complement of 638. Though the *Birkenhead* has been located, no one has yet raised the coin.

The Grosvenor Treasure – Myth?

On 4 August 1782, the homeward-bound East Indiaman *Grosvenor* went aground near the mouth of the Umsikaba River in South-east Africa. Most of the crew and passengers reached safety but only a handful survived the trek southwards. At the time the exact location of the wreck could not be discovered. It was about a century later that the legend of the *Grosvenor* as a treasure ship began to grow. Estimates of her cargo varied wildly, but one writer affirmed that she carried 19 boxes of precious stones, 720 bars of gold and 1,450 bars of silver. The Grosvenor Recovery Syndicate was set up in 1905, the first of many enterprises to seek the East Indiaman's treasure, but little was achieved. Later attempts involved several prominent personalities, including Sir Arthur Conan Doyle. Over the years, cannon, ballast, some coins and various naval and personal articles have been recovered. Professor P. R. Kirby, who has probably researched more thoroughly than anyone else the documents in the *Grosvenor* case, believes that little more is likely to be found. He suggests that the ship was carrying a consignment of uncut diamonds (one story states that this was buried ashore by one of the survivors) and a modest amount of coin, but that the rest of her cargo was perishable. Nevertheless, no amount of cold fact will cool the ardour and optimism of those who wish to believe in the great *Grosvenor* treasure.

World War II Treasures

The Tide of War

War and plunder go together like eggs and bacon. The biggest robbery in history was perpetrated by soldiers. It was in June 1945, immediately after the end of the conflict in Europe. Some German local officials in Bavaria offered to show some of the victorious Americans where the reserves of the Reichbank were concealed. They took US army officers to a cave on Klausenkopf mountain, near Einsiedel. There, the astonished soldiers saw stack upon stack of gold bars. In all there were seven hundred and twenty-eight of them and they were valued then at £3,518,334. It was a fortune so immense as to tempt any man to dishonesty. The conditions were also ideal for the execution of a major crime. The country was in a state of total confusion. Troops and armoured vehicles were everywhere. Bands of homeless Germans wandered the countryside. Fugitive Nazis were at large. Traditional government had broken down and had not yet been replaced by a system operated by the armies of occupation. A few ingots could easily have been smuggled away from their hiding place. But that was not enough for US captains Robert Mackenzie and Martin Borg. They planned and executed the robbery of the entire cache – truckloads of gold. Mackenzie was eventually brought to trial, but his accomplice disappeared from Switzerland in 1946. And much of the gold disappeared with him.

Much has been written and many legends have grown about the concealed hoards of the Second World War. As year succeeds year it becomes increasingly difficult to distinguish fact from fiction. Yet to see these stories in their true perspective we must go back even further in time. The world of the 1920s and 1930s was a world in turmoil; economic and political upheaval were accompanied by the clash of cultures. For example, the gradual Soviet expansion into the Ukraine was accompanied by the deliberate and systematic looting of art treasures. Mundane economic considerations were not the only reasons for this plunder: the Marxist conquerors were bent on removing all traces of the region's indigenous culture, particularly its religious heritage. Between 1928 and 1933 the Russian authorities sold 1,087 tons of Ukrainian works of art on the international market for $19,312,000 in gold. Many are the stories of precious or holy objects removed from the probing Bolsheviks and hidden away. When in 1939–40 the Soviet army occupied the Western Ukraine, the following items were removed from a church in Mykhailivsky Sobor: an eighteenth-century gilded gate, a golden chandelier, silver and gold chasubles and rings, and a picture of the Virgin studded with one hundred and fifty-eight diamonds. Their whereabouts is still unknown.

Adolf Hitler and his fanatical adherents believed that they and their master race represented the summit of human achievement. By a somewhat dubious logic they argued that this gave them the right to the

The Chequered History of a Royal Crown

The Crown of St Stephen of Hungary is so old that its origin is obscure. According to legend it was given by Pope Sylvester II to the first king of Hungary in the year 1000. Some scholars date it slightly later but there is no doubt that it was manufactured in the eleventh century and that it has always maintained a central place in the folklore and affections of the Hungarian people; it might be said, without exaggeration, to embody the soul of the nation. It is also of incalculable value: the golden circlet is garnished with fifty-three sapphires, fifty rubies, one emerald, and eight hundred and thirty-eight pearls. The other elements of the regalia are an eleventh-century jewel-encrusted sceptre and a fourteenth-century orb.

St Stephen's crown has certainly symbolized the tumultuous history of his nation. In 1301 it was given for safe-keeping to Prince Otto of Bavaria. He was a poor guardian and the crown turned up some years later in a marsh. In 1440 it was seized by the Emperor Frederick III when he conquered Hungary. It returned home in 1452 and a special hereditary guard was appointed to keep it. This did not prevent it being captured by Suleiman the Great of Turkey in 1524 or being removed to Vienna in 1703 and 1784. In 1848 an abortive nationalist revolt against the Austrian emperor led by Lajos Kossuth resulted in the loss of the regalia once more. Kossuth took the precious regalia with him when he fled in 1849, and buried it at Orsova near the frontier. It remained concealed for several years. In 1916 a new home was found for it in the Palace of Buda and a new Crown Guard was formed.

There it was safe – until the Second World War. In 1945 the Red Army occupied Hungary and the regalia disappeared. In May of that year some American soldiers in Bavaria apprehended a group of Hungarian fascists who had with them an iron-bound chest which, they claimed, held the regalia. But when the box was opened it proved to be empty. The patriots were interrogated and finally confessed the hiding place of the crown, orb and sceptre. They were in an oil barrel, sunk in a marsh near the Bavarian village of Mattsee. The place was searched and the precious objects were found. And then they disappeared from public view. Over the next twenty years various guesses and 'revelations' were made about the whereabouts of the insignia. Then, in October 1965, an article in the small US local newspaper the *Wichita Eagle* declared that the Hungarian treasures were concealed in America, in a place known to the State Department. The government admitted that it did, indeed, have custody of the insignia and would not return it to the communist dictators currently ruling Hungary. Claims and protests followed but any further move had to await the growth of détente. It was not until 1977 that President Carter decided on a gesture of goodwill to the Soviet bloc. But it was a very low-key gesture: the US Secretary of State, officially on 'holiday' in Europe, handed over the Crown of St Stephen and its accompanying relics to officials in Budapest. There was no ceremony and very little publicity to mark the end (?) of the treasure's adventures.

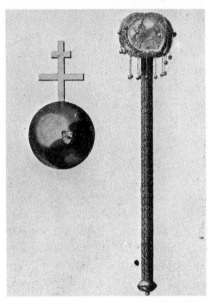

cultural heritage of the lands they conquered. In the early years of German expansion they attempted to give some legality to their plunder of the museums and fine houses of Europe. For instance, in 1937, when a pretext was needed for the removal of the Crown of Charlemagne and certain medieval royal regalia from Vienna, the Nazis had recourse to a fifteenth-century decree by the Emperor Sigismund. Hitler's plans were nothing if not grandiose. He intended to make his own home town of Linz into the cultural centre of the Third Reich and, indeed, the cultural Mecca of the world. He had his own staff of art historians and experts who examined every private and public collection of art and antiquities. Each object was photographed and its description dispatched to the Führer so that he could decide whether or not it was worthy of his personal Xanadu.

This systematic looting and cataloguing went on until the last days of the war. At the end of 1942, Germany's over-extended frontiers began to buckle. There followed several months of withdrawal and retrenchment, but by the close of 1943 British and American forces were advancing through Italy and Greece and the Russians had turned the eastern front. Despite this mounting pressure, the Nazis continued to devote transport, armed guards and administrative personnel to the acquisition of artistic treasures. Works of art from Neapolitan collections were stored at Monte Cassino, the scene of a long and bloody Allied siege. When the stronghold fell in 1944, the Germans removed their precious loot to the Vatican. During the same retreat the Nazi 362nd Infantry Division removed three hundred and seven paintings from the great galleries of Florence and hid them at various locations in the South Tyrol. The work was done hastily, and months later advancing Allied troops found the precious objects stored in conditions which could not but be detrimental to them. A number of paintings, for example, were roughly crated and stacked in a garage at Campo Tures.

In a different category from *objets d'art* and antiquities is the looting of cash, bullion and articles of intrinsic value from banks and private houses. The Second World War was the first total conflict in the history

In 1944 some German soldiers stationed at Salonika in Greece were digging some field works when they discovered what turned out to be an early fourth-century female statue. The Nazis carried out a great deal of unauthorized excavation, using local labour, but this was one of their more important finds. They used the discovery as an opportunity for propaganda: they handed it over to the Greek authorities to demonstrate how sensitive they were to national heritage, unlike the Allies, who, they claimed, were currently raping the public and private collections of Italy. However, shortly afterwards, the statue somehow found its way to Vienna.

National Treasures Go Underground

'Deep in the heart of the mountains somewhere in Britain there lie buried in caves the most priceless treasures...' So began one wartime newspaper report describing the concealment of thousands of masterpieces of painting and sculpture removed to places of safety to protect them from the ravages of war, and from the grasp of Adolf Hitler.

It was an immense operation. Every piece had to be carefully packed, catalogued and transported to its secret destination. But much more than that was entailed: the atmosphere in the underground chambers had to be carefully regulated. Centuries-old masterpieces are sensitive to very slight variations of temperature and humidity, so the haste necessary to the successful conclusion of the operation had to be contained while heating and humidifying plants were installed. Then, away the trucks rumbled, with their police or army escort, to those caves deep in the Mendips, the Cheviots, the Pennines and elsewhere.

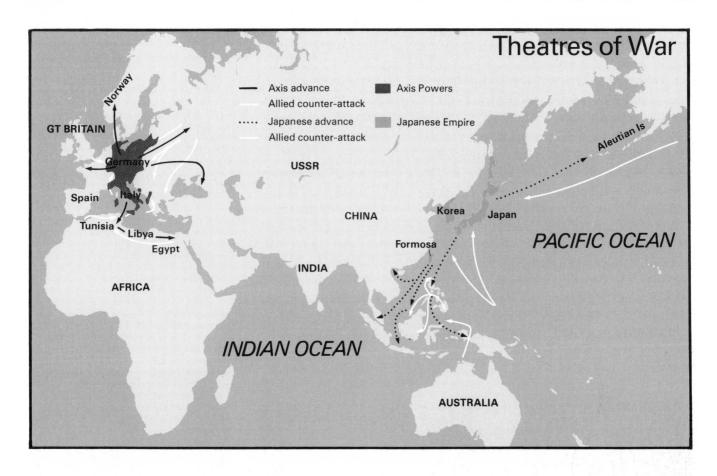

Theatres of War

Axis advance
Allied counter-attack
Japanese advance
Allied counter-attack
Axis Powers
Japanese Empire

Norway
GT BRITAIN
Germany
Spain Italy
Tunisia Libya
Egypt
AFRICA
USSR
CHINA
INDIA
Korea
Formosa
Japan
Aleutian Is
PACIFIC OCEAN
INDIAN OCEAN
AUSTRALIA

of the planet. It involved every member of the committed nations and it covered much of the surface of the globe. It was hugely expensive to all participating countries and, therefore, it was a prime task of every advancing army to possess reserves of gold, silver and currency in order to support its own war effort and to deny such valuables to the enemy. When the Japanese advanced through Malaya and Singapore in 1941–2 they accumulated plunder which, some years ago, was estimated to be worth almost £3,000,000,000.

At the conclusion of the war the victorious powers spent years recovering loot from various hiding places. The British and Americans set up special commissions to restore treasures to their rightful owners. It was a long, difficult and not entirely successful operation. In those territories under Soviet control the situation was simpler: all war loot became the property of the state.

So much for the 'official' story of the Second World War treasures. It is against this background that the hundreds of stories of private hidden hoards and military plunder must be seen. Citizens throughout Europe and Asia buried their precious objects to prevent them falling into the hands of the conquerors. Generals enriched themselves and then concealed their loot when the tide of war turned against them. Private soldiers carried off personal trinkets. For example, a number of Italian paintings known to have been housed at Monte Cassino were never recovered. Greed, fanaticism, political idealism – the years 1939–45 provided them with ample scope. And one result was the unprecedented number of treasures looted, concealed, recovered, concealed again or lost, perhaps for all time.

Long after the war, little treasures continued to turn up. In 1961 workmen demolishing houses at St Mary Axe in the City of London found an old wall safe. Inside were £1 and £5 notes done up in bundles whose bands were stamped with the date 1944. The face value of the notes was £5,500.

On the Trail of Nazi Treasure

King Peter escaped in the nick of time. His treasure did not. The ruler of Yugoslavia stayed as long as possible in his country but in March 1941 he was forced to flee before the advancing Wehrmacht. Acting on information received, the Nazis stormed up the steep scarp leading to the monastery of Nicsic at five o'clock one morning. They went from room to room, hoping to find the king. At last they came upon a chamber containing a table on which were the remains of a hastily consumed breakfast. They had missed Peter II by only a few hours. But Patriarch Gavrilo, the head of the Yugoslav Church, was there and the Germans bullied him, believing that he knew the whereabouts of the king's gold. The old man led them down the mountainside to a solid iron door set in the rock. The Germans rushed in, only to find themselves in the monastery's larder. In the cool, dry interior were sacks of flour and sugar, and hams suspended on hooks. But closer examination revealed large chests, packed to the brim with gold ingots. Peter had brought the bullion to this

Long before 1939 the wholesale persecution of the Jews had begun throughout Nazi-controlled territory. This included the confiscation of valuable possessions. Many such Jewish treasures as these books were discovered at Rosenberg Castle, near Hungen, in 1945.

It took US army officials months to sort out the Jewish treasures at Rosenberg Castle and convey them to a safe refuge prior to attempting to locate their rightful owners.

hiding place preparatory to flying it to Cairo. Instead, the gold travelled northwards to the heart of the Fatherland, its consignment meticulously noted in Reichsbank records, like so much other loot. Those records were discovered, at the end of the war, in a salt mine.

On 7 April 1945 a patrol of American GIs was enforcing the curfew in the little market town of Merkers in eastern Germany. They found the local midwife hurrying to a patient. They gave the *frau* a lift in their jeep and she surprised them by saying, 'I suppose you have come for the gold. It's over there.' The surprise of the soldiers was nothing to the shock that some of their comrades received when, acting on the woman's information, they carried out investigations the next day. They were directed to a salt mine. They descended some ninety metres to the galleries and soon found a newly bricked-up opening. Behind it was a huge steel door. When that had been forced open a staggering sight met their eyes. An interconnected series of chambers had each been devoted to a different kind of plunder. One contained bundle upon bundle of banknotes, another works of art, a third canvas sacks packed with bar gold. Also among these underground treasures were the Reichsbank files, which

Vast quantities of silver and jewellery stolen from wealthy Jews were also discovered at Rosenberg.

These silver crowns found at Rosenberg had their part to play in synagogue ritual and the silver knobs were fixed to the scrolls of the Torah, the Jewish law.

were of inestimable value to the Tripartite Commission for the Restitution of Monetary Gold, set up in 1947 to restore Nazi loot to its rightful owners.

But before the bullion, paintings, jewellery, church furnishings and other precious objects could be returned they had to be found. This was why Operation Rattle was set up. It was headed by three army majors who all happened to be peacetime art experts; their task was to locate all hidden hoards in the British sector of occupied Germany and to liaise closely with their American opposite numbers. In over two years the small British unit uncovered eighteen hundred tons of looted artefacts, from the skull of Neanderthal man to French impressionist paintings. They came from castles, caves, dugouts and holes in the ground and they were conveyed to a single depot at Grevenbroich in the Rhineland. Here for a while an incredible motley of fabulous works of art 'rubbed shoulders' – an eleventh-century madonna from Essen Cathedral, a self-portrait by Rembrandt, a tenth-century illuminated codex of the four gospels, and the document recording the marriage of King Henry VIII to Anne of Cleves.

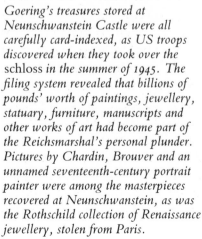

Goering's treasures stored at Neunschwanstein Castle were all carefully card-indexed, as US troops discovered when they took over the schloss in the summer of 1945. The filing system revealed that billions of pounds' worth of paintings, jewellery, statuary, furniture, manuscripts and other works of art had become part of the Reichsmarshal's personal plunder. Pictures by Chardin, Brouver and an unnamed seventeenth-century portrait painter were among the masterpieces recovered at Neunschwanstein, as was the Rothschild collection of Renaissance jewellery, stolen from Paris.

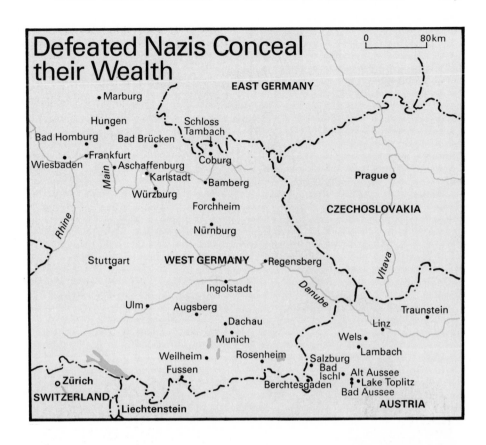

Yet even more treasure came from the American Zone. In Bavaria and Austria there were hundreds of caches. The most impressive was at Neunschwanstein Castle, Füssen. The location of this hoard was revealed by Reichsmarshal Hermann Goering, Hitler's chief of air staff, who had amassed an immense personal collection of looted art treasures. In the closing days of the war he gave orders that as much as possible was to be removed from his *schloss* near Nürnburg and conveyed to a safe hiding place near the Swiss border. At Neunschwanstein the Americans found a jumble of precious objects, many of them still in packing cases. They came from all over Europe – jewellery, pistols, snuff boxes, porcelain, furniture, statuary, paintings: all were of the highest craftsmanship.

About four-fifths of the Nazis' plundered treasures were eventually recovered. Of the remainder, some was undoubtedly appropriated by soldiers – on both sides – and by civilians. Some of it found its way via the black market into private collections. And some still lies concealed, either forgotten about or, if legend is to be believed, guarded by a secret society pledged to the eventual revival of National Socialism. Certain unexplained incidents of the 1950s add colour to the popular belief. In 1955 the body of a young man was found in the forest near Salzburg. He was shot between the eyes and a pistol lay close by. But suicide had to be ruled out when it was discovered that the fatal bullet did not match up with the gun. Shortly afterwards two climbers were stabbed to death in the same area. Near by there were holes in the ground from which chests or boxes seemed to have been removed. These murders occurred in an area where strong local rumour asserts that a band of Hitlerites buried large quantities of gold in the closing stages of the war. Whatever the truth behind these events may be, it seems clear that for some people the plundered treasures of the Second World War continued to hold a fatal fascination long after hostilities had ceased.

Secrets of an Austrian Lake

For years after the end of the Second World War, strong and persistent rumours connected Lake Toplitz, in the Austrian Alps, with Nazi treasure. Many individuals searched its chilly depths and one diver was killed. It was not until 1963 that a properly equipped salvage operation was mounted. It was sponsored by a German illustrated magazine. The salvors operated from a raft moored in the middle of the lake. They used television cameras and underwater lamps to probe the murky depths. After several days, during which the diving platform was moved by stages across the surface of the water, some objects were seen among the mud and rocks of the lake bottom. They appeared to be crates. Frogmen went down and soon the first of the boxes, rotten but intact, was brought to the surface. What was in it – gold bars, antique silver, uncut gems? No, as the lid was prised off the treasure-hunters found themselves gazing down at bundles of paper. They were banknotes – British five-pound notes of the type in circulation during the 1940s. They were large, austerely printed black on white, and their total face value ran into several million pounds.

What was British currency doing at the bottom of an Austrian lake? The answer reveals one of the more bizarre pieces of Nazi strategy. During the war they made many excellent forgeries of British and American banknotes. They were to be used as ammunition in a form of economic warfare. The theory was that if they could be smuggled into the Allied homelands in sufficient quantities and circulated there, they would undermine the economic system, causing such chaos that the supply of armaments would be considerably hampered. The scheme would have been very difficult to put into operation and it is probably for this reason that it was abandoned. But the forged currency was not dumped in Lake Toplitz until the closing stages of the war.

Secrets of an Austrian Salt Mine

Salt mines seem to have been favourite hiding places for Nazi treasures, probably because they were spacious, dry and cool – as well as secret. Alt Aussee salt mine in the Austrian Tyrol, near Salzburg, was the principal depository of items destined for Adolf Hitler's great Linz collection. Here, examples of every type of craftsmanship mastered by human genius were stored. They had been taken from all over German-occupied territory and they were carefully warehoused – at least they were carefully warehoused during the early years of the war. Row upon row of wooden tiers was constructed. They were numbered and divided into sections. On these shelves the precious objects were placed. Each item was meticulously noted in a ledger. However, once the Nazis were in retreat, looted treasures sent from the endangered areas began to flow into Alt Aussee so rapidly that the system broke down. Crates of uncatalogued works of art were piled indiscriminately wherever there was space.

The rich haul made by the US army at Alt Aussee in 1945 posed complex problems for the finders. Not only was there the enormous task of locating the owners of all the objects – owners who in many instances had been killed or had fled during the recent hostilities – but there was also the difficulty of security. At the beginning everything was moved to Frankfurt. But this was too close to the Iron Curtain, so pieces for which claimants could not rapidly be found were conveyed to the safety of bank vaults in London. The cost of all this was considerable. Fortunately, few of the items had suffered damage, a fact for which the strict rules laid down by the German High Command were responsible. Since Hitler's Aryan philosophy placed the master race at the summit of human cultural achievement, it followed that the guardians of the white man's heritage had to discharge their responsibilities diligently. During the Second World War few significant works of art were lost or suffered serious harm as a result of looting. Many important masterpieces were, of course, lost through military action.

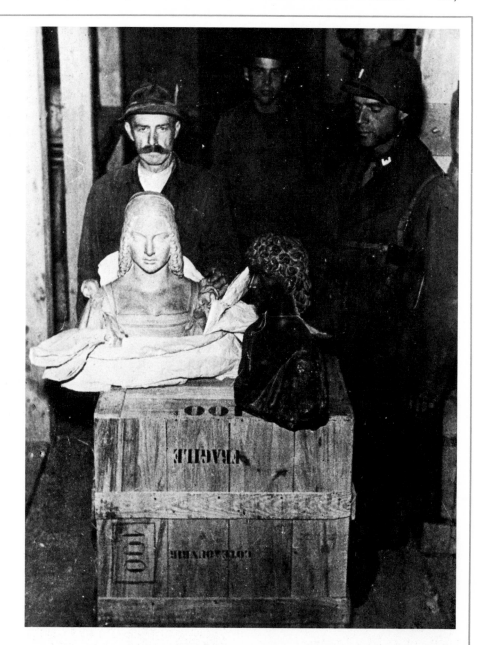

Fugitive Millions

Wartime plunder can be a means of ensuring a very comfortable future for the plunderer but it can also become a liability, threatening the very existence of that future. When a defeated general or political leader is forced to flee, his heavy, cumbersome loot may be an embarrassment and one which he is obliged to dispose of hurriedly. This happened to many fugitives in the closing stages of the Second World War.

Benito Mussolini, the Italian dictator who took his country into the war as an ally of Germany, was overthrown by his own people in July 1943 and imprisoned. However, he was rescued shortly afterwards by Nazi paratroopers and set up in some style as leader of a puppet regime called the Republic of Salo in North Italy. His guards were all Germans and their leader was Captain Otto Kisnat. When his protectors were pushed out of Italy, Mussolini's fate was sealed. He and his mistress got as far as the village of Dongo, near Lake Como, where they were caught by partisans and summarily shot in April 1945. Most of Il Duce's staff escaped, including Kisnat. He was, as he later claimed, carrying the ex-dictator's personal wealth. It was in the form of jewellery, which was relatively easy to transport, and it was packed in two large suitcases. But they hampered Kisnat's escape, so he dumped them in Lake Como during his flight northwards. The ex-bodyguard made his confession to Italian police in 1957 and an official search was immediately made for the treasure. It was unsuccessful.

Erwin Rommel was probably the most brilliant of Hitler's generals. In February 1941 he took over the command of German forces in North Africa, where he earned the nickname of the Desert Fox. Within a year he commanded Libya, most of Tunisia and part of northern Egypt. His Afrika Korps overran all the towns in this area, many of them ancient flourishing commercial centres where Arab and European traditionally met to do business. Considerable loot was accumulated in the form of gold, ivory, jewellery and works of art. But Rommel was eventually defeated at El Alamein in November 1942 and after this victory the Allied forces swept westwards along the coast; soon Rommel's army was confined to Tunisia, where it was gradually squeezed by a two-pronged Allied advance. In March 1943, Rommel was recalled to Germany, and within two months the war in North Africa was over. But not only the General had safely escaped to Europe; the treasure was flown out in the last days before a total Allied air and sea blockade was established. It was taken to Corsica, an island under German military control. From there it disappeared. The most reliable story is that it was taken out into the Gulf of Bastia aboard a German vessel on the night of 18 September 1943 and there dumped in thirty fathoms.

There have, of course, been many attempts to locate Rommel's treasure, some of which are spiced with cloak-and-dagger mystery. In the mid 1960s an ex-Nazi soldier came forward who claimed to have been involved in the concealment of the loot. He interested an American consortium in diving for it, but when the wide expanse of water supposedly covering the six iron chests was reached, his memory proved to be decidedly defective. The later disappearance of this man in mysterious circumstances suggested to some people that he had been silenced by a neo-fascist cell whose members had appointed themselves guardians of the treasure.

The career of Benito Mussolini is, in
many ways, a pattern of the rise and
fall of dictators. As a younger man
(above left) in the early years of the
century he was an ardent socialist and
pacifist, a champion of the people and
their democratic rights in the face of
imperialist, capitalist power groups.
Once in power (1922), his principles
evaporated and Il Duce (above right)
led Italy on a career of aggressive
expansion designed principally to
bolster his own prestige. Corruption
and the misuse of power brought him an
immense personal fortune and it is part
of this which is believed to have been
thrown into Lake Como during
Mussolini's flight in 1943.

Field-Marshal Erwin Rommel was,
in the opinion of many, the finest of
Hitler's generals during the Second
World War. The 'Desert Fox' earned
the respect of his opponents in the
North African campaign. Eventually
the Axis forces were outmanoeuvred
and pinned down in Tunisia. When
defeat was inevitable the Nazi leaders,
according to legend, shipped their loot
across to Corsica in the hope of
contributing to the war effort. It never
reached the mainland.

Generalfeldmarschall Rommel setzte seine Be-
sichtigungsreise im Westen fort und überzeugte
sich auch von der Stärke und Schlagkraft der
deutschen Verteidigungsanlagen an der nieder-
ländischen und belgischen Küste. Zur Besichtigung
von Marineanlagen an der Scheldemündung begab
sich Generalfeldmarschall Rommel an Bord eines
Vorpostenbootes   PK-Aufnahme von Kriegsberichter Jesse

Treasures of the Tiger

They called him the Tiger of Malaya. Tomuyuki Yamashita was a fierce, aggressive, dedicated soldier, feared as much by his own men as by the enemies of Japan. When his country entered the Second World War, Yamashita was given command of the attack on European imperial bases in the South-east Pacific. His army rampaged through the Malay Peninsula and, subsequently, occupied the Philippines. As he progressed, the Tiger amassed a fortune in war loot – gold, silver, platinum, jewellery, and paper currency. He kept his plunder with him in several trucks wherever he went and was still in possession of it all when the tide of war turned in 1944. His army steadily retreated before the advancing Americans but was not defeated. The Tiger was still holding out in the mountains of northern Luzon at the end of the war. He surrendered on 2 September 1945. Five and a half months later he was condemned for war crimes and hanged. But where was the celebrated Yamashita treasure? The General himself gave no indication as to its whereabouts, and it is widely believed that he deposited his loot in several caches along the line of his retreat. But there are other versions of the legend. According to these much of the loot never left Malaysia but was concealed there for possible later use by Yamashita himself or the imperial cause he served.

The Tiger of Malaya, caged at last. Yamashita (facing camera) was undefeated in battle but surrendered after his country laid down its arms. Here he is depicted enjoying a prison meal with other captive Japanese officers. A few months after this picture was taken he was executed for war crimes. He never revealed the whereabouts of the enormous war plunder he had accumulated in Malaya and the Philippines.

Yamashita hoped that his loot could be got back to Japan to help sustain the war effort. Another attempt was made to convey millions of pounds' worth of precious metal to the imperial treasury aboard the Awa Maru *(see next page). Nothing came of these plans. The Japanese dream of Asian domination ended in the nightmare of Hiroshima and Nagasaki. Even Japan's own gold reserves, at the time worth some £125,000,000, fell into American hands.*

Attempts to locate the Tiger's treasure have naturally not been lacking. According to one American journalist, writing in the mid 1970s, the leading loot-hunter of that time was no less a person than Ferdinand Marcos, the Philippine President, who was the principal backer of a syndicate called 'Leber' which, with the aid of old maps, was seeking 172 caches left by the Tiger. Marcos denied the story and his story was supported by Minoru Fukumitsu. This American-born Japanese *had* carried out a search for Yamashita's treasure, an official search. In 1953 he was given access to Japanese and US documents and allowed to interview three hundred witnesses, some of whom were on the General's staff. His researches produced a map which located a hoard at Kiangan, two hundred miles north of Manila. Fukumitsu dug at the specified site and discovered nothing. Yet there certainly had been a large amount of valuable plunder. What had happened to it?

Perhaps the clue lies in a Japanese press report of August 1978. It carried a statement by Masujiro Wada, a sixty-two-year-old citizen of Nagoya who claimed to have been one of five guards set by Yamashita to keep the treasure, or part of it. According to him, a large box of gold items – cups, cigarette holders, bars, plates, necklaces, bracelets, rings, and other objects – was handed over at Kuala Lumpur in 1945 to 'an Australian major with a red moustache'!

National Wealth Beneath the Waves

Legends abound about supposed lost hoards and buried treasure of the Second World War. Unfortunately, when closely examined, most of these stories appear to be without foundation. This is not because many precious items were not hastily concealed during the panic of impending disaster, but because usually too many people were in the know. Most caches of loot were recovered by the authorities or dug up by official salvors soon after the end of hostilities. However, of the whereabouts of two Second World War treasures there is no doubt.

At the entrance to Manila Bay lies the small island of Corregidor, upon which stands a formidable ancient fortress. It was to this place, in 1942, that the Philippine national treasury was brought. The Japanese were advancing steadily and it could not be long before the capital fell into their hands. In February the gold was got away: five and a half tons of ingots were loaded aboard the USS *Detroit* and conveyed, via Pearl Harbor, to America. The paper currency was later burned. This left 15,792,000 silver pesos, at that time worth almost £5,000,000. The enemy was drawing rapidly closer and there was no means of saving the money. The harbour commander therefore decided to sink it in the deepest part of the bay. In the last days of April 1942 the minelayer *Harrison* made a number of night-time sorties and dumped 2,632 boxes in about eighteen fathoms. The defenders, however, had reckoned without the Japanese talent for extracting information. The new masters of the Philippines soon learned the whereabouts of the silver and began salvage operations, using prisoners of war as divers. But the workers gave their conquerors the minimum possible cooperation, and by the end of 1942 only $2\frac{1}{4}$ million pesos had been raised. Before the war ended a gang of private American treasure-hunters appeared on the scene. They salvaged perhaps half a million pesos before being warned off by the authorities. Later, official expeditions recovered the bulk of the treasure, but it is estimated that about 1,176,000 pesos still lie on the floor of Manila Bay.

A large consignment of Japanese war loot lies in thirty fathoms of water at the bottom of the Formosa Straits. In the early months of 1945 the freighter *Awa Maru* was allowed by the Americans to make three mercy missions to South East Asia, ferrying Japanese wounded back to their homeland. However, the captain also loaded his hold with an immense quantity of loot, intending to smuggle it to Japan to resuscitate the war effort. An unofficial inventory lists the following items among the *Awa Maru*'s cargo: twelve tonnes of platinum, forty cases of art treasures, 150,000 carats of uncut diamonds, forty tonnes of gold bullion, 2,000 tonnes of tungsten and 3,000 tonnes of tin. The *Awa Maru* was three-quarters of the way home when she encountered the US submarine *Queen Fish* on 1 April 1945. Whether what followed was an accident or whether the American navy had discovered the real purpose of the ship's mission has never been quite clear. In any event, the *Awa Maru* was torpedoed fourteen miles off the Chinese mainland. She took to the bottom her precious cargo – and 2,008 human beings. A number of salvage operations have been mounted to find the *Awa Maru*, none of them successful. If the treasure is raised in the near future the salvors could find themselves with a considerable problem on their hands: there are thousands of people still living who might have legitimate claim to many of the plundered items.

When the Awa Maru was sunk she carried to the bottom of the ocean millions of pounds' worth of precious metal that might have enabled the Japanese to prolong the war in the Pacific. Thus finally died the dream of one man, the late Commander-in-Chief of the combined fleet, Admiral Isoruku Yamamoto (opposite left). His genius had engineered Japanese victory from Pearl Harbor until 18 April 1943, when his aeroplane was shot down by US fighters on the island of Bourgainville (opposite right).

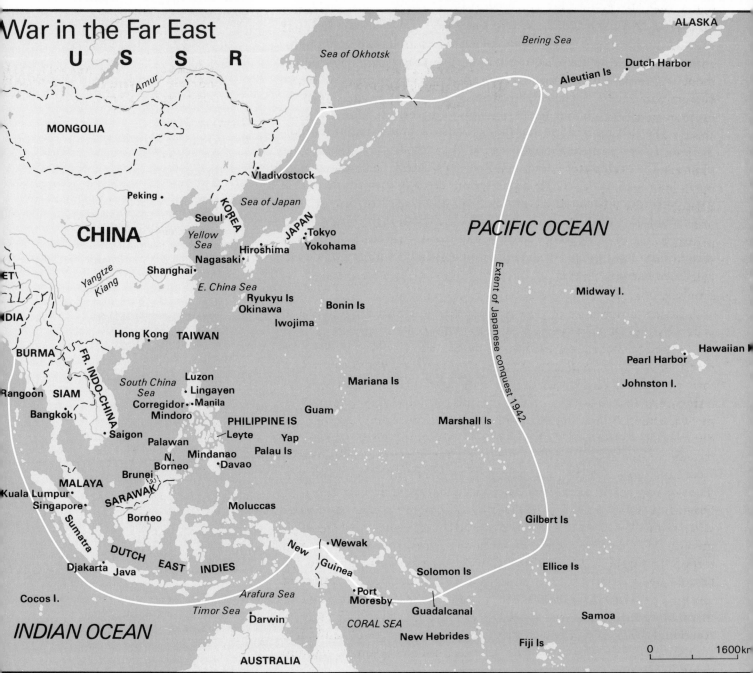

War in the Far East

ALASKA

U S S R

MONGOLIA

Amur

Sea of Okhotsk

Bering Sea

Aleutian Is

Dutch Harbor

• Vladivostock

Peking •

Sea of Japan

KOREA

Seoul •

CHINA

Yellow Sea

JAPAN

•Tokyo
Yokohama

Hiroshima •

Nagasaki •

Shanghai •

Yangtze Kiang

E. China Sea

Ryukyu Is
Okinawa

Bonin Is

Iwojima

PACIFIC OCEAN

Midway I.

Hong Kong TAIWAN

ET

DIA

BURMA

FR. INDO-CHINA

Extent of Japanese conquest 1942

Hawaiian I

Pearl Harbor

Johnston I.

Luzon
South China Sea   • Lingayen

Rangoon SIAM
Corregidor • Manila

Bangkok •

• Saigon

Mindoro

PHILIPPINE IS

• Leyte

Palawan

Yap

Guam

Mariana Is

Marshall Is

Kuala Lumpur •

Singapore •

N.
Borneo

Brunei

MALAYA

SARAWAK

Borneo

Mindanao
• Davao

Palau Is

Moluccas

Gilbert Is

Sumatra

DUTCH EAST INDIES

New

• Wewak

Guinea

Solomon Is

Ellice Is

Djakarta Java

Cocos I.

Arafura Sea

Timor Sea

• Port
Moresby

Darwin

CORAL SEA

Guadalcanal

New Hebrides

Samoa

Fiji Is

INDIAN OCEAN

AUSTRALIA

0   1600km

Finders and Seekers

The Phoenix Treasure

There are those who seek for buried treasure, with or without success, and there are those who find it quite by accident. The story of the Boscoreale Treasure involves men from both categories. The village of Boscoreale lies in the quiet Campanian countryside near the peak of Vesuvius. In 1876 one of the modest landowners of the region was excavating the foundation of a new wall when he discovered some amphorae and a pattern of ancient stonework. He was immediately excited. Archaeological exploration of nearby Pompeii had been in progress for over a century, during which time many interesting – and valuable – finds had been made. Unfortunately, only a corner of the old building appeared to lie within Signor Pulzella's property, so he approached his neighbour for permission to dig on the adjoining land. This was stoutly refused and thus the excavations came to an abrupt end.

So matters remained for almost three decades. By then the original actors in the drama were dead, and Pulzella's family had a new neighbour, Vincenzo de Prisco. He began serious digging towards the end of 1894 and soon uncovered the ground plan of a large Roman villa, one which had obviously been engulfed by volcanic ash at the same time as Pompeii. The discoveries of human and animal remains told the pathetic story of the last minutes of the villa's inhabitants before tragedy overwhelmed them in 79 AD.

The celebrated skeleton goblets from the Boscoreale Treasure. Nothing is known about these macabre relics. Perhaps they were memorials of some dead loved one. There was certainly a sinister appropriateness about their discovery in the ruins of a house which death visited so suddenly and horribly.

This pleasingly simple vase from the Boscoreale Treasure is decorated with foliage and birds.

The mistress of the house had died upon her bronze-framed bed. Her body still bore her jewellery of gold and topaz. A slave lay sprawled in a nearby corridor with the few coins which constituted his fortune. Many household and personal items were discovered, all of archaeological interest and some of intrinsic value.

On Easter Saturday 1895 the workmen were waiting for Signor de Prisco to pay them their wages. Having nothing else to do, they decided to try opening the entrance to the storage tank below the villa's wine-pressing room. Where a wooden trapdoor had once existed there was now only a hole part-filled with a pile of ash. However, when they had removed this they discovered that the vault beneath was clear of encumbrance. One of them, a man called Michèle, slipped through the opening to see what he could find. In the dim light he saw the remains of a man. When death overtook this Roman he had been crouching over some objects he had dropped and which still lay scattered about him, objects with the unmistakable gleam of gold – a chain, bracelets, earrings, and coins, hundreds upon hundreds of coins. Passing beyond the fallen figure, Michèle could just discern, against the cellar's end wall, a pile of utensils – bowls, cups, basins, ewers and dishes – fashioned in what he knew to be age-blackened silver.

Michèle had to think quickly. Once he let his workmates know what he had found, they would be down helping themselves with greedy enthusiasm. He stood to gain more by secrecy. He staggered back to the entrance, gasping and calling to his friends to pull him up. Once out, he reported that the air was too stale to allow the vault to be examined immediately. But later, when he was alone with his employer, he revealed all. The two men returned at dead of night and removed the Boscoreale Treasure (the entire portable wealth of a well-to-do Roman family). De Prisco sold the gold and silver to a Neapolitan dealer and paid Michèle handsomely for his discovery – and his silence.

Perhaps he paid too well. Soon afterwards the labourer went on a drinking spree and began boasting of his discovery. Word reached the Italian government, but de Prisco and the dealer were by then safely in Paris. Forty-one choice items from the Boscoreale Treasure were offered for sale to the Louvre and, with the aid of Baron de Rothschild, were bought for the then staggering sum of half a million francs. Most impressive is the first-century silverware, including a splendid table service.

Interestingly, a similar treasure was discovered in similar circumstances at Pompeii in 1930. Doctor della Corte, carrying out excavations in one of the more impressive dwellings, the 'House of Menandro', also discovered an underground chamber. The family treasures brought to light there included a silver table service embossed with representations of the Labours of Hercules. But there was also a wealth of personal jewellery, coins and magnificent luxury items.

The terrible tragedy of the eruption of Vesuvius in 79 AD has ironically preserved for posterity a number of beautiful pieces of silverware from the finest period of Roman craftsmanship. The ewer and dishes shown here, with their mythological figures in raised relief, are among the loveliest items of the Boscoreale Treasure.

Two more magnificent items from the Boscoreale Treasure.

The Hen and Chicks

Discovered treasure often brings out the worst in people, and nothing illustrates this better than the story of the Hen and Chicks (or, to give them their Romanian name, the *Closca cu Pui*). They were three gold brooches of barbaric design lavishly set with emeralds, garnets, sapphires, turquoises and pearls, which formed part of a hoard of Visigothic treasure discovered near the Transylvanian village of Petrossa in 1837. In the spring of that year two quarrymen, Ion Lemnar and Stan Avram, were cutting limestone from the hills high above their home when they saw, within a cleft, the glint of something that was not rock or earth. When they had made a hole big enough to crawl through they found a pile of gold ornaments, many encrusted with jewels. They were heavy objects containing a large amount of metal, some wrought in that crude and ebullient style which typifies the Gothic conquerors of the fourth and fifth centuries, others of a more refined, Byzantine workmanship. There were twenty-two pieces in all – brooches, torcs, dishes, collars, ewers and bracelets – with a combined weight of over thirty kilograms. They constituted the greatest buried hoard discovered up to that time, and in all probability they dated from the end of the fourth century AD.

The peasants, of course, realized nothing of the treasure's antiquity or value. The mountains were alive with spirits, vampires and demons. What goblin or wizard might own this treasure and what vengeance might he exact if they tampered with it? Yet eventually cupidity obviously conquered superstition. They bundled the ancient objects together, wrapped them in cloth and, taking care not to be seen by their neighbours, hurried home. They concealed the treasure in their house.

Occasionally, they made use of items to meet their domestic needs: a strip of gold was torn from a dish to plug a hole in an iron pot; a golden chain was exchanged for a bottle of liquor. Otherwise the hoard remained unmolested – a secret pleasure and a constant anxiety. Then came another shock. They were told to evacuate their home; it was scheduled for demolition in furtherance of a road improvement scheme. Lemnar and Avram were forced to take their kinsmen Nicholas and George Baciu into their confidence, and George hid the treasure in his house. A secret shared is a secret no longer. Rumours began to spread. At length they reached the ears of unscrupulous men. The first was Anastasius Verussi, a master mason. He persuaded them to let him take one of the torcs to Bucharest 'for valuation'. In fact, his real intention was to acquire the hoard as cheaply as possible. Verussi reported back the verdict of his fictional experts and obtained most of the treasure for £50. Tragically, Verussi had little more understanding of the treasure's artistic or intrinsic value than did the original finders, and he broke up some of the pieces and hammered others into more convenient shapes. Believing the gems to be of little worth he prised many of them out of their settings and threw them on to a rubbish pit, where they were discovered by children. That was his undoing. A sharp-eyed official noticed peasant children playing with emeralds and pearls, and questioned them closely.

Agents of the Ministry of the Interior now descended on Petrossa and confronted the conspirators with their crime. The original discoverers immediately cracked, and yielded up their few remaining pieces, while Verussi was forced to lead the inquisitors to a hiding place in the bank of the river Calnau. Here they found nine articles. This brought the total number of objects in official hands to twelve out of the original twenty-two. Verussi persuaded the agents (or perhaps bribed them) that the rest of his cache had been washed away in a spring flood. Certainly this unscrupulous rogue was the only conspirator to benefit from the discovery of the *Closca cu Pui.* Avram, Lemnar and the Bacius were beaten and thrown into prison. Before long, Avram and Lemnar died there. But when we hear of Verussi, some years later, it is as an established businessman of considerable importance.

The Hen and Chicks and their companion pieces were lodged in Bucharest Museum; they constituted one of Romania's proudest treasures. But their adventures were far from over. One night in 1875 a man called Pontczesco concealed himself in the room above that in which the treasure was housed. He tore up the floorboards, broke through the ceiling and made off with the entire hoard. In order to conceal it successfully – in the back of his piano – he had to inflict further damage on some pieces. Fortunately the police discovered it before the thief had time to dispose of it. During the First World War the treasure was moved further east for safety, to the Moldavian town of Iasi, not far from the Russian border. It escaped the Germans, but not the Bolsheviks. Sometime during the upheaval of the Russian Revolution the *Closca cu Pui* disappeared; it has never been seen since. Perhaps it was melted down to finance the workers' cause. Perhaps it still lies concealed, once more entombed by familiar earth and rock. Either way, it is now immune to the greed, violence and idealism of men.

The only picture which survives of the now lost Visigothic treasure, the Hen and Chicks. The discovery of these gold, gem-encrusted brooches brought misery and death to the peasants who discovered them in Romania almost 150 years ago.

Jewellery of a Nubian Queen

A decade after Howard Carter opened the tomb of Tutankhamen, other archaeologists made a series of discoveries further up the Nile which were scarcely less stunning and arguably more important to the world of historical scholarship. When the original Aswan Dam was scheduled to be heightened in 1933, the Egyptian Department of Antiquities set in hand an urgent campaign to rescue as many sites as possible from the impending flood. Among them were groups of tumuli on either side of the Nile at Ballana. Walter Emery, who supervised the excavation, expected to find graves of Nubian people of the Roman period – people who lived on the southern fringe of the empire. He also expected that they would have been well rifled by ancient tomb-robbers.

There was, indeed, evidence that plunderers had been at work but they had obviously been thwarted by the hard-baked mud of which the mounds were built; the chambers beneath were, for the most part, intact. And what treasures met the excavators' eyes! One of the ancient tribesmen had been accompanied into death by his animals. The skeletons of forty-six dogs were found with silver bells on their collars, and around the remains of a horse lay beautiful silver and jewelled harness. Further into the tomb, Emery discovered silver plates and bowls, golden rings, seals, earrings and a superb necklace. There was a bronze standing lamp in the form of a statue of Apollo, a gaming board of wood, inlaid with ivory, complete with dice and counters, and a treasure chest inlaid with

One of the most exciting archaeological finds of the twentieth century was made at Ballana on the Nile in 1933–4. An official Egyptian excavation of the Nubian tombs of the Byzantine period discovered that the graves had largely escaped plunder. The body of a king still lay where it had been placed with a massive jewelled silver crown on his head. His queen was surrounded by precious objects: silver ewers, bracelets, necklaces, anklets and earrings. She too had an impressive silver crown, set with carnelians.

JEWELLERY OF A BYZANTINE - NUBIAN QUEEN:
MORE TREASURES FROM A MYSTERIOUS EGYPTIAN CEMETERY.

A SILVER CROWN SET WITH CARNELIAN; FOUND ON THE HEAD OF A NUBIAN QUEEN OF THE BYZANTINE PERIOD: A MASSIVE TREASURE FROM AN INTACT ROYAL BURIAL. (10 IN. HIGH.)

GRACEFUL VESSELS OF SILVER FOUND WITH THE QUEEN'S BURIAL AT BALLANA: TWO OF THE MANY BRONZE AND SILVER VESSELS WITH WHICH THE CHAMBER WAS STORED. (12 IN. HIGH.)

ONE OF THE MANY MAGNIFICENT BRACELETS FOUND ON THE QUEEN'S ARMS: A SILVER EXAMPLE, SET WITH CARNELIAN, BERYL, AGATE, AND GARNET. (4½ IN. AT HIGHEST PART.)

JEWELLERY OF THE QUEEN: SILVER EARRINGS; A TOE - RING DECORATED WITH A FLY AMULET; AND (BOTTOM LEFT) A FINGER-RING WITH INSET JEWELS.

A SILVER BRACELET FROM THE QUEEN'S ARM: TREASURE FROM A ROYAL TOMB WHICH WAS FORTUNATE IN ESCAPING SPOLIATION BY ROBBERS. (4½ IN. ACROSS.)

WE are able to give on this page further illustrations of the remarkable treasures found in a Byzantine-Nubian cemetery at Ballana, near Abu Simbel, Upper Egypt, already dealt with in our issues of February 25 and June 24, 1933. The excavations were undertaken by the Department of Antiquities of the Egyptian Government, which is engaged in an Archæological Survey of Nubia, and, in so far as the larger tombs are concerned, were completed last season. This winter attention was directed on the smaller tumuli, all of which were plundered in ancient times, and yet amply repaid excavation, and upon one

A SILVER ANKLET ADORNED WITH LIONS' HEADS FROM THE QUEEN'S ANKLE: A DISCOVERY IN ONE OF THE FEW TOMBS AT BALLANA THAT WERE FOUND INTACT. (4 IN. ACROSS.)

NECKLACES OF SILVER AND GARNET FOUND ENCIRCLING THE QUEEN'S NECK: PART OF THE ROYAL TRAPPINGS WITH WHICH HER MAJESTY PASSED TO THE LOWER WORLD. (ONE-THIRD NATURAL SIZE.)

royal burial which by good fortune had remained intact. This chamber had been built on a higher level than the other tombs, and so had escaped the robbers' attention. It was the burial of a queen. The body had been partially destroyed by water, but the silver and jewelled treasure which clothed it — crown, earrings, necklaces, bracelets, rings, anklets, and toe rings — were in good preservation, and formed the largest complete find of jewellery yet made at Ballana. As mentioned in our previous issues, the discoveries relate to a mysterious half-Christian, half-Pagan Nubian tribe, perhaps the Nobatæ, of the early Christian era.

The rich variety of goods in the Ballana graves, as well as being a feast for the eyes, tells us a good deal about this little-known kingdom. A bronze lamp holder in the form of a statue of Apollo reveals the cultural and commercial links existing with the Roman Empire. A most intriguing find is the gold arrow guard which the king used to protect his left hand. There were several crowns covered in gems and carving. There was an entire set of silver horse harness. All gave ample testimony of the wealth and power of these forgotten rulers.

panels of painted ivory. All these items came from the graves closest to the river, which were the first to be excavated.

Subsequent excavations on the west bank proved to be scarcely less exciting. Emery returned in March 1933 for a last brief season of excavation before the sites disappeared for ever below the Nile flood. He found the tombs of a Nubian king and queen. Each consisted of a complex of four chambers, some containing the bodies of slaves, together with tools, utensils and weapons of bronze, iron, silver and earthenware, all carefully stacked. The royal couple themselves were decked with earrings, necklaces, rings, bracelets, anklets and toe rings. Most impressive of all, however, were the crowns – massive, heavy circlets of solid silver, thickly encrusted with gems, and bearing representations of the Egyptian gods.

Who were these rulers, resplendent in death as in life? No complete answer can yet be given, but the Ballana discoveries furnish us with a number of clues. They speak to us of a turbulent society inhabiting the remotest corner of an empire where various cultures merged. In an earlier epoch Nubia had long been under Egyptian control, and many articles bore representations of Isis, Khnum and others of the ancient gods. But Roman deities also figured prominently in the treasure, as did the Christian symbol of the cross. The kingdom of Meroe flourished in lower Nubia after the decline of Egyptian power but it, too, collapsed about 340 AD. The new dynasty may have come from a people called the Nobatae who retained the Meroitic royal insignia but came under increasing influence from the north until, about 540, they accepted Christianity. Sometime in those two centuries lived and died a wealthy king and queen who passed into obscurity until they and their treasure were rediscovered by twentieth-century archaeologists.

The Well of Sacrifice

Edward Thompson fought his way through the jungle of Yucatán with few companions, little money and a complete belief in the existence of a treasure which most people dismissed as legend. He drew his inspiration from *Relaciónes de las Cosas de Yucatán*, a book by a sixteenth-century Catholic archbishop of the Spanish province. In describing the customs and beliefs of the Mayan people, the writer referred to a sacred well at Chichén-Itzá which was associated with the most appalling rituals. To propitiate the water god, virgins were sacrificed and precious objects flung into the well's slimy depths. The report was dismissed by scholars as the biased account of a Christian missionary anxious to present the indigenous culture in the worst possible light. Water, they pointed out, was very scarce on the limestone plateau of central Yucatán. The natives would not be so foolish as to pollute their only source with bodies and other matter which would decompose.

Thompson was a young American working at the US consulate at Mérida in the closing years of the nineteenth century. Mexican archaeology was in its infancy and there were lost cities, jungle-choked temples and burial sites in plenty to fascinate anyone interested in the country's pre-Columbian past. But Thompson, after visiting many Mayan centres, remained obsessed by the gruesome legend of Chichén-Itzá. He had seen the sacred *cenote* (a water hole formed by the collapse of the limestone roof into an underwater stream). It was unprepossessing – a murky, stagnant pool surrounded by the luxuriant vegetation of the humid jungle. Yet it was to that spot that he was determined to return with the equipment and skills necessary to probe its secrets. He spent years obtaining the backing and arousing the interest of archaeological bodies in the USA. He took diving lessons and bought suits and pumps. He acquired a mechanical grab, accumulated enthusiastic companions and, in 1904, he returned to Chichén-Itzá.

The *cenote* was about sixty metres across, and its smooth rock sides descended, by Thompson's computation, to approximately twenty metres beneath the surface. At one side there was a stone platform. It was from this, Thompson calculated, that the priests of Chac had flung the maiden brides chosen for their master. In order to narrow the area of search he had a tree bough cut, about the size and weight of a human body. He fixed a rope to this and cast it repeatedly into the well. This gave him a circle beyond which it would have been impossible for the sacrificial victims to have fallen. Over the spot he fixed his dredge, operated by a hand winch. The steel jaws descended into the pool and buried themselves in the centuries-old accumulation of sludge at the bottom. The workmen bent to the winch handle and up came the bucket. On the edge of the *cenote* it deposited a mass of slime and half-rotted vegetation. Eagerly Thompson sifted through it. Nothing. Time after time, day after day the grab scooped muck from the depths of the well. No precious object, no shred of evidence of ancient rituals emerged. Thompson's faith began to falter:

> I began to get nervous by day and sleepless by night. 'Is it possible,' I asked myself, 'that I have let my friends into all this expense and exposed myself to a world of ridicule only to prove, what many have contended, that these traditions are simply old tales, tales without any foundation in fact?'

In addition to the cenote at Chichén-Itzá, explorers discovered the remains of ornately carved temples, and even a seated stone figure marking the grave of a high priest.

The first hint that he was right and the sceptics wrong was when he dredged up some balls of yellowish-white resin. When exposed to the camp fire they smouldered and gave off a sweet smell. They were pieces of incense. And incense meant ritual. Then, one by one, up came the treasures. There were parts of human skeletons. There were gold discs, rings and animal carvings. But the bottom of the well was pitted with holes and it was clear that many items were eluding the dredge. Thompson decided to dive, sharing the work with a Greek sponge diver called Nicholas whom he had hired for the purpose. They found themselves working in a large pit scooped out of the mud by their dredging operations. Visibility was *nil* and the threat of the mud walls collapsing on them was ever present. But they did probe the *cenote*'s floor more efficiently, bringing up objects of jade, gold and gold–copper alloy, weapons of metal and stone, and even fragments of fabric. The treasure, shipped by Thompson to Cambridge, Massachusetts, for display in the Peabody Museum, was impressive in its intrinsic value and even more so in the information it conveyed about the ancient Mayan civilization.

But the sacred well had not yielded all its secrets. Other expeditions were made to Chichén-Itzá, culminating in an attempt by professional salvors working for the Mexican National Institute of Anthropology and History to drain the *cenote* in 1967–8. This failed, but by pouring in chemicals the excavators managed to clear the water. Using air-lift and suction-pump equipment, the team discovered carved stone from the original temple, skeletal remains which suggested that not only young women had been sacrificed, and over 1,100 artefacts of gold, silver and jade.

The Quest for Vilcabamba

'The lost treasures of the Incas' – ever since the sixteenth century men have been talking about them, writing about them and going in search of them. Francisco Pizarro and his *conquistadores*, in the first flush of triumph, extracted millions of pounds' worth of gold from the rulers and priests of the great Andean empire. Most of that they acquired by holding the Lord Inca, Atahualpa, to ransom. Treasure flooded in from cities and temples throughout the land to save the life of the god-king. After Atahualpa had been treacherously put to death, his subjects, fully realizing now the greed and faithlessness of their adversaries, hid their ancient treasures and sacred relics. In succeeding decades and centuries the Spaniards located and looted many hoards and religious sites. But not all – or so the legends insist.

At Cuzco, Pizarro's envoys discovered the immensely rich principal shrine of the sun god, completely sheathed with plates of gold and filled with precious ornaments and ritual objects. Orders were given that everything of value was to be sent to Cajamarca. Much of it was, but somewhere on the mountain road the priests diverted part of the llama train and hid their most sacred relics. Many serious quests have been made for this treasure. One set of adventurers tried to drain Lake Urcos, south of Cuzco. Other seekers have contemplated plumbing the depths of Lake Titicaca and another lake near Sorata, but these deep, steep mountain pools defy even the most sophisticated equipment, and the local people can also be defiant: one Sorata expedition came to a halt when the Indians threatened revolt. Explorers pursuing the great golden

Machu Picchu, the most dramatic of all the 'lost' Inca cities. Scholars seeking the last Inca stronghold believed for many years that this was it. But Hiram Bingham was among those who thought otherwise. Pressing deeper into the Andes in search of Vilcabamba, he at last found the remains of overgrown temples and dwellings.

Hiram Bingham's expeditions unearthed the ruins of a number of ancient villages and buildings of the Incas. When his men cleared the jungle from the great rock of Yurac-rumi, Bingham was able to examine it and identify it as Chuquipalta, the chief shrine of the lost Inca kingdom of Vilcabamba.

The quest for lost Inca treasures

statue of the Inca Huayna Capac among the dizzy heights and tortuous tracks of Azongaro were forced back by rocks, boulders and other missiles.

Most persistent of all, however, are the legends of a lost city cut off by high mountains and thick jungle where descendants of the last Inca ruler established an independent state and 'enjoyed scarcely less of the luxuries, greatness and splendour of Cuzco ... For the Indians brought whatever they could get from outside for their contentment and pleasure'. From the mid eighteenth century onwards explorers, undeterred by the appallingly difficult terrain, have sought the last stronghold of the Incas. Since 1800 no less than fifteen major expeditions have set out to find it. The most important were those led between 1909 and 1915 by the American archaeologist Hiram Bingham. It was he who discovered the most dramatic Inca city remains, those of Macchu Pichu (see opposite). Pressing on beyond this site, Bingham located at Chuquipalta a shrine to the sun god and knew that he had found the last great centre of Inca worship. Bingham and later explorers mapped out a complex of ancient towns, long since swallowed up by the jungle. But no one found any treasure. As late as 1963 a group of archaeologists, convinced that even greater wonders still lay deep in the rain forest, were dropped by parachute thirty miles beyond the previous excavations. But they found nothing. It seems that Vilcabamba, the last Inca stronghold, is to be identified with the place now known by the Indians as Espiritú Pampa – 'the Plain of the Spirits'. Here, far up the Pampaconas River, hopelessly choked with vegetation, are the outlines of streets, palaces and temples of exquisite workmanship. But, alas for human greed, Vilcabamba, discovered by Bingham in 1911, was a burned city. Careful research in Spanish sources reveals the sad fact that it was destroyed by the Incas themselves in the face of invasion in 1572. The Indians, so the record runs, destroyed their idols, storehouses, homes and places of pleasure, 'setting fire to all that they could not take'. But perhaps they did take their treasure and perhaps at some spot now covered by jungle ...

The Headline Makers

Scarcely a month passes without someone, somewhere, retrieving buried or sunken treasure. In 1967 a Danish farmer, Aage Bang, was tilling his fields when his plough scattered dull silver over the glistening earth. He had stumbled upon an incredible hoard of 40,000 fourteenth-century coins. In the same year an English farm worker, Peter Beer, engaged in much the same task near Maidstone, Kent, found a gold cross mounted with red stones. It was of a similar age to the coins found in Jutland. It, too, had once been the property of a wealthy man, perhaps a bishop or abbot making his pilgrimage to Canterbury. Meanwhile, across Europe, a Hungarian peasant woman was congratulating herself on her good fortune. She had accidentally discovered 1,396 Byzantine gold coins dating from the fifth century AD.

Take another year at random – 1974. A man in Michigan, USA, dug up $384,000. No owner was traced, and it was generally assumed that the money was the proceeds of a crime. The discoverer was allowed to keep half of his find. On the other side of the world some Chinese labourers digging a well literally stumbled upon the terracotta army that formed part of the imperial burial at Mount Li. And an English schoolboy goggling off the Devon coast saw a cannon on the sea bottom. It turned out to be a fine seventeenth-century bronze saker, worth £7,000.

Not all treasures consist of precious metal and gems or even of ivory, jade, ancient marble and terracotta. In December 1976 the British press was running the story of a pile of papers conjectured to be worth half a million pounds. During reconstruction work in the basement of a London bank – Barclays of Pall Mall – a brass-studded trunk was discovered. It had not been lost so much as forgotten about for over a hundred and fifty years. It had once been the property of a young man of good family and profligate habits, Scrope Beardmore Davies. This gentleman moved freely in social and literary circles and was the friend and intimate of many prominent men and women, among them the poets Byron and Shelley. Davies kept up a lively correspondence with these literary giants, who lived much of their life abroad, and acted as an unofficial agent for them with London publishers. The poor Davies was eventually forced to leave the country to escape his gambling debts and it was then that he deposited the trunk with his bank for safe keeping. It contained all his private papers – letters, bills, notes and sketches – and is a rich mine of information about contemporary customs, events and per-sonalities. Much more important, though, are the manuscripts. They include an original in Byron's own hand of part of his epic *Childe Harold's Pilgrimage* and two hitherto unknown poems by Shelley. Any monetary value put upon this unique collection is purely arbitary. Its full import-ance will only emerge gradually as scholars work on it.

From that same year, 1976, comes the delightful story of little Gary Fridd. He was just nine years old and he was fishing for tadpoles – without permission – in a stream on Lord Bolton's land at Gilling West, Yorkshire. Suddenly, he noticed something much more interesting than baby frogs: a rusty old sword. Proudly he carried it home, and his parents took him along to the local museum to show it to the experts. Their excitement was as great as Gary's when they realized that his find was a ninth-century silver-mounted weapon in a remarkably fine state of preservation. The discovery was reported, and a coroner's jury sat to

Great Spanish treasure riddle

THE STATE of Florida has been accused of losing more than £200,000 worth of treasure taken from a sunken 17th century Spanish galleon.

The loss came to light after a salvage company beat the state government in a court fight over ownership of £1.1 million worth of treasure found in the Nuestra Senora de Atocha which sank off the Florida Keys in 1622.

The state, which claimed the find was made in its territorial waters, had been holding the treasure — including gold coins and a huge emerald since 1973. Now the salvage firm is taking the state back to court to try to recover the losses.

THE SUNDAY EXPRESS August 11 1974

OVERSEAS NEWS

Watergate man uncovers a tale of hidden gold

from HENRY LOWRIE: Washington

A FEW words among the millions said and written during the Watergate investigation have brought to light a strange story of a Jesuit priest, a band of massacred Indians and a treasure in gold and jewels reported to be worth 225,000 million dollars.

The words were spoken by John Dean, former counsel to ex-President Nixon, when he told the Senate judiciary committee of a meeting between F. Lee Bailey, one of America's top criminal lawyers, and the then attorney-general, John Mitchell.

According to Dean, Bailey told Mitchell he represented people who knew where there was a cave containing 100 tons of gold bullion. He wanted Federal immunity for his clients for unspecified crimes—presumably illegal possession of gold and trespassing on federal lands—during the gold search.

But even without its Watergate back-drop, the original ingredients of the story were bizarre enough for any fictional adventure.

THERE was Philippe La Rue, the handsome, adventurous son of a wealthy French nobleman, who became a Franciscan monk when a love affair went sour. He emigrated to Mexico in 1797. In the early eighteen hundreds he and his forty-strong colony were massacred by Spanish dragoons.

THERE was an Apache Indian chief, Victorio, said by some to be greater than the famed Cochise and Geronimo, who was wiped out with 300 of his warriors by the United Cavalry in 1880.

AND THERE was Milton Noss, a hunting guide, brawler and alleged con-man, shot to death in 1949 by his partner in the gold search.

Deerhunt

According to local legends La Rue led his group to a rich gold vein, the Soledad Mine, after he had heard about it from a dying soldier he had befriended.

If he found it he did a first class job in mining it, refining it and hiding it before being wiped out by the Spanish. For only the legend existed until 1937, when Noss, serving as a deer hunting guide, came across a mine shaft under a flat rock.

When the deer hunt was over, Noss with his wife Ova, went back. He scrambled down the shaft and found a series of caves hundreds of feet deep.

Mrs. Noss, who is now 78, has said since the shooting of her husband this partner had acted in self defence that he had found the gold. With it were church records, boxes of manuscripts, 27 human skeletons and jewels, probably hidden by Victorio, who may also have looted the original Soledad mine.

When Noss tried to blast open a blocked passage in the caves all he did was to produce a cave-in that sealed the treasure inside.

There the matter seemed to rest until John Dean was testifying before the Senate Watergate Committee.

Gold sample

Bailey had approached John Mitchell because Victorio Peak, renamed after the Indian chief, is within the United States Army White Sands missile range. Secretary of the Army, Howard Callaway, refused to let treasure seekers on to the range and said there was no gold there anyway.

But Bailey said his group knew where the gold was hidden. The lawyer refused to identify his gold hunter but said they had produced a sample gold bar to support their story.

When the army denied the gold hunters permission to enter the missile range, New Mexico Governor Bruce King said the whole thing was off.

But Lee Bailey, who never takes no for an answer, flew to Albuquerque in New Mexico and won a court decision giving his clients two days to prove they know where the stuff is hidden.

If they can't do it within that time limit Bailey will move to a higher court.

He told me — "We are not giving up. Imagine all that gold just lying there! How can you give up on that?"

But even if the mine there is another legal snag. Mrs Noss has filed a claim in Santa Fe claiming that whoever finds the gold it is hers anyway.

ON THE TRAIL OF THE DEATH CURSE MINE

Apache Junction, Arizona

ALL round loomed the hostile grey peaks of Superstition Mountain.

Alone in the craggy wilderness, with only an Indian Thunder God for company, I kept remembering the warnings the townsfolk had given me: "Watch out for Crazy Jake—he's got a gun. And beware of the Apache curse."

A rattlesnake slid for cover beneath a rock as I nervously trod the narrow trail in the footsteps of a thousand men who have tramped the great canyons of Superstition Mountain with the gleam of gold lust in their eyes.

I had joined the search for the legendary Lost Dutchman Mine.

Back in the Golden Nugget bar in Apache Junction, tobacco-chewing old - timers had cackled gleefully as I set out with my pick and shovel.

"Lookee here sonny if you find the Dutchman you high-tail it back here and buy us all a beer, y'hear? They'll accept gold nuggets over the bar. Oh, yessir!" And

Still looking . . . Prospector Doc Rosecrans has been searching for the mine for 30 years.

they slapped their thin thighs with delight at the thought.

For almost 100 years Apache Junction has played sceptical host to an endless stream of treasure hunters in search of the Lost Dutchman Mine.

The dusty Arizona desert town, some 35 miles east of Phoenix has seen them all . . . the dreamers, the drifters, the desperate. And the dead.

Ghostly

And when the lightning flashes over Superstition Mountain they swear you can hear 'the ghostly laughter of Jake Walz, the Old Dutchman himself.

Walz was an immigrant prospector who arrived in this area in the 1870s.

He vanished among the enveloping cliffs of Superstition Mountain and emerged with a sack full of gold ore and the claim

WAY OUT WEST with Plain JOHN SMITH

that he had found a mine with an 18-inch streak of gold running right through it.

But a curse of death was on the gold.

Almost 30 years earlier the mine had been discovered by Mexican cattle baron Don Miguel Peralta.

He sent a force of 400 men to bring out the precious ore. But the Apaches resentful of this invasion of the lands where their Thunder God dwelt, massacred them in one bloody afternoon.

A young Indian girl who was thought to have led Walz to the mine had her tongue cut out by the Apaches for revealing the secret of the sacred mountain.

Walz himself shot several men who tried to follow him into the mountain. And when the old Dutchman died in 1891 at the age of 83

he took the secret of the mine to his grave.

So today a small army of prospectors still comb the canyons and gold fever runs high.

Try to approach the camp of one miner called Crazy Jake and the barrel of a rifle is pointed straight between your eyes.

The lust for gold can do strange things to a man," explains 62-year-old 'Doc' Rosecrans, who spent 30 years as a "Dutchman hunter."

Feuds

"We've had people killed up on Superstition because of feuds. One guy from Honolulu shot his partner because he thought they'd found gold. Others commit suicide because they get despondent."

Doc lives in the cluttered one-room shack he built as his "temporary" home near the mountain base in 1946. He has a small mine on his property. But his heart is set on finding the Dutchman.

Doc Rosecrans reckons the wealth side of finding the mine wouldn't be so important as being able to go round and say: "Hell, feller, y'know who I am. I'm the guy that found the Lost Dutchman Mine."

The bachelor Doc— "this ain't the kind of business you get married in"—stared at the wooden floor of his small cabin, the shelves crammed with rock samples and maps. "I'll keep looking."

He paused. "Mind you, it can get kind of weird up there in the hills . . ."

And he shivered slightly in the evening gloom as he looked across the desert to Superstition Mountain where a Thunder God stands guard over the forbidden secrets of the Lost Dutchman Mine.

Treasure-hunts and treasure-finds are part of the stock-in-trade of modern journalists. They know that for every person who goes looking for treasure there are thousands who are fascinated by the idea of hidden wealth. And so headlines like these are common. 'On the Trail of the Death Curse Mine' leads into a colourful account of Arizonan prospectors who have searched for years for the Lost Dutchman gold mine, one of the many

pay loads with which American legend abounds. According to the story Jake Walz, a Dutch pioneer, found the rich vein of ore deep in hostile Apache country but died without passing on his secret. Now hopefuls imbued with the same spirit roam Superstition Mountain, feuding among themselves, jealously guarding from encroachers those claims which as yet have revealed little or no gold. Other headline stories are equally sensational.

A legend about Basing House, Hampshire affirmed that in 1645 the then Marquess of Winchester had concealed £3,000,000 worth of gold before surrendering to the besieging army of Oliver Cromwell. In 1963 a metal-detector survey indicated metal on the site of the old chapel. Weeks of digging (left) produced no treasure. Four years later (below) a Danish farmer, Aage Bang, ploughed up some old pots full of about 40,000 medieval silver coins from many countries, later valued at 6,000,000 kroner. The Fishpool Hoard of fifteenth-century gold coins and jewellery caught the public imagination in 1966. The Nottinghamshire workmen who discovered this £250,000 treasure (bottom) failed to report it immediately, and received only a token reward.

decide whether or not it was treasure trove. 'No,' said the representative of the Crown. The sword had almost certainly been lost by its original owner and not deliberately concealed. As no one else, after eleven hundred years, could possibly have a claim to it, it belonged to the boy who found it. Then, enter the hard-hearted lawyers. Gary had been trespassing, they insisted, and therefore had no right to the ancient and doubtless valuable relic. There was, of course, a local outcry but one which Lord Bolton himself hastily silenced. As soon as he knew the full details he commented, 'I would hate to see a fairy story have a sad ending', and he ordered the case to be dropped. At a subsequent auction the Anglo-Saxon sword was bought by the Yorkshire County Museum for £10,000, most of which went into a new bank account for a little boy who had become a celebrity overnight.

Just as track- and field-event records continue to be broken although one might think the limits of human athletic achievement have already been reached, so unexpected treasure finds are made month in and month out when it seems that the supply must be virtually exhausted.

In 1978, Mr Roland Morris followed up his remarkable work on the *Colossus* and the *Association* by discovering the legendary 'Dollar Wreck' in Gunwalloe Cove, Cornwall. Ever since this unnamed Spanish treasure ship sank in the 1780s men have been trying to locate her amidst the sand and swirling currents of this treacherous stretch of coast. Morris's men succeeded and are sanguine of eventually bringing up silver coins, packed by the hundredweight in leather sacks.

Norfolk is a county already rich in Roman treasures but, in June 1980, yet another hoard was discovered. Near Thetford seventy-seven pieces including jewellery and thirty-three silver spoons were dug up. They date from the early fifth century, the last days of imperial rule.

At the same time came news that one of the greatest potential treasures of all had been located. The *Titanic* lies two miles down on the floor of the North Atlantic under pressure of 6,000 lb per square inch. Her exact position was hitherto unknown, and the salvage of her strongroom contents – including tons of bullion and coin – considered quite impossible. Now a costly American expedition claims to have found her and there is talk of raising her with the aid of liquid nitrogen or getting at her valuable cargo using a complex system of machines and underwater cameras.

The Water Newton Hoard

Alan Holmes certainly hit the headlines in 1975. This young amateur archaeologist from Peterborough was exploring a field belonging to a farmer at Water Newton, Huntingdonshire (now Cambridgeshire). He owned a metal detector, but the newly ploughed land was unsuitable terrain for it, so he was relying on his eyes. He was hoping to find pieces of Roman pottery to add to his collection. It was no random search that he was engaged upon. The ground beneath him was the site of the old Roman town of Durobrivae; various finds had been made there before, culminating only a few months previously in the discovery of a pot containing two pieces of silver and thirty gold *solidi* of the fourth century AD. His eye was caught by what seemed to be the edge of an earthenware jar. Closer investigation showed it to be dull metal – lead or pewter, he thought. Digging carefully with his fingers, Mr Holmes found a hoard of dishes, plates and small vessels, some damaged by the plough. He took his cache home, largely out of curiosity, for the objects seemed to have no value or interest. He put it in his garden shed and it was a few weeks before he mentioned the discovery to an archaeologist. Then the excitement began. The pieces were easily recognized as silver, and expert opinion dated them to the early fourth century. Closer examination revealed the Christian symbols and inscriptions on several items. One beautiful bowl carried a Latin verse which reads in translation, 'I, Publianus, your servant, honour your holy sanctuary, O Lord.' The other items, less immediately impressive but even more interesting to the historian and archaeologist, were a collection of personal plaques or medallions. They were in the shape of stylized leaves stamped with Christian symbols. One had an inscription: 'Anicilla has fulfilled the vow which she promised.' Clearly these were items to be hung on chains round the neck or fixed to the clothing to declare the wearer's devotion to the Christian God. The Water Newton Hoard was the earliest deposit of Christian silver ever discovered. It must have been secreted by its owners at the time of Diocletian's persecution (303–5 AD) or during a provincial purge carried out by pagan officials in Britain. At an inquest in September 1975, Holmes' twenty-five pieces of silver were declared treasure trove and acquired for the nation by the British Museum for £39,000. Mr Holmes used part of his reward to open his own shop selling treasure-hunting equipment.

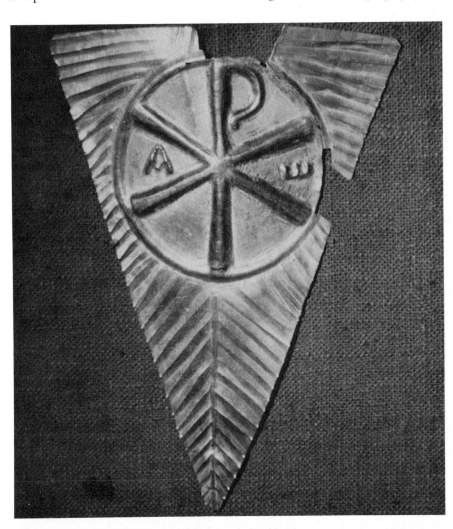

Treasures Still to Find

To numismatists the word 'Vigo' suggests a rather common coin of the reign of Queen Anne. To treasure hunters it means one of the largest caches of gold and silver still held by the sea. In September 1702 the seventeen ships of the Spanish treasure fleet, heavily laden with rich cargo from the Americas and the Orient, lay in Vigo Bay on the north-west corner of the Iberian peninsula. There they were located and attacked by an Anglo-Dutch force of 150 vessels. Too late, the order was given to scuttle the ships. Although some exploded or were burned to the waterline, the attackers were able to plunder their way through floating and half-submerged vessels at will. They left several weeks later with £25,000,000 worth of bullion and merchandise. In England the silver and gold were sent to the mint and a special issue of coins was struck with the word 'Vigo' beneath the Queen's head. So many of these pieces were made that nowadays it is the coins of Anne's reign without the inscription that are the more valuable. The triumphant allies took six prizes of war. HMS *Monmouth* left Vigo towing the *Santo Cristo de Maracaibo*, the

The name of Paul Kruger, the Boer leader, is linked with one of the legendary treasures of South Africa. As British forces closed in on him, he dispatched a consignment of gold and diamonds by sea to Europe. The ship foundered on the Natal coast.

largest and most heavily laden of the Spanish galleons. On the way out of the harbour the prize struck a rock and sank rapidly. Many salvage operations have been attracted to Vigo, and most of the bullion from the other vessels has long since been raised, but the gold and silver of the *Cristo de Maracaibo* still lies at the mouth of the bay beneath seventy metres of sea and several more of mud.

An equally valuable wreck lies off the coast of South Africa. This is the *Dorotea*, which foundered in 1898. The second Boer War was in full spate and it was not going well for the Afrikaners. As the British advanced across the frontier of the Boer republics, the Transvaal leader, Paul Kruger, assembled as much as possible of his country's reserves of gold and uncut diamonds and transported it to the port of Laurenço Marques for shipment to foreign banks. The treasure was entrusted to three small vessels, none of which was destined to complete its journey. On one the crew turned pirate, beached the ship and stole the gold. A second foundered in a storm off Delagoa Bay. She sank in deep water, and her position is unknown. The third was the barquentine *Dorotea*, small and in need of repairs. As there was no time for delay she had to sail as she was. Off Cape St Lucia she ran into a gale, which tore away her sails and rigging.

The quest for the Basing House Treasure continued unabated for many years. In 1965 the owners called on the army for assistance, and frogmen from the Royal Engineers descended into a thirty-metre-deep well in a vain search for the Civil War hoard.

'The Royal Treasure of Dorak'

What became of the 'Royal Treasure of Dorak'? Did it ever exist? Does it exist now? Is it hidden? Dispersed? The story of this strange hoard is a fascinating one. In 1958 a British archaeologist was travelling on a train in Turkey. Suddenly he was stunned to notice that the only other occupant of his compartment, an attractive young woman, was wearing a solid gold bracelet that seemed to be of Bronze Age origin. When he asked if he might see it, the lady gladly obliged and commented nonchalantly that she had several more at home. The girl's name was Anna Papastrati, and she invited him to her house in Izmir where the archaeologist was staggered to discover a pile of golden jewellery and other artefacts which he dated at about 2500 BC. Miss Papastrati told him, quite openly, that the treasure had been illegally excavated from a grave at Dorak, near Troy, and permitted him to make sketches. The archaeologist excitedly reported his adventure to colleagues and, with Miss Papastrati's permission, published his sketches. That was probably a mistake. When the Turkish authorities heard of the Dorak Treasure they stopped the Englishman continuing his work, and there were rumours that he had smuggled the artefacts out of the country. Of Anna Papastrati no trace could be found. The ancient gold of Dorak has never been seen again.

Turkey — land of plundered treasures

The crew escaped in lifeboats, abandoning the *Dorotea* to her fate. She broke in two on the reef and sank in fairly shallow water. There have, of course, been many salvage attempts but all have been bedevilled by breakers, rough weather and sand.

According to impeccable documentary sources, a Jacobite treasure awaits discovery on the shores of Loch Arkaig in the Western Highlands. In the spring of 1746 a ship left France with £35,000 in *louis d'or* to aid the cause of Charles Edward Stuart, the Young Pretender. By the time it arrived, in early May, the bloody battle of Culloden had already been fought and Bonny Prince Charlie's remaining supporters were taking refuge in the hills. The bulk of the money was carried to Achnacarry House at the eastern end of Loch Arkaig to be used by Jacobite chiefs who planned a second uprising. But the English forces moved too fast for the rebels, obliging them to flee, concealing the gold in two major caches. One parcel was buried 'in the wood about a mile from Lochiel's house at the foot of Loch Arkaig'. The other was disposed around the other end of the lake. One bag was put 'under a rock in a small rivulet, the other two parcels in the ground at a little distance'. Of those who knew the secret of the treasure, some sailed to France with the prince shortly afterwards, never to return. Others were captured and executed. Thus, it would seem, at least some of the Loch Arkaig caches are still there.

The tomb of Attila the Hun; General Monck's Treasure in the Firth of Tay; the £10,000,000 worth of gold and gems in the wreck of *Las Cinque*

Chagas, off the Azores; the Singer Hoard of southern Texas – the list of more or less well-documented treasures is endless. We have space for only one more. As well as being a narrative of lost wealth, it may also be regarded as a cautionary tale. In 1939, Dr Watkinson of Hartlepool, Co. Durham, died. In his will he left £10,000 to his only son. It was a considerable sum but it reflected only a fraction of the old man's wealth, most of which lay in his collection of diamonds. Furthermore, there was a condition attached to the inheritance: 'All my jewels are to be put in a box and thrown into the sea two miles north of Hartlepool.' The son contested the will. The advent of war lengthened still further the un-hurried processes of the law, and it was 1948 before judgement was given. Dr Watkinson's will was upheld. Therefore, a boatload of solemn officials made their way to the prescribed area and watched a fortune sink into the North Sea. And the good doctor's reason for arranging this bizarre event? 'I have noticed that jewels are a source of disloyalty, treachery, violence and injustice, and for this reason I consider it a duty to promote the disappearance of such articles for they tend to corrupt human nature.'

Prince Charles Edward Stuart, the Young Pretender – loyal Highlanders put their fortunes at his disposal when he made a bid for the crown in 1745. Money came from France to back his cause. But the cause was lost and so was much of the Prince's treasure.

The Quest Goes on

Divers have found a wreck. It is on a coral bank five miles out in the Red Sea. It could be a ship which foundered in 1917 while on a secret mission delivering gold to Britain's Bedouin allies under the leadership of Lawrence of Arabia. But there is not much time to find out. This stretch of territorial water is due to be handed over by Israel to Egypt soon. It is a small salvage outfit – one American, two Israelis, and a German. Initial dives bring up plates with the name *Dunraven* on them. Lloyd's have no information on a vessel of such name. Perhaps the word on the crockery has no connection with the ship. The search continues. A rival salvage team arrives and has to be warned off. It is difficult to break into the rear portion of the ship, completely overgrown with coral. One of the men makes a conjectural drawing of the vessel, and his colleagues argue over it: 'It's too early to be a 1917 wreck'; 'No, it could have been still in service'; 'It must have lain on top of the reef and been stripped before it sank'; 'No, there is still gold in there.' They all want to believe they have found a treasure ship. They twist every piece of evidence to make it fit that hypothesis. They find a copper name plate – DUNRAVEN. Why have Lloyd's no information on her? 'Because she sank before 1886 when Lloyd's registers start'; 'No, because she was on a secret mission, working under a false name.' Conjecture abounds; work goes on; hope is maintained; optimism reigns. At last, conclusive evidence from the Public Records Office in London: SS *Dunraven*, built at Newcastle in 1873, lost in the shales of Dubal 1876, carrying a cargo of cotton bales which was salvaged before the ship went down. The divers move off to another site. No luck on this occasion. Perhaps next time ...

It is not only in the materialistic West that men get the treasure bug. On Mount Akagi, north of Tokyo, there lives a Japanese family whose members have been seeking a hidden hoard for three generations. The supposed three-trillion-yen treasure was concealed in 1868 when the existing government was overthrown by adherents of the Emperor Meiji. The Mizuno family is convinced that the wealth of the defeated *shogun* is buried on their land, and a century of digging has brought to light one golden statue and the gate from a shrine. The present owner devotes most evenings to his excavations. He has to work for his living by day – until he finds treasure. Not far away, another hopeful fortune-seeker, Mr Izawa, is looking for the site of a medieval warlord's treasure

Japan's troubled history – with frequent periods of warfare between powerful territorial magnates – has left the islands studded with caches of loot and personal treasure buried at times of crisis. The villagers of Churui in Hokkaido have been digging for years for a hoard of bandit plunder believed to have been concealed two hundred years ago. Another treasure is on the site of Matoba Castle, 100 kilometres north of Tokyo. It probably consists of oval gold coins and square or round silver ones. Mr Izawa is seen standing in the vicinity of the treasure site. (Top) Mr Mizuno digging for yet another hoard.

Treasure exists – but how to find it? For many thousands of enthusiasts the modern answer is 'with a metal detector'. The rapidly growing craze for 'T.H.ing' is attracting adherents in several countries. But indiscriminate use of metal detectors, as well as being socially obnoxious, is unlikely to lead to success. There is no substitute for patient background research in public and private archives to seek clues to possible buried hoards and to check the reliability of local legends. In Japan Mr Izawa has been seeking a medieval hoard for many years. He uses ancient documents for his research.

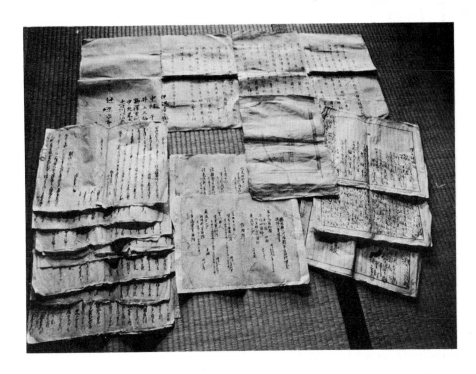

house. He has an ancient parchment in his possession which gives clues to the location of this building. Systematic digging has failed to lead Izawa to the gold – so far.

Most of this activity is harmless. Those whose greed and enthusiasm carry them to the brink of eccentricity are little danger to their neighbours or their environment. It is not so with all treasure-seekers. Throughout the history-rich countries of the Third World desperate men pursue buried wealth as a means of filling empty bellies. We have touched on the activities of *huaqueros* and *tomboroli* and have seen how the ready market provided by collectors and museums guarantees the continued existence of the ancient craft of tomb-robbing. But there are countries where the treasure-hunter is a very sinister being indeed. In Thailand one of the essential tools of his trade is the submachine gun. In India antiquity smugglers dissatisfied with the state of the market have been known to diversify their business interests – they have taken to kidnapping antique dealers and art experts.

From the denizens of the Asian criminal underworld to the devotees of the West's fastest growing hobby would seem to be a very long step indeed. But the distance is much shorter if we believe some of the opponents of 'T.H.ers' (as initiated treasure-hunters call themselves). They are people who 'destroy or damage highly important archaeological structures in search of loot'; who 'often act outside the law by trespass and by stealing objects to which they have no title'; and who 'sometimes pretend to be members of responsible national or county bodies'. These claims were made in a poster devised and displayed by the Council for Kentish Archaeology in 1977.

The treasure-hunting craze began with the development of the modern metal detector from wartime landmine discovering equipment. It has been in full swing now for more than a decade, and there are probably over five million devotees in Europe and North America. The number of companies manufacturing metal detectors – retailing at between £15 and £1,000 – is large, there is a proliferation of magazines produced for followers of the new hobby, and most centres of population boast at least one T.H.ers club. Every treasure-hunter hopes to make a major find, and

DIG

British treasure-hunters are represented by DIG – Detector Information Group. It is the contention of this body that, apart from the activities of a minority of 'cowboys', archaeologists have nothing to fear from metal detector users. Responsible 'T.H.ers' observe a code which includes the following points:

1 Always obtain permission before going on to any land.
2 Do not interfere with archaeological sites or ancient monuments.
3 Remove any finds with care and leave the site tidy.
4 Report all finds to local museums or similar authorities.
5 In the event of important archaeological finds being made report them immediately and do not proceed without expert advice.

They claim that metal detectors only work effectively on objects in the upper levels of the soil so that there is little likelihood of positive signals leading to extensive digging. They suggest that some archaeologists are guilty of arrogance in demanding exclusive right of excavation on any land, and claim that some landowners would rather have 'T.H.ers' than archaeologists on their fields. They give instances of sites such as a medieval pavement at Westerfield, Suffolk, which would never have been discovered were it not for the activities of treasure-hunters. They reject the suggestion that they are only interested in money and refer to the many items donated by 'T.H.ers' to the local museums.

such hopes are kept alive by the journals: 'He Found £8,000 Worth of Coins in his Lunch Break'; 'The Family Hobby that led to a £25,000 fortune in Roman Coins'; 'Graham Couple's Hobby Offers Rewards'; such are the headlines which whet the appetites of grocers, housewives, schoolboys, accountants, policemen and the multitude of other ordinary folk who have been bitten by the treasure bug. Most of them settle for much more modest discoveries – single coins, old keys, lost jewellery, badges and buttons. Many afficionados have discovered that the research, which is a vital part of any treasure hunt, is the most exciting part of the game. They enjoy reading up local history, pursuing information through museums and archive offices, and building up an understanding of the past. Seaby's, the London numismatic dealers, report a considerable interest in old coins as a result of activity with metal detectors. Large numbers have been brought into their offices in recent years and, as a result, over twenty hitherto unknown coin types have been recorded. There are, of course, some T.H.ers whose electronic equipment does locate items of real value. There was the boy who found gold and silver communion plate in a Tipperary bog, and the two men who located in Wiltshire the largest hoard of Roman coins ever discovered in Britain. In Texas, in 1971, T.H.ers discovered $350,000 in cash and jewels (the proceeds of a robbery), and more recently a treasure-hunting club pinpointed a hitherto unknown Anglo-Saxon site at Martham, Norfolk.

There ought to be no clash of interest between archaeologists and treasure-hunters. T.H.ers should respect digs in progress and potential sites. The professionals should welcome the metal detector fraternity to their excavations as observers and, where possible, assistants, and they should not assume exclusive rights to the heritage of the past. But as soon as words like 'ought' and 'should' appear in the argument it moves into the dimension of ethics – and, as we have seen, buried treasure and morality are seldom close companions. Some T.H.ers tear precious objects from the soil and completely destroy their stratigraphical context. Some archaeologists pocket finds for private gain. Some museum curators compete to buy antiquities they know to have been illegally looted. And all this is because of the fascination treasure holds for everyone. Scholars may claim to be immune to considerations of financial value but they habitually spend astronomical sums of public or private money in the acquisition of precious objects. And when museum authorities wish to commend their collections or gain extra funds do they not do so by staging exhibitions with such glittering titles as 'Treasures of Tutankhamen', 'The Wealth of the Roman World' and 'The Gold of El Dorado'?

Criminals, emperors, peasants, adventurers, academics, businessmen – there is scarcely a category of the human species with which our foray into the subject of buried treasure has not brought us into contact. Men have traversed every kind of earthly hell to obtain it. They have forsaken all in its pursuit. They have risked even the displeasure of the gods and the perdition of their immortal souls to acquire it.

Bell, book and candle shall not drive me back,
When gold and silver becks me to come on . . .

(Shakespeare, *King John*, II, iii)

Buried treasure, it seems, tells us as much about ourselves as about those civilizations to which it originally belonged.

STOP

'Stop Taking Our Past' is a campaign begun in 1979, supported by leading British archaeological societies, and aimed at curbing the activities of treasure-hunters, whom it accuses of damaging the nation's heritage for motives of personal gain. Specific objections to 'T.H.ers' are:

1 Many operate metal detectors without permission, and are guilty of illegal trespass.
2 Many remove objects from private or public property without permission, which is theft.
3 Many operate without permission on archaeological sites, now specially protected by the Ancient Monuments and Archaeological Areas Act, 1979.
4 The removal of 'treasure' frequently destroys archaeological evidence.
5 Amateur attempts to clean antiquities removed from the ground often damage the articles irreparably.
6 The rapid growth of treasure-hunting encourages the unscrupulous dealer in antiquities.
7 Piecemeal and careless digging hampers the work of archaeologists who are concerned to reconstruct an accurate picture of the nation's past.

The organizers of STOP instance many examples of irresponsibility by 'T.H.ers'. For example, the discovery and removal of the Mildenhall (Wiltshire) hoard of Roman coins in 1978 in itself destroyed important archaeological evidence. But the site was immediately invaded by clandestine excavators who dug wildly, destroyed part of a Roman floor and hopelessly jumbled evidence of not one hoard, but two.

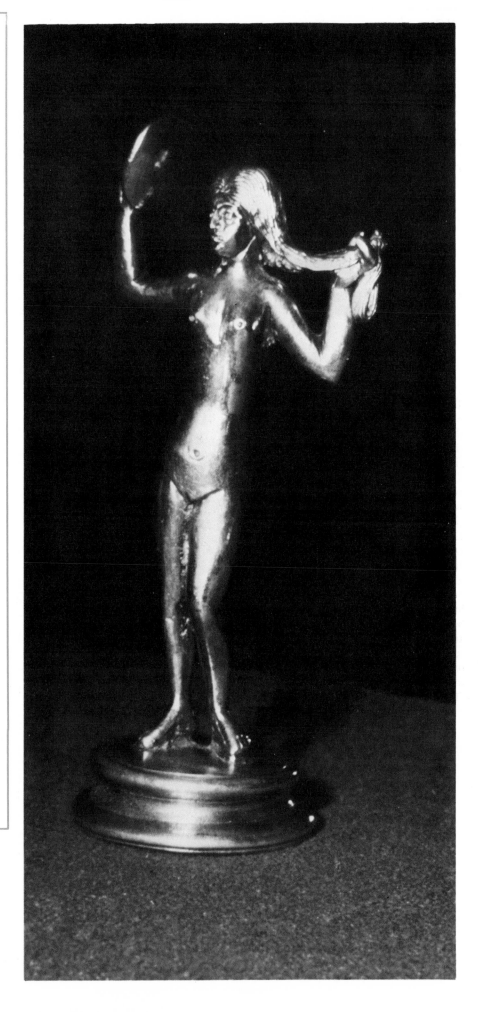

The lovely little statuette of Venus from the Kaiseraugst Treasure. 'Treasure, like beauty is in the eye of the beholder.'

Select Bibliography

Archaeology and Archaeologists
Baumann, H., *The Land of Ur*, Oxford 1969
Birley, R., *Vindolanda, A Roman Frontier Post on Hadrian's Wall*, London 1977
Blegen, C. W., *Troy and the Trojans*, London 1963
Borovka, G., *Scythian Art*, London 1928
Brackman, A. C., *The Luck of Nineveh*, London 1980
Bray, W., *The Gold of Eldorado*, London 1978
British Museum catalogue, *Frozen Tombs, The Culture and Art of the Ancient Tribes of Siberia*, London 1978
—, *Treasures of Tutankhamen*, London 1972
—, *Wealth of the Roman World, Gold and Silver AD 300–700*, London 1977
Ceram, C. W., *Gods, Graves and Scholars, the Story of Archaeology*, London 1971 revised edition
Coggins, C., 'Archaeology and the Art Market', *Science*, 21 January 1972
Cunliffe, B., *Iron Age Communities in Britain: An Account of England, Scotland and Wales from the 7th century BC until the Roman conquest*, London 1974
Davel, L., *Memoirs of Heinrich Schliemann*, London 1934
Fagan, B. M. (ed.), *A Short History of Zambia*, Oxford 1966
Hawkes, J., *Atlas of Ancient Archaeology*, London 1974
Higgins, R., *The Aegina Treasure – An Archaeological Mystery*, London 1979
Hoffman, M. A., *Egypt Before the Pharaohs*, London 1980
Hooker, J. T., *The Ancient Spartans*, London 1980
Johnson, S., *Later Roman Britain*, London 1980
Johnstone, P., *The Sea-craft of Prehistory*, London 1980
Laing, L., *Celtic Britain*, London 1979
Laing, L. and J., *Anglo-Saxon England*, London 1979
Leca, A.-P., *The Cult of the Immortal: Mummies and the Egyptian Way of Death*, London 1979
Minns, E. H., *Scythians and Greeks, A survey*, Cambridge 1913
Philips, P., *The Prehistory of Europe*, London 1980
Posnansky, M., *Prelude to East African History*, Oxford 1966
Powell, T. G. E., *The Celts*, London 1980 edition
Royal Academy catalogue, *The Genius of China*, London 1973
Sandars, N. K., *The Sea Peoples, Warriors of the Ancient Mediterranean, 1250–1150 BC*, London 1978
Schliemann, H., *Mycenae, A Narrative of Researches and Discoveries at Mycenae and Tiryns*, London 1976 reprint edition
Tatton-Brown, V. (ed.), *Cyprus BC, 7,000 Years of History*, London 1979
Trump, D. H., *The Prehistory of the Mediterranean*, London 1980
Wacher, J., *The Coming of Rome*, London 1979
Wellard, J., *The Search for the Etruscans*, London 1973
Willets, R. F., *The Civilization of Ancient Crete*, London 1977
Woolley, C. L., *Excavations at Ur*, London 1955

Marine Archaeology and Sunken Treasures
Allen, G. and D., *Clive's Lost Treasure*, London 1978
Arnold, J. B. (ed.), *Beneath the Waters of Time: Proceedings of the Ninth Conference on Underwater Archaeology*, Austin (Texas), 1978

Bass, G. F., *Archaeology Under Water*, London 1970
—, *The Cape Gelidonya Wreck*, London 1973
Beater, J., *Pirates and Buried Treasure*, London 1959
Blair, C., *Diving for Pleasure and Treasure*, New York 1968
Boxer, C. R., *The Portuguese Seaborne Empire 1415–1825*, London 1969
Burney, J., *History of the Buccaneers of America*, London (n.d.)
Clarke, A. C., *The Treasure of the Great Reef*, Sydney 1973
Cooper, G., *Treasure Trove, Pirates' Gold*, New York 1970
Cotton, E., *East Indiamen*, London 1937
Course, A. G., *Pirates of the Eastern Seas*, London 1966
Cousteau, J.-Y., *Diving for Sunken Treasure*, London 1971
Davis, J., *Treasure, People, Ships and Dreams*, San Antonio (Texas) 1977
Deas, W. and Laler, C., *Beneath Australian Seas*, Sydney 1970
Earle, P., *The Wreck of the Almiranta*, London 1979
Edwards, H., *Islands of Angry Ghosts*, London 1966
Esquemeling, J., *The Buccaneers of America*, London 1893
Eunson, K., *The Wreck of the General Grant*, London 1974
Flemming, N. C. (ed.), *The Undersea*, London 1977
Gibbs, J. A., *Pacific Graveyard*, New York 1970
Goldsmith, F. R., *Treasure Lies Buried Here*, New York 1963
Gosse, P., *History of Piracy*, London 1968 edition
Harding, C. H., *Trade and Navigation Between Spain and the Indies in the Time of the Hapsburgs*, London 1918
Horner, D., *The Treasure Galleons*, London 1973
Howlett, A., 'The Mystery of Captain Kidd's Treasure', *Wide World Magazine*, October 1958
Jameson, J. F., *Privateering and Piracy in the Colonial Period*, London 1923
Johnson, C., *Lives of the Most Notorious Pirates*, London 1724
Kirby, P. R., *The True Story of the Grosvenor, East Indiaman*, London 1960
Larn, R., *Cornish Shipwrecks, The Isles of Scilly*, London 1971
Lonsdale, A. L. and Kaplan, H. R., *A Guide to Sunken Ships in American Waters*, New York 1977
McDonald, K., *The Treasure Divers*, London 1978
McKee, A., *History Under the Sea*, London 1978
Marsden, P., *The Wreck of the Amsterdam*, London 1974
Martin, C., *Full Fathom Five, Wrecks of the Spanish Armada*, London 1975
Marx, R., *Pirate Port*, London 1969
—, *Shipwrecks in Florida Waters*, London 1972
—, *Treasure Fleets of the Spanish Main*, London 1965
Meylach, M., *Diving to a Flash of Gold*, New York 1970
Morris, R., *HMS Colossus*, London 1979
—, *Island Treasure*, London 1969
Nesmith, R. I., *Dig for Pirate Treasure*, New York 1968
O'May, H., *Wrecks in Tasmanian Waters*, Sydney 1975
Owen, D. I., 'Excavating a Classical Shipwreck', *Archaeology*, April 1971
Parry, J. H., *The Spanish Seaborne Empire*, London 1967
Peterson, M., *History Under the Sea*, London 1976

Potter, J. S., *The Treasure Divers of Vigo Bay*, New York 1963
—, *The Treasure Diver's Guide*, London 1960
Rackl, H.-W., *Diving into the Past: Archaeology under Water*, London 1973
Schurtz, W. L., *The Manila Galleons*, London 1959
Scott, D., *The Egypt's Gold*, London 1958
Slack, J., *Finders, Losers*, New York 1967
Sotheby sales catalogue, *Association Treasure*, London 4 July 1969
—, *Association Treasure*, London 28 January 1970
—, *Hollandia Treasure*, London 8 April 1972
—, *Shetland Islands Treasures*, London 8 November 1973
Snow, E. R., *Mysteries and Adventures Along the Atlantic Coast*, London 1948
Sténuit, R., 'The Treasure of Porto Santo', *National Geographic Magazine*, August 1975
—, *Treasure of the Armada*, London 1972
Stirling, N. B., *Treasure Under the Sea*, New York 1975
Taylor, J. du P. (ed.), *Marine Archaeology*, London 1965
Throckmorton, P., *Diving for Treasure*, London 1977
Tucker, T., *Treasure Diving with Teddy Tucker*, New York 1970
Wagner, K., *Pieces of Eight*, London 1966
Walter, R., 'Undersea Treasure Stolen', *New York Post*, 30 September 1971
Wilkins, H. T., *Captain Kidd and his Skeleton Island*, London 1935
Williams, M., *Sunken Treasure*, London 1980
Winston, A., *No Purchase, No Pay . . . The Great Age of Privateers and Pirates, 1665–1715*, London 1970

Treasure and Treasure-hunting
Adam, N., 'The Treasure They Buried Again', *Observer*, 12 November 1972
Andrew, W. J., 'Buried Treasure: Some Traditions, Records and Facts', *British Numismatic Journal*, 1905
Ayloffe, J., 'An Account of the Body of King Edward the First . . . in the Year 1774', *Archaeologia*, 1775
Bankes, G., *The Story of Corfe Castle*, London 1853
Beard, C. R., *The Romance of Treasure Trove*, London 1933
Bethwell-Gosse, A., *The Knights Templars*, London 1897
British Commission on Preservation of Works of Art, *Works of Art in Austria*, London 1946
—, *Works of Art in Germany*, London 1946
Bunt, C. G. E., 'The Ramsey Thurible and Incense Boat', *Apollo*, 1930
Cabanne, P., *The Great Collectors*, London 1963
Carley, W. M., 'Some of the Looters of Archaeological Sites Now Turn to Murder', *Wall St Journal*, 30 November 1971
Cassou, J., *Le Pillage par les Allemands . . .*, Paris 1947
Chamberlin, E. R., *Preserving the Past*, London 1979
Charroux, R., *Treasures of the World*, London 1966
Cockett, M., *Treasure*, London 1973
Coggins, C., 'The Maya Scandal', *Smithsonian*, October 1970
del Mundo, F., 'Yamashita Treasure Hunt', *International Herald Tribune*, 30 May 1978
de Villefosse, A. M. A. H., 'Le Trésor de Boscoreale', *Académie des Inscriptions et Belles Lettres*, 1899
Esterow, M., 'L'oeuvre d'art la plus volée . . .', *Histoire pour Tous*, January 1968
Evans, A. J., 'On a votive deposit of gold

objects found on the north-west coast of Ireland', *Archaeologia*, 1897

Eyre, C., *The History of St Cuthbert*, London 1849

Fowler, G., 'The Loss of King John's Treasure', *Proceedings of Cambridge Antiquarian Society*, 1952

Furneaux, R., *The Money Pit Mystery: The Costliest Treasure Hunt Ever*, New York 1972

Gaskill, G., 'They Smuggle History', *Illustrated London News*, 14 June 1969

Graham-Campbell, J. and Kidd, D., *The Vikings*, London 1980

Grant, J., *A Pillage of Art*, London 1966

Greenwall, J. H., 'On the trail of Europe's Stolen Treasures', *John Bull*, 16 November 1957

Guardian, 'Japanese Treasures Seen', 9 August 1978

Hale, A., 'The Help Yourself Treasure Chests', *Sunday Times*, 17 December 1972

Hall, A. R., 'The Recovery of Cultural Objects Dispersed During World War II', *Dept of State Bulletin*, 27 August 1951

Hemming, J., *The Conquest of the Incas*, London 1970

Hope, W. H. St J., 'The Loss of King John's Baggage Train in . . . October 1216', *Archaeologia*, 1906

Hopkirk, P., 'Treasure Hunters Take Antiquities', *The Times*, 27 October 1969

—, 'Mycenaean Treasures Plundered from Tombs are Smuggled out of Cyprus', *The Times*, 16 August 1971

Howe, T. C., *Salt Mines and Castles*, London 1946

Hughes, J., 'The Army Brought Back the Skull and 1,800 Tons of Treasures', *The Soldier*, March 1948

Illustrated London News, 'Jewellery of a Byzantine–Nubian Queen', 11 June, 16 July 1932; 25 February, 24 June 1933; 10 March 1934

London Museum catalogue, *The Cheapside Hoard of Elizabethan and Jacobean Jewellery*, 1928

McFadden, E., *The Glitter and the Gold*, New York 1971

Mellaart, J., 'The Royal Treasure of Dorak', *Illustrated London News*, 28 November 1959

Meyer, K., *The Plundered Past: The Traffic in Art Treasures*, London 1973

—, *The Maya Crisis: A Report on the Pillaging of Maya Sites*, New York 1972

Odobescu, A. J., *Le Trésor de Pétrossa*, Paris 1900

Paige, C., 'Amateur Threat to Digs', *Guardian*, 6 July 1971

Porter, J. S., 'Discovery of Roman Coins and Other Articles near Coloraine, Co. Derry', *Ulster Journal of Archaeology*, 1854

Reinhold, R., 'Looters Impede Scholars Studying Maya Mystery', *New York Times*, 26 March 1973

Report of the American Commission for the Protection of . . . Historic Monuments in War Areas, 1946

Roxan, D. and Wanstall, K., *The Jackdaw of Linz*, London 1964

St Clair, W., *Lord Elgin and the Marbles*, London 1967

Sichynsky, V., *Destruction of Ukrainian Monuments*, New York 1958

Simmon, K., 'Italy's Tarquinia: What the Tomb Raiders Missed', *New York Times*, 12 March 1972

Simon, M., *The Battle of the Louvre*, London 1971

Smith, J. L., *Tombs, Temples and Ancient Art*, London 1956

Stall, W., 'Treasure Hunt Begins on US Missile Range', *International Herald Tribune*, 21 March 1977

Treue, W., *Art Plunder*, London 1960

Trevor-Roper, H., *The Plunder of the Arts in the Seventeenth Century*, London 1970

Turner, D., 'Brief remarks . . . illustrative of . . . Treasure Trove and the Invocation of Spirits for the Discovery of Hidden Treasure, in the 16th Century', *Norfolk Archaeology*, 1847

Vermeule, E. and C., 'Aegean Gold Hoard and the Court of Egypt', *Illustrated London News*, 21 March 1970

Walter, R., '$1 Million Vase: Magistrate Goes to Looted Tomb', *Observer*, 3 March 1973

Wilkins, H. T., *A Modern Treasure Hunter*, New York 1948

Worsley, F. A., 'Searching for Long-Buried Pirate Treasure with Gold and Silver Indicating Instruments', *Illustrated London News*, 10 March 1934

Index